The
EVERYTHING.
Dreams Book

Dear Reader:

Nothing is more powerful, more intricate, or more exciting than the study of dreams. Through careful analysis and introspection, and with a little work, you can see past the signs and symbols of your dreams right into your true self—your hopes, wishes, and desires. It's that simple and that scary. By choosing to investigate your nighttime fantasies, you can conquer the fears of your waking life and transform memory and desire into fate. What could be better? What's stopping you from being the best you can be? Learn about yourself from your dreams, and change your spiritual karma. Change your life.

From the moment I started writing this book, my dreams became more intense, more vivid. I remembered each one of them, and they continue to guide me now toward the future. They're becoming more powerful because I'm letting myself remember. Intention is everything. Have the strength to believe. Do your homework now, and you'll learn what you can achieve in the best of all possible worlds. Go for it!

Best wishes,

Jenni Kosarin

The EVERYTHING® Series

Editorial

Publishing Director	Gary M. Krebs
Managing Editor	Kate McBride
Copy Chief	Laura M. Daly
Acquisitions Editor	Gina Chaimanis
Development Editor	Katie McDonough
Production Editors	Jamie Wielgus
	Bridget Brace

Production

Production Director	Susan Beale
Production Manager	Michelle Roy Kelly
Series Designers	Daria Perreault
	Colleen Cunningham
	John Paulhus
Cover Design	Paul Beatrice
	Matt LeBlanc
Layout and Graphics	Colleen Cunningham
Series Cover Artist	Barry Littmann

Visit the entire Everything® Series at *www.everything.com*

THE
EVERYTHING®
DREAMS
BOOK

2ND EDITION

What your dreams mean and how
they affect your everyday life

Jenni Kosarin

Adams Media
Avon, Massachusetts

An Everything® Series Book.
Everything® and everything.com® are registered trademarks of F+W Publications, Inc.

Published by Adams Media, an F+W Publications Company
57 Littlefield Street, Avon, MA 02322 U.S.A.
www.adamsmedia.com

ISBN: 1-59337-336-8
Printed in the United States of America.

J I H G F E D C B A

Library of Congress Cataloging-in-Publication Data
Kosarin, Jenni.
The everything dreams book / Jenni Kosarin.—2nd ed.
p.   cm.
(An everything series book)
Rev. ed. of: Everything dreams book / Trish and Rob MacGregor. c1998.
ISBN 1-59337-336-8
1. Dream interpretation. 2. Dreams. I. MacGregor, Trish, 1947-
Everything dreams book. II. Title. III. Series: Everything series.

BF1091.M315 2005
154.6'3--dc22
2005009554

This book is available at quantity discounts for bulk purchases.
For information, please call 1-800-872-5627.

*For Pussycat, who will have all her best dreams
come true this year. You're ready for them!*

Contents

Acknowledgments

To Paul and Donna Kosarin, who have always been my dream-catchers. Thank you for the extra research and support! A special and warm thanks to Gina Chaimanis, whose talent and guidance makes her indispensable (and just a great gal). To Katie McDonough, who makes anyone look good. Wow. Hats off, too, to Jamie Wielgus. Thank you! Thank you, also, Laura Daly—you've been a star with my other books as well! And to Kate McBride, who is charming as well as incredibly gifted. Thank you all!

Top Ten Things You Will
Learn about Dreams

1. Prophetic dreams are rare, but they can be big—even *global*! You can dream about a world event before it happens.

2. Telepathy can happen in waking life and in dreams—among friends, family, and even strangers.

3. Regardless of whether you believe in reincarnation, these real-life stories illustrate that past lives can be experienced again in dreams!

4. From Freud to modern-day psychologists, you'll find out what master dream-researchers say about the translation of dreams.

5. You can make predictions and learn how to change your future by finding truth in coincidences between dreams and waking life.

6. You can face your fears and control your dreams once you interpret them.

7. We all have nightmares, but why? You'll discover what to do to push the boogeyman away.

8. Can we really leave our bodies and travel while we sleep? Of course we can, and you'll learn how!

9. Lucid dreaming is when you know you're dreaming. Once you master it, you can change your life!

10. Dreaming about sex shouldn't be taken literally, just as dreaming about death doesn't mean you're going to die. You'll learn all about it!

Introduction

▶ You wake up. You're a bit startled. You've been dreaming. Was it a nightmare? A good dream? You wonder for a few moments what it all means and then put it out of your head as your day begins. Yet tidbits of the dream linger on. You're dying to know if there was a message somewhere in there for you. Now you can figure it out.

With this book, you have a new scenario. You wake up in the morning from the same dream. This time, you remember it in its entirety. You jot it down, interpret it, and then realize it addresses some of the major concerns in your life. With practice, you can do this kind of analysis. And it's more powerful than any therapy in the world.

Let's give an example. Janet has a dream about a big, spooky Gothic house. As you'll discover, in most cases, when you dream about *any* house, you're actually dreaming about yourself, or your "self," as Swiss psychologist Carl Jung called it. Jung believed that dreams like this can indicate how you feel about your life. In fact, since the rooms can be what make up your self, it's important to remember what the rooms in the house were like. In other words, the rooms are your various facets, your parts.

The ground floor is the self you present to the world, the way other people see you. For Janet, the ground floor was expansive, quiet, gracious, and warm. In her dream, the house had a wide staircase, which represented the accessible way she offers her advice and care to other people.

In Janet's dream, she was also confronted with a heavy, rusted metal door. This was most likely a reference to her heavy emotional stuff—the old thoughts and feelings she should have cleared out years ago. Yet, in her dream, the door didn't appear to be locked. This was a good sign that to deal with everything, all she had to do was open the door and walk right through.

Janet woke up the moment she should have gone through the door, proving that sometimes it's easier to wake up than to deal with our issues. It also puzzled her that there were no other people in the dream. This indicated that the journey into the house was essentially a journey into herself, and one she needed to take alone.

A Freudian psychologist would translate this dream as a sign that Janet has some terrible childhood secret, probably related to her sexuality. To a Jungian psychologist, the metal door might symbolize beginnings and endings. The only interpretation that really matters is Janet's—what makes sense to her. This is *her* dream from *her* unconscious. It doesn't get more personal than that.

That's what this book is for. Read through it. Understand how to analyze your dreams, and then use the information that works with *your* dreams—with *you*. Most dream researchers agree that we can use our dreams as tools for better understanding ourselves—for dealing with and solving the problems in our waking lives. We can use dreams to enhance relationships, gain insight into a health issue, and even obtain career guidance.

By following the instructions for recalling, recording, and interpreting dreams, you can avoid letting important dreams slip away and gain new perspective on your life. Even if you already recall and record dreams, you'll discover new ways to decipher and understand them. You'll also pick up new ideas about lucid and out-of-body dreams. With practice, you'll learn how to program dreams and adventure into new worlds. You can meet up with friends, departed loved ones, and intriguing strangers. You'll find out how to search through past lives and peek at future events. Your destiny is waiting for you to shape it. Bend and change fate!

Chapter 1

Translating Basics: The Meaning of Dreams

Nothing is more intriguing than the study of dreams. While unique to each person, dreams are still a universal link to the far reaches of our psyches and beyond. Across the globe, regardless of race, language, or religion, we all dream. There is no question that dreams have significance. What do they mean? This chapter investigates the different types of dreams and why we have them.

Understanding Dreams

The many different kinds of dreams can all be categorized in distinct ways. Even so, a particular dream can be a combination of two or even three different kinds of dreams. So how do you tell the difference? There are five main categories of dreams:

- Release dreams
- Wish dreams
- Prophetic (psychic) message dreams
- Astral dreams
- Problem-solving dreams

As you progress through this book, you'll learn more about the nature of dreams and where they come from. You'll discover how categorizing your dreams is the most important step toward understanding them.

Studies have shown that all humans dream, but so do all animals—even your pets! All birds and mammals dream. Strangely enough, cold-blooded animals are the only ones that don't dream.

Release Dreams

Even though fear, insecurity, frustration, and angst often cannot be expressed during waking hours, some part of you always needs to be heard. Your regrets, worries, and concerns—things you find too difficult to deal with consciously—go straight to your subconscious and come through in release dreams. Release dreams are typically jumbled. They have no sequential order and can frequently be classified as nightmares. When you're being chased or running away from something evil, you are usually having a release dream. Experts say that the monster or demon you're running from is actually yourself. Do you want the release dream, the nightmare, to go away? Confront the part of your life that needs work, and these evil beings will leave you alone.

Wish Dreams

Many people confuse wish dreams with prophetic message dreams because wish dreams seem to be showing you a part of your life that hasn't already happened. This makes the dreamer wonder if the dream will soon come true. But this isn't the case with wish dreams. A wish dream puts you into a situation you may have been imagining or fantasizing about. For example, you might win the lottery or get the promotion you've been hoping for in a wish dream.

A good way to distinguish a wish dream from a prophetic dream is that prophetic dreams always have a logical order. The action in the dream happens in the sequence it would in real life. If your dream is jumbled and doesn't make much sense, it's probably not a prophetic dream.

ALERT!

Pay close attention to your wish dreams! Sometimes you may not even consciously know what you want. But your subconscious knows, and it can help you discover it in your dreams.

Prophetic (Psychic) Message Dreams

Prophetic message dreams unfold logically, with events that happen in sequential order. Many psychics also say that prophecy dreams only happen in color and that they're incredibly vivid as well. Here's an interesting tidbit: You don't have to be psychic at all in order to have a prophecy dream. If fact, many people who are psychic or incredibly intuitive in their waking hours may never have a prophecy dream, while those who have prophecy dreams are not necessarily psychic in waking life. Prophecy dreams can be confusing because they usually deliver a warning, but the dreamer is not always given enough information to take action. Be patient if this happens to you. Ask out loud for more assistance just before you go to sleep the next night, and the next, until you get it. Never dismiss your dreams. If you get a warning that something may happen to your brother in his car, for example, make sure you tell him to be careful driving. Even if he thinks you're nuts, you'll still feel better later.

Astral Dreams

Regardless of whether we remember them, we all have astral dreams, or "visits," as they're sometimes called. Our departed loved ones and our personal spirit guides, who help us along with life choices, actually visit with us. Because there are no limits to space or time in the dream or spirit world, we can find ourselves walking along the Seine in Paris with an old friend who died several years ago or in Alaska, dog-sledding with Great-Granddad. Some other types of dreams may feel like astral dreams. This can happen when we wish a person into the dream when his spirit is not really there.

Here are two ways to recognize a true astral dream. First, the events in astral dreams, like prophetic dreams, happen in sequential order. Second, spirits are by nature happy with where they are, and they want you to know that. If for some reason you feel in your dream that a spirit is evil, or even just sad or angry, you are combining a release dream with an astral visit.

ALERT!

A release dream can kick in when you have an astral visit from someone you love who has died. Out of fear, grief, or shock, you may push him away in your dream, even though he's trying to tell you he's okay. Spirits are always happy beings! Dreamers are the ones who are afraid.

Problem-Solving Dreams

Did you ever go to sleep trying to figure something out and then wake up with a clear understanding of the answer? The term "sleep on it" really does have significance. Sometimes our subconscious knows the solution to a problem we're having and can dig it up more readily than our waking mind. But there's something else. Astral and problem-solving dreams can combine to give us information that certainly never existed in our conscious minds in the first place. Whether or not we remember it, some information is given to us through outside sources—from astral visits. For proof, just look at the countless geniuses in history who simply "happened" upon their inspiration in nighttime dreams.

Dreams Through Time

Did you know that the famous artist Paul Gauguin came up with subjects in his paintings from his dreams or that Albert Einstein formulated the theory of relativity from a vision he had while he slept? Thomas Edison's light bulb and Mendeleyev's periodic table were inspired by dreams as well. Coincidence? Not a chance!

One inventor wrestled for years over a small but vital detail he needed to complete a machine he was building. But the detail eluded him like a mirage that vanished when he got too near. One night, though, he dreamed he had been taken captive by savages who were attacking him with spears with eye-shaped holes at the ends. When the inventor awoke, he realized the nightmare had provided the solution to his problem: the eye of the needle belonged near the point! With the help of his dream, Elias Howe was then able to complete his invention: the sewing machine.

FACT

Even Hollywood has been influenced by inspirational dreams. Many stars throughout history have been motivated by their nighttime visions. According to reliable sources, Ingmar Bergman's movie *Cries and Whispers* was inspired by a dream.

The history of dreams is rich with stories, like this one, that illustrate the incredible fertility of our nighttime dreams. Physicist Neils Bohr had a dream that planets circled the sun attached to pieces of string. He then developed his theory about the movement of electrons, and *bam*! The model of the atom was born. Richard Bach, the author of *Jonathan Livingston Seagull*, actually dreamed up the second half of his book eight years after he'd written the first half.

The English poet Samuel Taylor Coleridge dozed off one afternoon after taking opium as a sedative. The last words he read before he fell asleep were "Here the Khan Kubla commanded a palace to be built." Coleridge awoke three hours later with several hundred lines of poetry in his head. He quickly wrote the opening lines of "Kubla Khan: Or, A Vision in a Dream":

In Xanadu did Kubla Khan
A stately pleasure-dome decree:
Where Alph, the sacred river, ran
Through caverns measureless to man
Down to a sunless sea.

After completing fifty-four lines, Coleridge was interrupted by a visitor. When he returned to his work an hour later, the inspiration had vanished "like images on the surface of a stream." Dreams are fleeting—they need to be written down.

Those who research sleep and dreaming say that ten minutes after waking, we've already forgotten nearly 90 percent of our dreams. That's why it's so important to write them down right away!

A dream about a snake helped the German chemist Friedrich August Kekule complete his quest to comprehend the molecular structure of the chemical compound benzene. The atoms, dancing in his dream, suddenly turned into one snake with its tail in its mouth. When he woke up, "as if struck by lightning," he realized that the structure he was searching for was shaped like a ring.

A Little History

The ancient Egyptians sought to decipher dreams in terms of prophecy. A papyrus dream book from around 1500 B.C. explains a variety of dream symbols. If you dreamed, for example, that your teeth were falling out, it meant your relatives were plotting to kill you.

In ancient Greece, dreams were believed to be conduits to a higher power. People sought curative dreams by sleeping in temples with snakes, which symbolized healing. In the second century A.D., Artemidorous, a Greek soothsayer, proved to be so skillful as a dream analyzer that he won Freud's admiration many centuries later. Artemidorous's books on dreams were preserved for nearly a thousand years and were actually still being used in the 1700s, in the early period of Rationalism.

Oneiromancy, the study of divining the future through dreams, is thought to have originated with the Romans. They considered dream happenings to be just as real as warnings that happened in everyday life.

Renaissance heroes essentially dismissed the importance of dreams. Shakespeare, despite Hamlet's eloquent soliloquy on the nature of dreams, called dreams "the children of an idle brain." The poet John Dryden wrote dreams off as indigestion and infections of the blood. This general bias against dreams persisted into the nineteenth century, when dreams came to be viewed as the consequence of an external stimulus. Rain on a rooftop, for example, was thought to trigger a dream about the roof of a house falling in. Beyond the literal translation of the external stimulus, it was believed that dreams held no meaning. Then Freud came along. (See Chapter 2 for Freud's interpretation of dreams.)

Prophecy—Beware!

How can you decipher information you're receiving in a prophetic dream? Many times you'll get a number, but you won't know if it's a date, a measure of time, or even an amount of money. Once again, unless your subconscious combines them with release dreams (due to fear or anxiety), prophetic dreams usually happen in color and in sequential order. Here are just some of the techniques you can use to translate symbols in your dreams.

Metaphors

Metaphors are figures of speech that substitute one image with another to suggest a connection between the two: "buried in work" is a metaphor. When you recognize a metaphor in your dreams, it can help a perplexing image take on meaning. For example, when you dream about people who aren't in your life anymore, think about what they represent to you. If Bert from your office is a gossip, his appearance in a dream might refer to gossip.

Here's another example. A woman who had been reading tarot cards before going to bed dreamed that she was at a turnstile in a subway station. The token she put in didn't go through. A hand reached into her vision and held out a vividly colored tarot card—Strength—which she then inserted into the slot. The turnstile began to move and she was able to pass through with ease. The turnstile, she felt, was a metaphor for how she was about to undergo a "turn" or change in her "style" of doing certain things; hence, "turnstile." The Strength card practically proclaimed that she possessed the inner resources to make the change successfully. Deep down, she knew she could handle it.

Edgar Cayce said, "All dreams are given for the benefit of the individual, would he but interpret them correctly." Some significant dream metaphors for your life might be "in the dark" (a secret or the truth is hidden from you) or "turbulent waters" (usually indicating a relationship on the brink of disaster).

Puns

Another way to decipher meaning is to think of a dream as a pun, or a play on words. For example, a dream of Bob Hope bouncing along on a pogo stick, moving off into the distance, might seem outrageous and nonsensical. However, a look at the dream elements as a sort of pun reveals a message: Hope springs eternal. If a bizarre image or random person ever appears in your dreams, thinking of the situation as a pun could help expose its true meaning.

Archetypes: From Myths to Movies

An archetype is a symbol or theme that rises from a layer of the mind common to all people. Carl Jung called this layer the collective unconscious, and he believed that we each give these symbols and themes our own individual stamp. Archetypes are prevalent in mythology, folklore, and religion. The hero, for instance, is a common theme in mythology that has been transferred to forms of modern media, such as movies.

From Apollo to Zeus, King Arthur to Luke Skywalker, the hero follows a standard pattern. First he is cut off from his roots—what mythologist Joseph Campbell terms his "call to adventure." For Luke Skywalker, this happens with the murder of his aunt and uncle. Next, the hero sets out on a journey of self-discovery—a rite of passage in which he must confront and overcome villains, disasters, and challenges to awaken a power within himself. For Luke, this awakening is his contact with the Force.

Movie Archetypes

In *The Wizard of Oz,* Dorothy is cut off from her roots by the tornado that whisks her house off the ground. On the yellow brick road she encounters tricksters, witches, and innumerable challenges. She overcomes her fears when she accepts the friendship of her traveling companions—the Scarecrow, the Tin Man, and the Cowardly Lion—who are on their own heroic journeys.

The hero, of course, always reaches his goal. Luke Skywalker saves the universe from Darth Vader's evil empire and discovers his true heritage. Dorothy reaches the wizard. But the goal isn't the end of the journey; the hero must return to his ordinary life with his new wisdom and enrich the lives of everyone around him.

You may not consciously recognize an archetype when you encounter it in a dream, but it will resonate at some level inside you. Jung called this sensation a "click"—a feeling of rightness.

Archetypes Equal Transformation

In the following dream, the archetypal figure literally jumps out at the dreamer:

I walk into a room with four doors and a raised platform in the middle with a gargoyle-like devil in the middle of the platform. The room is filled with light. I don't feel afraid. I walk around the room, closing three of the doors, then walk out the fourth door and shut it behind me. Now I'm in a room filled with smaller gargoyle-like creatures. Suddenly, they begin to transform into human beings. I look back at the large gargoyle in the other room and he too is transforming into human form.

Vicki, a librarian, had been going through changes in her life when she had this dream. She was in the process of leaving behind her old self, which she described as a typical bland Iowa schoolmarm. The new Vicki was discovering other parts of her personality, deeper areas that she had previously feared. The dream made sense to her and was easy to interpret.

QUESTION?

What are some more classic archetypes you may dream of?
Water or a dog can represent your mother. The sun can indicate your father. A tree might signify your intellect. A snake can point to your sexuality or healing.

The platform in the room was an altar, and the gargoyle was the devil—the darker elements of her personality. The fact that the room was brightly lit was significant to her. In order to become a whole person, she was illuminating her dark side. The fact that the gargoyles changed into humans signified that we all have a dark side that needs illuminating.

What Do You Believe?

Archetypes always relate to a higher meaning. Always look for the big picture before you start going into details. Then, when you're finished pinpointing the general meaning of an archetype, relate it to how you feel about that meaning. Does it make sense for you?

The Snake Symbol

Read the following dream and see how you would react toward a dream of this nature. Before reading the translation of the dream that follows, try to decipher what it could mean and why the dreamer may have dreamed it. This dream is called "Snakes":

I'm walking in tall grass, grass that brushes my knees. I hear rustling around me and pick up my pace, anxious to get to the clearing I can see just ahead. I know the rustling is caused by snakes.

The rustling gets louder, like the cacophony of a thousand crickets screaming for rain. I start running. I'm still running when I reach the clearing and run right into a bed of snakes. They are everywhere, writhing, slithering, rattling. But even worse than the snakes is the realization that I'm barefoot and that the only way I'm going to get out of this is to walk through them. So I walk. And I make it though the bed of snakes without getting bitten.

In the ancient Greek and Roman cultures, snakes were symbols of the healing arts. In the Bible, the snake symbolizes temptation and forbidden knowledge. In fairy tales, the snake is often a trickster—wise but wily. The ancient symbol of the snake swallowing its own tail represents the way nature feeds on and renews itself. Jung considered snakes to be archetypal, representing an awareness of the essential energy of life and nature.

The woman who had this dream was in the process of breaking away from a Catholic background. She wanted to explore areas her religion would call heretical. Therefore, she needed to apply her beliefs and feelings at the time she had the dream to this particular archetype. What could it mean?

She interpreted the dream to mean that the prospect of this exploration was somewhat frightening for her, but that she would complete it without harm. She felt the dream was confirming her belief that the exploration was a necessary step in her growth as a human being.

On another level, though, she felt the dream was pointing to a situation at work, one in which she was surrounded by "snakes in the grass"—a pun that probably indicated malicious gossip. Since the snakes didn't bite her, she figured she would survive whatever was being said about her.

ALERT!

You have to pay attention to what a symbol means to you! A seagull, for example, indicates freedom, independence, peace, and hope. But if birds frighten you, or if you simply don't like them, then ignore the dream dictionaries. Apply every situation and symbol to you.

Even though the snake is considered an archetypal symbol, in this case the most relevant meaning to the dreamer concerned her daily life. She didn't need a psychologist to interpret the dream for her. Once she'd remembered it and written it down, the pun "clicked" for her. She knew what the dream was referring to. Pay attention to your gut when translating your dreams. You'll find the solution. Guaranteed.

Chapter 2

The Dream Experts

You spend about a third of your life asleep. That means that in a lifespan of seventy-five years, you sleep the equivalent of twenty-five years. That's a lot of time to spend dreaming! Yet it wasn't until fairly recently that scientists have begun to understand the processes and functions of dreaming. This chapter explores what happens while we sleep and what the experts have to say about your dreams.

Reality Versus Fantasy: The Basics of Sleep

Dreams make up about 20 percent of our sleeping life. The average lifetime includes well over 100,000 dreams. In the course of a typical night, you pass through four phases of sleep that can be distinguished by the frequency of brain waves, eye movements, and muscle tension. The four phases are as follows:

- **Beta:** You're awake.
- **Alpha:** You're in a relaxed state, with eyes closed, on the boundary between waking and sleeping. You may enter the REM stage here.
- **Theta:** You are asleep, perhaps still in the REM stage.
- **Delta:** You're in the deepest level of sleep, beyond the REM stage and too deep for dreams.

The Beta Level

In this first stage of sleep, the rhythms of the brain are in the process of shifting from beta, your normal waking consciousness level, to the alpha stage, where brain waves oscillate between eight and twelve cycles per second. Your heart rate, blood pressure, and body temperature drop slightly. Your muscles begin to relax, and you experience drifting sensations. "Hypnogogic" images—surreal scenes that usually concern your last thoughts before turning out the light—may flit through your mind. These hypnogogic images are often vivid and psychedelic. Though brief, the images can be as meaningful and significant as longer dreams in deeper stages of sleep.

The hypnogogic state—the state between waking and sleeping—also refers to the time when you just start waking up from your dreams. It is in this period when we have hallucinatory images.

The Alpha Level

In the second stage, called alpha, you experience a deepening of the drifting sensation as you fall into a light slumber. Theta waves are now included in your brain-wave pattern, characterized by rapid bursts of brain activity. On an electroencephalogram (EEG), these waves appear as spindles and are believed to signify true sleep. Yet people who are awakened during this phase report they weren't asleep, but were "thinking."

Most of your dreams occur during the alpha stage. If you watch someone sleeping, you can actually see him dream because his eyes move back and forth beneath his eyelids. This period of rapid eye movement, or REM, usually lasts for several minutes. Twenty to forty-five minutes or so after the sleep cycle begins, the spindle pattern of brain waves is replaced by large, slow delta waves. Delta waves indicate the plunge into deeper stages of slumber.

The Theta Level

In the theta stage, the EEG consists of 20 to 50 percent delta waves, as compared with the fourth stage, called the delta stage, in which the EEG registers more than 50 percent delta waves. People who are wakened during this phase are usually disoriented and incoherent and only want to go back to sleep.

FACT

In the fourth stage of sleeping, the delta level, there are no eye movements at all. Strangely enough, this stage—when we're in the deepest level of sleep—is when sleepwalking can occur. Most people who sleepwalk don't remember that they've done it at all.

The Delta Level

In the delta stages, the high rate of delta waves can go on for periods ranging from a few seconds to an hour. In grown men, for instance, it takes about ninety minutes to complete the sleep cycle. Once this first delta stage is complete, the cycle begins again but in reverse—from delta, you revisit theta, then alpha.

When you enter the alpha stage while already asleep, your reactions are different. Your blood pressure rises, your pulse quickens, and your brain waves are similar to those during the waking state. Except for REM and twitches in your fingers and toes, your body becomes virtually paralyzed. If you are awakened during the REM period, you'll probably remember most of whatever you're dreaming.

The first REM period lasts from five to ten minutes, and then you go through the cycles of sleep three or four more times. Each time the REM stage is repeated, it lasts longer and the time that elapses between stages is considerably shorter. The final REM stage can last as long as an hour.

In practical terms, this means that if you sleep seven hours, then half your dreaming time will occur during the last two hours. If you sleep an additional hour, that eighth hour will consist almost entirely of dreaming. This, however, is only an average. People who need fewer than eight hours of sleep may simply be more efficient sleepers.

About 4 million people in this country suffer from insomnia. A sleep disturbance disrupts more than your sleep. If you don't dream as you should, you can suffer physically, emotionally, and spiritually. Make sure to get the sleep you need!

Edward Cayce: The Prophet

Most of us go to sleep at night, surrender to our dreams, and then wake up in the morning and get on with our lives. We may or may not mull over our dreams, or explore their symbolism, their tales. It's our choice. But for a grade-school dropout from Kentucky named Edgar Cayce, the dreams and visions that rose from sleep *were* his life.

Edgar Cayce (1877–1945) has been called the greatest seer of the twentieth century, yet he was never on television, never sought publicity, and never wrote a best-selling book. However, for many of his sixty-seven years,

Edgar Cayce did extraordinary things in his sleep. He diagnosed illnesses with astonishing accuracy and recommended treatments. His methods were completely unorthodox for his time, but they have gained enormous support in the years since his death. With nothing more than an individual's name and geographic location, he could give a detailed description of the person's physical condition and then prescribe certain therapies, about which he claimed he knew nothing in his waking life.

Cayce also gave "life readings" to many of the people who consulted him for medical advice. These readings covered a vast range of topics, from spiritual matters to love and relationships to business, past lives, prophecies, and dreams. More than 14,000 of Cayce's readings are preserved at the Association for Research and Enlightenment in Virginia Beach, and more than 1,000 of these deal with dreaming.

Cayce, like Swiss psychiatrist Carl Jung, believed that many dreams hold psychic content. Both men dreamed presciently of their own deaths. Both dreamed about the rise of Hitler and the beginning of World War II long before it happened. But even more importantly, both of these men—contemporaries separated by half a world and totally different views of life—believed that our dreams are our most personal sources of self-knowledge.

FACT

Edward Cayce truly believed in the power of our dreams and our psychic power in them, whether or not we are psychic in our waking life. "Any condition is first dreamed before it becomes reality," Cayce claimed.

Cayce, like Jung, believed that dream symbols are highly individual, that each of us stamps common symbols according to our own perceptions and worldviews. Yet, through the readings that Cayce gave, common meanings emerged for certain symbols:

- **Animals:** Man's negative and positive qualities (the wilder the animal, the more primitive the emotion)
- **Boat:** Life's voyage
- **Fire:** Cleansing, wrath, or destruction

- **Fish:** Christ, spirituality, spiritual journey, or spiritual forces
- **Fishing:** Man's search for higher consciousness
- **House:** The body, the self
- **Mandala:** The inner state of the dreamer, a thrust toward wholeness
- **Mud or tangled weeds:** Need for cleansing, purification
- **Naked image:** Exposure or vulnerability to the criticism of others
- **Snake:** Wisdom, sex, or both
- **Water:** The unconscious, the source of life, or a spiritual journey

Cayce believed that dreams fell under four general headings: problems with the physical body, self-observation, psychic perception, and spiritual guidance. Jung's breakdown was more complex, a reflection of his slant as a psychologist. However, there are striking similarities in their beliefs about dreams and what they mean.

Although the two men never discussed the meaning of dream symbols, they may very well have obtained their meanings from the same source. Cayce called it "the universal mind," and Jung termed it "the collective unconscious."

Sigmund Freud: The Realist

Although his views today appear excessively fixated on sexual matters, Sigmund Freud (1856–1939) transformed the way people viewed their dreams. Suddenly, the metaphorical landscapes of our nightly sojourns assumed a personal, internal meaning. In the process, Viennese psychiatrist Freud led the way out of the repressive Victorian era in which any talk of sex was taboo. According to Freud, dreams were the expression of forbidden sexual longings that originated in childhood.

The hypnogogic state—the state between waking and sleeping—also refers to the time when you just start waking up from your dreams. It is in this period when we have hallucinatory images.

Like the ancient Greeks, Freud believed that dreams, once understood, could heal. The main difference between the two, really, was that the Greeks sought physical healing and Freud sought to cure emotional disorders. Although Freud maintained that most dreams were "wish fulfillment" for repressed sexual desires, Carl Jung disagreed with him.

This disagreement eventually led to a falling out between the two psychotherapists. Jung, who began as one of Freud's disciples, thought that sexuality was just one of several themes that appeared in dreams. He argued that dreams didn't disguise the unconscious—they revealed it. Jung eventually followed a path that was quite separate and distinct from Freud's.

Carl Jung: Meaningful Coincidence

Born in Switzerland, Carl Gustav Jung (1875–1961) is probably better known now, decades after his death, than he was during his lifetime. Once a disciple of Freud, he broke away from Freud's more literal translation of events in dreams. In fact, Jung's research pushed him far past the literal symbolism of dreams and well into the psychic and uncharted areas of man's psyche. He theorized the existence of a "collective unconscious," in which all men, regardless of race, religion, or background, are united by a common pool of knowledge and experience that often manifests itself in dreams.

QUESTION?

What does the collective unconscious contain?
It contains psychological archetypes: imprints, history, stories, and myths that our mind inherits when we are born. In other words, we don't create the archetypes—they already exist. Therefore, if we dream of an archetype, Jung says that it basically refers to the same thing for each of us.

Jung's exploration of esoteric realms—telepathy, precognition, astrology, the I Ching, tarot, poltergeists, and hauntings—led him to one of his most important theories. He found meaningful patterns in chance events, a phenomenon he referred to as synchronicity. Although such "coincidences" are outside the realm of cause and effect, Jung believed synchronicity was the manifestation of an underlying pattern in nature. For Jung, the phenomenon served as an explanation for precognition, as exhibited in the following dream.

In his autobiography, *Memories, Dreams, Reflections*, Jung speaks of a dream in which he was attending a garden party. His sister was there with a mutual friend from the town of Basel, a woman whom Jung knew well. In the dream, he knew the woman was going to die. But when he woke up, he couldn't remember who the woman was, even though the dream remained vivid in his mind. "A few weeks later," he said, "I received news that a friend of mine had a fatal accident. I knew at once that she was the person I had seen in the dream but had been unable to identify."

Many of his discoveries about the unconscious came to him initially through dreams, which were his richest source of information—his conduit to the deeper mysteries he studied for most of his life. His theories on the collective unconscious, archetypes, synchronicity, and dream interpretation essentially redefined psychology, deepening it and making it accessible to everyone.

In her book *Awakening the Heroes Within*, author Carol Pearson names twelve archetypes: the Innocent, the Orphan, the Warrior, the Caregiver, the Seeker, the Destroyer, the Lover, the Creator, the Ruler, the Magician, the Sage, and the Fool.

Jung, like the other dreamers cited in this chapter, understood that dreaming is an ancient art—a lost one that begs to be revived. The first step to reviving that art begins in Chapter 3.

Modern-Day Psychological Beliefs: Judith Orloff

In Western culture, psychiatrists do not profess to be psychic, even if they are. Why? Because they risk ridicule and open themselves to accusations of being charlatans, at best, and mentally deranged at the worst. But Judith Orloff, a Los Angeles psychiatrist, did exactly this when she wrote *Second Sight.*

Dreams in the Womb

Dreams have always been integral to Judith Orloff's life. "Dreams are my compass and my truth; they guide me and link me to the divine," she said. As a child, when her mother cautioned her not to talk about her predictions, dreams comforted her. As a rebellious teen, her dreams perplexed her. As a young adult, her dreams seemed to guide her, nudging her in particular directions.

Her earliest remembered dream, which she recalled under hypnotic regression as an adult, occurred while she was still in the womb, when her mother was five months pregnant. Fibroid tumors had grown on the outside of her mother's uterus and were pressing inward. She remembered hearing the noises of the surgery and waking in a dark, watery, alien place. She tried desperately to return home, but didn't have any idea where home was.

She began to dream of a small farmhouse. A blond woman, the woman's husband, and their two teenage sons came out to greet her. Orloff felt an immediate kinship with them, as though they were her real family. This same family, she said, kept her company until she was born.

Classic dream dictionaries tell us that dreaming of a prosperous farm foretells good health and monetary gain. Sometimes, though, you have to look at the symbolism in dreams and decide what it means to you—and you alone!

Retracing Life in Dreams

Orloff believes each of us has a "dream history." By tracing this history, regardless of how far back the dream goes, it's possible to fill in gaps in your life. This missing information often allows you to illuminate hidden memories that explain who you are.

Orloff classifies dreams into two distinct types: psychological and psychic, with various subcategories under each type. The majority of dreams, she says, fall under the first category.

In psychological dreams, anxieties, fears, and insecurities sometimes surface. They may come in the form of nightmares or may simply be unpleasant dreams. Guidance dreams also belong in this category—dreams in which you are advised on a particular course or given a solution to a problem.

Guidance Dream—A Story

Orloff cites a guidance dream she had about a problem with a colleague in which she was clearly cautioned to wait a few days before confronting the man. Despite the clarity of the message, she started to call his beeper, then changed her mind and phoned a friend first.

Her friend related a dream she'd had the night before about Orloff, in which they were sitting in a room with their meditation teacher. The teacher turned to her friend and told her to tell Orloff not to do anything right now, that she should allow some time to pass. Orloff was so struck by the message that she allowed several days to go by before confronting her colleague.

Judith Orloff says you must also listen to your body's responses. A chill, goose bumps, or a sudden hollowness in the pit of your stomach are all indications that a dream has hit on an answer you need.

When you're analyzing a guidance dream, you need to look for specific clues—something that grabs your attention. It might be a word, a phrase, or a particular image—or something else entirely.

There are two kinds of psychic dreams, according to Orloff: precognitive and healing. In precognitive dreams, the focus is on some future event that may or may not involve you personally. In healing dreams, you may receive guidance about how to deal with a physical problem. You may also experience what seems to be a metaphorical healing, though it actually affects you physically.

Modern-Day Miracles: William Brugh Joy

Personal transformation is rarely the same for any two people. But sometimes a physical threat serves as the catalyst that sets the entire process in motion. For William Brugh Joy, a life-threatening disease (chronic relapsing pancreatitis) in 1974 prompted him to abandon a thriving medical practice in Los Angeles. Within six weeks, his pancreatitis was cured, and he had already embarked on a transformative journey that, twenty-two years later, is still unfolding. Dreams have been and are an intricate part of his journey.

A dream, in fact, was the trigger that spurred Brugh Joy to write his first book, *Joys Way*. In the dream, he was signing his own medical chart and noticed that it was utterly disorganized. He straightened out the chart and realized his signature was odd. It was written last name first, as it would appear on a death certificate. To the right of his name were an asterisk and a note that directed him to "See box above." Written in the box, in red pencil and capital letters, were the words "*PLEASE HURRY!*"

To Brugh Joy, the significance of his dream was obvious. He needed to organize the transformational material he used with groups; he needed to clarify and summarize it. The eleven-chapter outline popped into his head one afternoon as he was falling asleep. A voice ordered him to get up and write down the organization of the book, so he did.

In his transformational workshops and conferences, Brugh Joy emphasizes dream interpretation. He stresses that the goal isn't merely to understand one particular dream or another but to achieve self-insight so that you can continue to interpret your dreams in the future. In this way, he is similar to both Jung and Cayce.

Brugh Joy states that "The best dream analysts are intuitive, and so are the best dream analyses." When you hit on the correct interpretation of a dream, Brugh Joy says, you feel a "zing" (the same term Orloff uses). Jung referred to this phenomenon as a "click." In both cases, it's an intuitive sense—a hunch that you're on the right track.

Joy—Dream Interpretation

With his own dreams, Brugh Joy uses seven different perspectives for interpretation:

- Physical
- Sexual
- Emotional
- Collective human viewpoint
- Higher creative viewpoint
- Mental
- Universal

Brugh Joy advocates the use of tarot cards as one means of analyzing dreams. "The Tarot operates primarily through the symbolic, nonrational aspects of consciousness—the same state from which dreams communicate." When you shuffle and lay out the cards in a particular spread, it's as if you're presented with a dream. Both are mosaics that form a pattern, and the patterns are what you interpret.

FACT

Though Jung and Cayce seemed to accept certain symbols as gospel, Brugh Joy believes that there are no absolute meanings for any dream symbol. He points out that water in one dream may represent the unconscious, while in another it may symbolize emotions.

Searching for Patterns

In his second book, *Avalanche*, Brugh Joy uses the term "pattern projections" for mosaics like those created with tarot cards. These patterns are evident in astrology and numerology and are, according to Brugh Joy, also evident in odd places, like clouds. He believes the deeper levels of the mind "can project onto the clouds a pattern that is germane to a question that has been posed." By learning to read patterns in this way, it becomes easier to interpret your own dreams.

Through dream interpretation, you open channels to the deeper parts of your mind and begin to perceive yourself and your life in entirely new ways. Once you're aware of these patterns, they sometimes manifest when you're awake. Brugh Joy cites a startling example from his own life, which happened in Hawaii.

The cards that make up the Tarot's Major Arcana are similar to Jung's famous archetypes. Cards such as The Fool, Death, The Empress, and The Sun are all good examples of universal symbols.

He was talking about angels with a young woman who had recently had a mastectomy. Although her prognosis was excellent, Brugh Joy sensed that she was orienting herself toward death. As they talked, a lone seagull swept past them, then flew straight up into the air and vanished. At that moment, Brugh Joy knew with utter certainty that the woman would die very soon. "An omen had been delivered through the very unusual flight pattern of the seagull. I cannot describe the extent to which this process is disturbing to my intellect or how the process actually works." The woman died within a year.

In a sense, these external patterns are analogous to the symbols contained in waking dreams (discussed in Chapter 10). At some point in your dream explorations, the things you learn begin to spill over into your waking life. Don't be afraid of this.

Chapter 3

Remembering Your Dreams

Sometimes dreams are so startling or vivid that you wake up in the middle of the night. At the time, you think, "I won't forget this one." But by morning, you have. Maybe you recall the flavor of the dream and nothing else. Maybe you only remember small parts, like flashes in a movie. This chapter describes how to remember your dreams so that you can interpret them and use them to your advantage!

Recalling Fantasies

The best way to remember dreams is to record them right after they end. If you don't usually wake up after a dream, try giving yourself a suggestion before you go to sleep to awaken after a dream. It is possible using this technique to recall four or five dreams a night. Remembering dreams just takes practice.

Take Note

Jot down your dreams on a bedside pad, or record them on tape. Your scrawls may be virtually indecipherable at first, but with practice you'll learn to write clearly enough so that you'll be able to transcribe the dream into a journal in the morning. The next best time to remember a dream is in the morning when you first wake up. Experts agree that the way you wake up in the morning has a lot to do with your preliminary recall of dreams.

FACT

Many people claim that because they don't remember their dreams, they must not have them. But it's a proven fact: Everybody dreams! The truth is, you can remember your dreams if you really want to. The more you practice, the more you'll succeed.

The key is to set your alarm about fifteen to twenty-five minutes early. Immediately press snooze and go back to sleep. You'll have your most vivid dreams during this time, and you should be able to remember them.

When you wake up for the second or third time, don't open your eyes. Just lie there for a few minutes, retrieving your dream images. If nothing comes to mind, move into your favorite sleep position. This might trigger some dream fragment that you had. "For some (as yet) unknown reason," writes Patricia Garfield in her book, *Creative Dreaming,* "additional dream recall often comes when you move gently from one position and settle into another."

Go with It

It's also best to avoid making any value judgments and just to write down your dream as if it were someone else's story. Later, when you interpret it, you might find that what seemed silly or outrageous or insignificant has far deeper meaning than you initially realized. At first, you may remember only bits and pieces—an image, a word, or a face. But with practice, large parts of your last dream will come to you. These parts, in turn, may trigger a memory of the dream before it. Eventually, this process will become automatic and as fundamental as brushing your teeth.

Reference points can sometimes help in the recollection of a dream. Quite often, our own thoughts and beliefs about our dreams are the biggest obstacles to recalling them. A dream may be so unusual, for example, that we wake up certain that we'll remember it—only to forget it within minutes of opening our eyes.

Sometimes, we may think that a dream is too silly or embarrassing to write down, or that it's not worth remembering. Do yourself a favor, and write down everything! Things will make sense later.

Remembering Exercise

To help identify the areas you would like to better understand through your dreams, try brainstorming to define key elements of your life. Once you recognize them, you'll have a better idea about what to request from your dreaming self. Start by going over these areas:

- **Consider your relationships.** What are your most intimate relationships generally like? Do you feel good or bad about your relationship with your spouse, significant other, or others who are important in your life? Can you identify any patterns in your relationships with your parents, siblings, other family members, or friends? What would you change, if you could? In a perfect world, what would your relationships be like?

- **Think about your work and career.** Is there anything you would like to change about your work? How much money would you like to earn, ideally? What is your ideal job? How do you feel about your boss and other coworkers?

- **Analyze your health/physical self.** Do you like the way you look and feel? If you could change anything about the way you look, what would it be? How is your health at present? Do you have any chronic problems? Have you been to doctors recently? What is your ideal version of yourself?

- **Reflect on your spiritual life.** What do you believe in? How do you feel about your spiritual life? How would you like to develop, spiritually?

- **Explore other thoughts on your life in general.** In six months, where would you like to be? What about in a year, or in five years? Is there anywhere you're looking for guidance?

Keeping a Dream Diary

A dream journal is an integral part of dream exploration. A notebook will do, but a bound journal is even better. Many bookstores now sell bound journals with blank pages inside. Some are specifically designed as dream journals and include a place for the date and time of the dream, the dream itself, and your interpretation.

If your bedside writing isn't clear, transcribe your dreams later into a permanent notebook or onto a computer file. If you use a laptop, keep it near the bed and type in your dreams when you wake up. Keep the journal and a penlight handy on a nightstand, on the floor, or even under your pillow. If you jot down your dreams during the night or tape them, set aside a time to transcribe them into your journal.

Jog Your Mind

When you describe the dream, include as many details as possible. The interrogatives—who, what, where, when, and how—act as excellent guidelines when collecting details. Were you alone? If not, who was with you? Friends? Family? Strangers? What activity, if any, were you or the others engaged in? Was it day or night? Dark or light? Where were you? How did the dream "feel" to you? Was it familiar? Odd? Pleasant?

A dream journal is like a portal to another side of you, like the hole Alice fell through on her way to Wonderland. We have to remember our dreams in order to decipher and understand them!

How Bright Is Your Dream?

Author William Brugh Joy attributes particular significance to the lighting in a dream. If a dream is brilliantly colored and vivid, it reflects what he calls the "superconscious" state, the more evolved areas of consciousness. In Brugh Joy's own life, these types of dreams were nearly always prophetic. If the light in a dream is soft or shadowy, in sepia tones like an old photograph, or if it's in black and white, it emanates from less evolved areas of consciousness. Dreams that are even darker originate from the deep unconscious.

If you're not getting enough sleep, recalling your dreams is going to be much more difficult! Make sure you get the sleep you need, or exhaustion will interrupt your REM level of dreaming!

When you record a dream, one of the details you should include is how you feel when you wake up. What is your dominant emotion? Exhilaration?

THE EVERYTHING DREAMS BOOK

Fear? Sadness? Happiness? Sometimes, when you go over the dream later, you may remember more details. When attempting to recall dreams, also jot down whatever you were thinking about at the time you went to bed. It may provide a clue to the meaning of the dream.

You might not always remember the specifics of a dream. You'll only remember that you *have* dreamed. Then, later that day or several days later, something in your waking environment will trigger your memory of the dream. When this happens, be sure to note the event or experience that prompted the recollection—it may provide vital clues about the dream's meaning or significance.

Meditation and Dream Recall

Because meditation makes you aware of other states of mind, it can be another means of assisting your dream recall. When your conscious mind is quiet, symbols and images can flow more freely from the intuitive self. The technique you use depends entirely on what feels most natural to you. A walk in the woods or on the beach can serve just as well as ten or twenty minutes of sitting quietly after you wake up.

If despite all efforts you still can't remember your dreams, the problem might lie in your "invisible beliefs." Perhaps, in your heart of hearts, you're afraid to remember or to know what you dream about. Examine your beliefs honestly, and you might be able to uncover the obstacles to your remembering.

Help Yourself to Remember

The best time to suggest to yourself that you will remember your dreams is when you are in a slightly altered state, because your mind is more open. As you drift to sleep at night, tell yourself that you will recall the most important dream you have that night. If you have a specific question, tell yourself you'll remember the dream that answers that question. Repeat this request several times as you fall asleep. Make sure that your journal and a pen are within reach.

During quiet moments throughout the day, you should also remind yourself that you're going to remember your dreams. If you have particular questions, phrase them to yourself. Experiment with different methods until you find the one that works best for you. It helps if you sincerely believe you can receive answers through your dreams.

Facing Your Fears

We're constantly guided by our dreams, whether we remember them or not. Once you begin to recall your dreams with ease, it's possible to request dreams that will guide you and even give you hints of future events related to particular issues—relationships, health, career, or something else. Or you may simply request a dream that you will remember. Called "dream incubation," the act of asking for a dream, for whatever purpose, is the healthiest method of facing fears.

QUESTION?

How does dream incubation help you face your fears?
By admitting your trepidation and asking for a specific dream, you've already done more than half the work toward acknowledging and thus ridding yourself of a problem.

Dream incubation was popular in many ancient cultures, including Mesopotamia, Egypt, Rome, and Greece. People often traveled to temples dedicated to specific gods, where they spent the night in hopes of receiving a dream that would heal, illuminate, guide, and provide solutions. In some temples, priests were available to help people interpret their dreams. Professional dream-seekers were even hired by those too ill or otherwise unable to travel to the dream temples.

Today, there is no recognized dream temple for seekers, but anyone can practice dream incubation right at home. The first step in dream incubation is to figure out the areas of greatest concern so you know what to ask for. Then you must decide which of the areas you want to focus on.

Some experts recommend writing your request for a dream on a slip of paper and placing it on your nightstand or under your pillow. By making a ritual out of your request, you are formalizing it. Most of the time, however, a sincere need and intent will suffice. And, of course, you have to remember the dream. But even the need to remember the dream can be included when you ask.

In her book *Breakthrough Dreaming*, Gayle Delaney suggests that you jot down five or ten lines about your request in your dream journal. Afterward, condense this into a phrase or question that states what you want to know. As you fall asleep, repeat this phrase or question to yourself.

ALERT!

Even if you don't remember anything the first time you try dream incubation, keep at it! With persistence, you'll recall a dream that addresses your concern. Be aware, however, that sometimes your answers might not be what you bargained for.

You Snooze, You Win

Working out your problems. Facing your fears. Asking for guidance. Receiving an astral visit from a departed loved one. Sleeping and dreaming are good for you, and they can help you accomplish many things. Even your nightmares help you release anxiety or face problems your conscious mind can't deal with in a waking state. Your dreams may be complex and difficult to decipher, but they'll become a lot easier to figure out once you've completed this book.

Sometimes you have to recall an image from a dream to remember that you've dreamed at all, and what you remember may not make any sense. Other times, the dream is there the moment you become conscious, and you can capture it in full detail. But until you become proficient in dream recall, you will generally only remember pieces or fragments.

The benefits of dreaming are never lost, regardless of whether you remember your dreams. According to a spirit named Seth who apparently channeled a book called *The "Unknown" Reality* through dream researchers Jane Roberts and her husband, Robert Butts, "Your dreams . . . constantly alter the chemical balances within your body. A dream may be purposely experienced to provide an outlet of a kind that is missing in your daily life."

In this book, Seth outlines specific ways to familiarize yourself with dream landscapes:

- Before you fall asleep, imagine that you have a dream camera with you.
- Give yourself the suggestion that you'll take a dream snapshot of the most significant dream of the night.
- Keep at it. Practice.
- Once you begin to obtain results, write out a description of each scene you remember. Include descriptions of how you felt at the time of the dream and how you feel as you record it.
- Note the weather conditions in the dream. Is it raining? Is the sun shining? Is there a pervasive gloom? These weather conditions will tell you a great deal about the inner state of your psyche.

Seth also adds, "Your dream snapshots will show you the kind of experiences you are choosing from your inner reality." It's important to pay attention to these. Record everything you can, and then go through it carefully and methodically.

Using a camera to view your dreams is a cue to your inner self that you're serious about dream exploration. By using this tool in your dream exploration, you'll become more aware of all your interior landscapes. In other words, giving yourself the hint that you want more information about your dreams is very effective.

Dream Meditation: The Ultimate

It is easy to achieve a meditative state in order to better understand your dreams. Begin by meditating five minutes a day, preferably in the morning. Choose a spot where you won't be interrupted and the distractions are minimal. Sit on the floor in a cross-legged position or, if that's uncomfortable, in a chair. Make sure your back is straight and that both feet are on the floor. Don't wear shoes or constrictive clothing.

Start by firmly stating your intent: to remember a dream or to expand on one that you recall only in fragments. Take several long, slow breaths through your nostrils. Watch your breath and let go of your thoughts. Inhale slowly through the nostrils, holding your breath—without tension—and count to seven. Slowly exhale with the tip of your tongue touching the roof of your mouth. Start over again and repeat this ten times.

Before yoga and Pilates were popular in the West, Edgar Cayce always said that he entered a meditative state through alternate nostril breathing: inhaling through one nostril, exhaling through the other, repeating, and then changing nostrils.

Relax your body, starting either with the top of your head or the tips of your toes. Feel all the tension being released from each part. Quiet your mind by turning off all your internal dialogue. Whenever you start thinking about something in general, gently release your thoughts and force yourself to return to a meditative state. Wait for an image or impression to come to mind. This will feel different than a thought. You may have a sense that it's a message from "elsewhere," a higher part of yourself. If this feels weird, ignore the rationalization and go with it.

You can also visualize yourself descending stairs or an elevator, and then going to a private movie theater. Focus on the screen and let go of your thoughts. Soon an image may appear relating to your concern.

Never meditate while you're lying in bed—you may fall asleep! Also, try to meditate on an empty or nearly empty stomach. You'll have a clearer head and you won't feel as groggy. Meditation requires focus.

Once you can meditate for five minutes, increase the time to fifteen or twenty. However, don't feel as if you have to stick to a particular time limit. In meditating to recall a dream, you'll probably feel more relaxed and centered, and you'll be able to remember dreams more easily. If you continue to have trouble, ask yourself before meditating why you're experiencing difficulty. The answer should come to you. We each have an inner voice that's useful to us. Use it.

Chapter 4

The Dream Interview

There are many steps in the process of dream analysis. Remembering your dreams is the first step. Figuring out what they mean is next. You have to understand how dreams work and how to obtain the important information from them. In this chapter, discover a foolproof method to getting the most from your nighttime visions.

How It Works

It's night. You're dreaming. You wake up but have no idea what that bear in the woods meant. You search and search your brain, or maybe you ask everyone you know, "What do *you* think?" It's not easy. During the day, we have our own problems, so we tend to dismiss our dreams or forget them easily. But understanding dreams is the first step to understanding your life. Through analyzing dreams, you can get a glimpse of your real hopes, fears, barriers, and wishes.

Thousands of years ago, the world sat up and took notice of dreams. Wars were predicted. Future kings were named. Dreams were reveled in and appreciated. However, as technology and modernization took hold across the globe, dream importance was diminished and dream interpretation was pooh-poohed. Dreams still hold meaningful significance, but dream study has unfortunately all but lost its place.

Thankfully, there are methods to be used. The dream interview works because it helps you to pay attention to your innermost thoughts. Many times, we don't want to deal with our feelings. We hide them and push them back. This is natural. Inevitably, though, they find their way into our dreams. The interview technique forces you to come clean. By gently probing your thoughts and the symbols that emerge, you're making a conscious effort to understand your deepest, darkest wishes and fears.

FACT

"I was not looking for my dreams to interpret my life, but rather for my life to interpret my dreams" (Susan Sontag, *The Benefactor*). First published in 1963, Sontag's novel is written in the form of memoirs. The main character is a man named Hippolyte who, after time, has trouble distinguishing real life from his dreams.

If the meaning of a dream continues to evade you, approach the analysis as if you were conducting an interview. Therapists use the interview technique to help patients uncover dream meanings. You don't need a therapist to try the dream interview technique. A trusted friend or a spouse can act as your interviewer, or you can do it yourself.

The Method

The first step in this technique is to name your dream. This will help you to distinguish the dream in your journal, and it might also help you to pinpoint a major image or symbol. The interviewer—whether it's a friend or yourself—must have the goal of finding the answers to the dreamer's questions about the dream. The dreamer should write out the dream so that you (as the interviewer) have it in front of you. Before you begin the interview, underline the words or images that strike you. Ask the dreamer to do the same. Use these words as triggers during your interview. Record everything.

Be Intuitive

If the dreamer goes off on a tangent, follow it. Don't try to push the dreamer back into the parameters you have defined for the interview. This is *her* dream, so follow the tangent and see where it leads. If the dreamer suddenly stops or seems uncomfortable with what she is saying, gently probe to discover her feelings. Strong emotions are often clues to the real heart of a dream.

In your dream interview, keep in mind that dreamer and interviewer are both explorers. Maintain your curiosity, your excitement, and your sense of adventure. And by all means, keep the mood playful!

Encourage Self-Interviewing

When conducting a dream interview, suggest that the dreamer interview himself in the future. Self-interviewing is a playful technique in which the dreamer alternately plays both roles. If you decide to interview yourself, compose your questions beforehand. If you go off on tangents, follow them. If you feel a strong emotion while writing your answers, then pause and explore the emotion. Are you angry? Fearful? Exuberant? Why?

Value Your Interview

Remember that your feelings about your dreams are important. It is *your* emotion about *your* dream—an intimate peek at your unconscious self. Even if you don't "solve" the mystery of a particular dream, you can still learn a lot from your responses during the interview.

The Senoi Tribe

Among the Senoi, a primitive tribe in the mountainous jungles of Malaysia, dream sharing is the pivot around which the rest of life revolves. According to researchers, each day begins with the members of the family, including children, sharing their dreams from the night before. Family members are asked about how they behaved in their dreams, and suggestions are given for correcting behavior and attitude in future dreams. Then the group suggests actions based on the events in the dreams.

Once the family dream-sharing is finished, the village council meets and the serious dream business begins. With each dream that's reported and discussed, the tribe's picture of itself becomes clearer. Symbols are analyzed, and each council member gives his opinion. People in the tribe who agree on the meaning of a particular dream adopt it as a group project.

"The Senoi people determine most activities of daily life from the interpretations and decisions that arise out of their council discussions," writes Patricia Garfield in *Creative Dreaming*. The dream actions of the Senoi are carried out, in positive form, in waking life. If, for instance, one person dreams that he's hostile toward another member of the tribe, then in his waking life he goes out of his way to be amicable.

Joy's Use of the Senoi Dream Practice

In his conference workshops, William Brugh Joy, author of *Joys Way,* encourages dream sharing. But since this practice isn't typical in Western culture, it can be a disconcerting experience for some people. Judith Orloff, who attended one of Brugh Joy's conferences and writes about it in *Second Sight,* initially felt intimidated. Out of a bunch of strangers, Brugh

Joy chose her to be the first person in the group to share a dream from the previous night.

FACT

The Senoi don't criticize or condemn dream actions. Instead, they suggest alternative behaviors. Any negative aspect is to be transformed. Fear is transmuted into courage. Danger is avoided, pleasure is harnessed, and a positive outcome is achieved.

Orloff couldn't remember any dreams from the night before, so she related a recent dream that had puzzled her. Brugh Joy proceeded to interpret the dream, and by the end, Orloff felt as if she'd been stripped naked. She was mortified. By the next morning, she was so angry she considered leaving the conference. She soon realized, though, that her anger meant Brugh Joy had touched a nerve and she had to take a closer look at everything he'd said. Her experience is cautionary. It's far more comfortable to share dreams with people you know and trust. On the other hand, a knowledgeable outsider such as Brugh Joy may offer a concise interpretation that you, or someone close to you, might not suggest.

Senoi Study

The British anthropologist H. D. "Pat" Noone first gathered information about the Senoi culture for his doctoral dissertation at Cambridge in 1939. Noone's brother Richard and Dennis Holman wrote *In Search of the Dream People,* which was published in 1972. In the years since, certain researchers have claimed that the Senoi culture described by Noone never existed as depicted. The issue is still being debated. But as Jill Morris notes in *The Dream Workbook,* "There is no dispute over the effectiveness of the techniques themselves."

Using the Dream Interview

The dream interview will always help you uncover how you truly feel. You have to record the dream and then highlight the basics. Included in this section are all the steps toward giving the dream interview and analyzing it.

Remember to always name your dream. We'll call the following dream "Valet Parking":

It's night. I'm in front of a restaurant, wearing a uniform. A car pulls up, I open the doors, and the passengers get out. I realize I'm a valet parking attendant. I slide behind the steering wheel and drive the car out into the lot to park it.

The lot is large, crowded with vehicles. I have to park at the far end, where there are a few empty spots. It's a long walk back to the front of the restaurant, and I feel vaguely depressed that I'm doing this sort of work. When I reach the front of the building, a wolf is trotting along beside me, a white wolf. The restaurant is gone and in its place is a library. I'm now wearing street clothes instead of a uniform. I go inside and the wolf accompanies me. No one objects to the wolf's presence.

I'm not sure why I've come to the library; I can't seem to remember. So I decide to check the new fiction shelf for something good to read. I find all of my books on the shelf, even the ones that are now out of print. I'm elated! I also find a book with my name on it that doesn't have a title, just a tremendous spiral on the front.

If a man dreams of a wolf, it sometimes refers to a crush he has on a particular woman and his desire to aggressively pursue her—as in the story of Little Red Riding Hood.

This dreamer, Ben, was a forty-eight-year-old suspense writer who was having money problems at the time of this dream. He was working on a novel that was quite different from his previous books. But since he was writing it on speculation, he needed other writing projects to pay the bills until the novel sold. He'd taken on a ghostwriting project, which paid well but took him away from his novel.

Highlighting the Basics

Once Ben had recorded the dream in his journal, he went through it and highlighted the most important items; that is, the setting, people, emotions, animals, major objects or symbols, and major actions. This is an important step. The technique was developed by dream therapist Gayle Delaney and her partner, Loma Flowers, directors of the Delaney and Flowers Center for the Study of Dreams. Ben listed the following:

- **Setting:** Outside restaurant, library, crowded parking lot
- **Time:** Night
- **People:** Me and other people whose faces are indistinct
- **Emotions:** Vague depression, elation
- **Animals:** White wolf
- **Major objects or symbols:** Cars, books, uniform and street clothes, spiral
- **Major action:** Parking cars, entering library, perusing new fiction shelf

Ben asked his wife to be the interviewer, and she worked from this list to devise questions. When doing this, Delaney recommends that you, the dreamer, pretend the interviewer is from another planet. In other words, get detailed. Make believe you don't know the person at all. This urges you, the dreamer, to give more detailed answers to the questions.

Ben also used a tape recorder to record the interview. He said it would be easier to write everything down, but since he writes for a living, he wanted to try a different format in the hopes that more information would turn up.

Some dream experts suggest recording at least 150 dreams and then looking for patterns and similarities. Chances are, you'll find many recurring themes and images to give you a clue into your hidden problems!

Ben's Interview: An Example

What are your dominant feelings in the dream?

Depression in the beginning—a kind of resignation to menial work as a valet parking lot attendant. I hate wearing the uniform. It smacks of regimentation.

Is there anything familiar about the feelings of depression in this dream?

No.

What sort of feelings does the restaurant elicit for you?

No feelings, really, just an awareness that it's associated with eating, food, that kind of thing. I think it represents sustenance.

How do you feel about the crowded parking lot?

Irritated that I have to drive so far to find a parking space.

In general, what did the cars look like?

I didn't notice. Nothing stood out about them. There were just a lot of them.

What do you think the parking lot represents?

The publishing business as it exists now has vastly changed since the 1980s. It's becoming more and more difficult to get published—that is, to find a parking space. These projects I've taken on are the equivalent of being a valet parking attendant.

In other words, I'm parking other people's cars—doing other people's projects—and that's why none of the cars stood out in any way. The restaurant symbolizes paying bills and putting food on the table as a result of these other projects.

How do you feel about the white wolf?

Delighted; surprised to see it trotting along beside me. I've always had an affinity for wolves. In a sense, they're my guardian spirits.

It's interesting that the white wolf appears at your side on your way back to the restaurant, which has turned into a library. What do you think that means?

The appearance of the wolf seems to be a signal that things in the dream landscape are about to change—and then they do. The restaurant is suddenly a library. Maybe it means things in my waking life are about to change, too.

QUESTION?

Does a recurring animal in my dreams have any significance?
Yes! Each of us has an animal spirit guide. If you have a real affinity for one particular animal, chances are that this is your helper while you sleep.

What do libraries represent to you?

Books. Knowledge. Pleasure. In my waking life, the new fiction shelf is usually my first stop at the library. I didn't expect to see all my books there, even the ones that have gone out of print.

What do you think that means?

Maybe that some of my older books will be in print again. I was elated to find all the books on that shelf.

What do you feel about the spiral symbol on the untitled book?

I think it represents the novel I've been working on between other projects. One of the titles I've been considering is *Spiral*.

Longhand Answers

Once you decide on your interviewer, offer him your list so he can devise questions to ask you. Try to give as much detail in your answers as possible, and capture all your responses, especially at first. You never know where the important information or the heart of the matter lies. Be sure to either use a tape recorder or take good notes so you can review the information later. Once you become proficient at dream interpretation, the interview technique will become second nature.

Veronica Tonay, a psychotherapist and lecturer at the University of California at Santa Cruz, warns not to put too much stock in any one dream. "Usually a series of dreams is more reliable for picking out themes," says Tonay. "You want to look for what is common in the dreams, such as something always blocking your way or threatening your chance to succeed. Then you should uncover how you are coping with this threat. What can you learn from what you are doing or not doing in the dream?"

Do I always have to write down everything?
No. You won't have to write out the entire interview or record it once you get good at the technique. But you might still want to do so with more complex dreams.

Children's Stories

Children's dreams often hold clues to the same anxieties and insecurities that plague their parents. Some kids will talk spontaneously about their dreams; other kids might have to be prodded. But one fact holds true for all kids: If they live in households where dream sharing is simply part of the family routine, they'll be more apt to remember and relate their dreams.

It's so important to ask your children about their dreams! Gently prod them into telling you how they feel about what goes on in their nighttime fantasies. You'll get real insight into how your children are developing.

Can you figure out what the next dream was telling the dreamer and her mother? The title of this dream is "Alligator":

Mommy and I are on a beach. It's hot. The sand burns my feet. The ocean is calm, real pretty. Mommy and I are going to go swimming. But I look back and see an alligator chasing us. It's coming so fast and I'm scared. I'm screaming. I don't want to be eaten up. We run and run, but the alligator comes faster and faster. Then the lifeguard kills it.

The dreamer was Jenny, a seven-year-old girl who lived in Florida. Her mother, Helen, had been divorced for a year or so from Jenny's father, who was considerably older. Jenny spent most weekends with her dad, and he and her mother were on friendly terms. Jenny appeared to have adjusted to the divorce.

Since Helen encourages her to share her dreams, "Alligator" was casually related over breakfast one morning. Helen's initial reaction was that it was a positive dream, but she wanted to explore it to be sure. Although she'd never heard of an interview technique with dreams, that's basically what she carried out right then, as she usually does with her daughter's dreams. The spontaneity of such an exchange could be even more important than the dream itself.

FACT

Through sharing their dreams, children learn that they are a very personal source of information. This can be good for self-esteem. They also learn that it's natural to remember, share, and pay attention to them.

It's important to interpret your dreams according to the circumstances of your own life. Always record the themes, metaphors, and symbols you gather from your dreams. Helen was able to do this with her daughter's dream about the alligator within seconds; she intuitively identified the metaphors and symbols based on knowledge of her daughter and their collective situation:

- **Ocean:** Represents Jenny's emotions. The fact that the ocean is calm indicates there aren't any upheavals inside Jenny right now.
- **Beach:** Represents the shore of their new world. Jenny feels comfortable in this new world until she looks back and sees the alligator. The act of looking back may indicate that in the past, she felt threatened by the move, the separation, and the divorce.
- **Alligator:** The threat. It chases Jenny and Helen along the "shore of their new life." But it doesn't catch them—doesn't eat them up.

- **Lifeguard:** He "guards life" by killing the threat. Jenny doesn't confront the alligator herself, but an adult male does it for her. Helen felt this indicated Jenny's sense of security about the role her father now plays in her life. She also realized she needed to nurture Jenny's self-reliance, so that she didn't always depend on an adult to fix things for her.

Dream Protectors

Sharing dreams with your children and others close to you not only helps you spot potential trouble areas, it also creates a special dimension to your relationship. One four-year-old, an only child named Megan, had a series of nightmares in which she was being chased by huge tigers, ugly monkeys, and aliens. For weeks she woke up crying every night and crawled into her parents' bed because she was afraid to stay alone in her room.

Children may start having nightmares after the age of two. Try to help even a very young child discuss and work through the fears that may be causing the nightmares. Shielding them from violent behavior—television or even parents fighting—will also help.

Her parents told her the usual things. The creatures and the aliens weren't real. They couldn't hurt her, and it was just a dream. But to Megan, the dreams *were* real. Megan's parents, who were redecorating the house at the time, put up a strip of unicorn wallpaper in her room. She loved the unicorns. She wanted to know all about them and to see one at the zoo. Her parents suddenly realized they'd found the answer to the nightmare problem. They suggested that the next time she had a bad dream, she should call on a unicorn to protect her from whatever was chasing her.

One morning at breakfast, Megan proudly announced that the night before she'd seen a unicorn in her nightmare. She'd called to it and the unicorn had galloped over. She'd climbed onto its back and it had flown her away. Now Megan is seven and has learned to create a variety of guardian creatures in nightmares. She is aware that her dream life is important, even if she doesn't yet know why.

Ask yourself, your child, or other important people in your life the following questions. Also see the section titled "Animals as Guides" in Chapter 14.

- What animal do you feel closest to?
- Has this animal appeared in any of your dreams?
- What were the dreams with the animal concerning?
- Were there other symbols in the dream?
- How did the animal help you, or what did it do in the dream?
- How can you apply what the animal did in your dream to your waking life?

Chapter 5

Healing Dreams

Nobody can argue that dreaming isn't good for you. But just how good for you is it? Dreams are where we work out and solve problems. Release dreams happen solely for that purpose. But studies have also shown that suggestions from the subconscious that happen in dreams can also heal you—even physically. In this chapter, find out how both methods work.

Snoozing Therapy

Imagine a world where, if you were sick, you could find a cure for your body based on what was going on in your mind. It makes sense. Your healer would work with you personally to understand the source of your disease. He or she would intuitively probe your beliefs about yourself and would help you to identify general and specific patterns in your unconscious. Herbs, body work, special foods, and visualization techniques would be recommended. The healer might also recommend intense dream work to galvanize the body's defenses.

True-Life Healing

Judith Orloff has studied healing dreams. One extraordinary case study she found was that of a female friend who had a lipoma, a fatty tumor, at the base of her spine. It was causing her considerable pain, but she was reluctant to undergo surgery. Instead, this friend dreamed that she inserted a three-foot syringe into her neck and worked it down her spine to the lipoma. In the dream, she then drained the lipoma.

Dream researchers say that people can have prognostic dreams—dreams that lead to a remedy for an illness—or pathogenic dreams—dreams that can actually cause sickness. Most experts say that the latter are extremely rare.

When she awoke, she remembered the dream. Immediately, she checked for the lipoma, feeling around her lower back. She couldn't find it. Shortly afterward, her doctor confirmed that the lipoma was, in fact, gone. The woman's recollection of the dream strengthened her belief in the power of dreams to heal. The experience convinced Judith Orloff as well.

Health in Dreams

The irony is you don't have to remember a healing dream to benefit from the effects. As William Brugh Joy, author of *Joys Way*, writes, "If we recognize that we are much more than we understand at the outer levels of consciousness, then we can see that the forces experienced in dreams may reflect healing and balancing processes that never reach the outer levels of our awareness, yet are profoundly important to the overall Beingness."

Also, it's important to pay attention to how you feel in a dream. Are you feeling rundown or alive and sprightly? Your subconscious probably knows before you do if something is wrong. It's always a good idea to get a checkup if you're feeling ill in your dreams. That is, of course, unless alcohol or nicotine enters the equation. Alcohol can sometimes influence your dreams; your body might react to impending hangovers by putting the information out into your dream world.

Your Body's Defense

Dr. William A. McGarey, director of the Association for Research and Enlightenment in Phoenix, points out an example of a woman who reported that she had the same dream on two successive nights in which she blurted out, "I have MS." McGarey researched the early symptoms of multiple sclerosis. "We took measures to stop it from developing," he says. "She is presently doing quite well."

FACT

Asclepius, the son of Apollo in Greek mythology, was known as the God of Healing. Because he held serpents sacred, people believed that if they dreamed of snakes, Asclepius himself had come to heal them.

McGarey's next example featured a dreamer named Toni, a woman who had requested a guidance dream about her parents' health problems. At the time, Toni had recently developed a humming in her left ear, but she wasn't thinking about it when she requested a dream concerning her parents.

Dream Meets Reality

This is Toni's dream. It's called "Healing":

I'm with a friend who is studying alternative health and I'm telling her about the annoying humming in my ear. She asks if I've ever heard of . . . a word I couldn't remember when I woke. I reply that I've never heard of this therapy, so she shows me how it works.

She takes a long object that resembles a stick of incense and inserts it into my left ear. Then she rolls it gently between her fingers and the stick slips in deeper and deeper. I hear a popping sound, then a liquid seeps out, a milky liquid. When I wake, the humming in my ear is gone.

Getting Physical

Toni felt the dream's message was twofold. It confirmed her belief that healing dreams were possible, and it indicated that her parents might be helped through alternative therapies. On the surface, these other therapies could seem absurd. Those who've seen them work, however, believe otherwise.

QUESTION?

Do dreams in which you're ill mean that you'll get sick in real life?
No, not necessarily. In fact, illness can symbolize how you feel mentally. Maybe you feel guilty or regret not doing something. Sometimes you feel sick in dreams when you don't feel good about what you're accomplishing in waking life.

It's interesting to note that the humming in Toni's ear returned a day after the dream, though to a lesser degree. According to the doctor, this was because of the equalizing pressure between the inner and outer ear, a process similar to what happens when taking off or landing in an airplane. But the root of the problem, Toni admitted, probably had to do with her need to find balance in her life—to "equalize" the various demands on her time.

Symbols and Signs

Hippocrates, the ancient Greek physician, believed that the body sensed the coming of disease and often warned the dreamer about it. He said the appearance of the sun, moon, or stars in a dream symbolized the dreamer's organic state. If the dream stars glowed brightly, it meant the body was functioning as it should. However, if the stars seemed dim or cloudy, or if some cosmic disaster occurred in the dream, it indicated that disease was forming somewhere in the body.

Hippocrates theorized that if such symbols were a portent of disease, then other symbols could be therapeutic. Hippocrates also believed that dreams were the one place where gods and humans could meet—for real. He said that if gods came to you in your dreams, they could alleviate suffering and heal illness.

Modern-day renowned medium and psychic Sylvia Browne also believes in visits from God or departed loved ones: "We know that while we sleep there's . . . no limit to where we can travel, from the far reaches of the universe to the intimate closeness of The Other Side."

Association with Symbols

Once you begin working with your dreams, you become more attuned to yourself and to your environment. Even if you can't recall your dreams at first, or you only remember them in bits and pieces, you may find yourself remembering a particular image during the day. Sometimes a conversation or a situation may trigger your recall.

When you start to recall symbols, try to associate them with something in your life. When you hit on something, associate that with something else, working your way back through your life until something clicks. Freud was the first to popularize this method of association.

The Power of Suggestion

When Louise Hay, author of *You Can Heal Your Life,* was diagnosed with cancer, her physician wanted to perform a hysterectomy as soon as possible. Hay resisted. She told him she wanted some time to work on the problem herself.

She completely revamped the externals in her life—nutrition, exercise, and work schedule. She then began to work with her beliefs through visualization, affirmations, and prayer. She created mental stages on which she spoke to the various people in her past who had hurt her deeply, and she saw herself forgiving them. She also experienced self-forgiveness by learning to love herself. Within six months, miraculously, her cancer was in remission.

One of Hay's most valuable contributions to alternative-healing literature is a list of physical ailments and diseases and their probable emotional cause. She also includes affirmations to help reverse the emotional patterns that cause them.

Your dreams reflect what's going on in your body; your body reflects the texture of your dreams. The inner is a reflection of the outer. This is just one important reason you need to pay attention to your dreams.

Visualization Techniques

Dr. Carl Simonton pioneered a program for treatment of cancer patients combining visualization and relaxation techniques. His first attempt was with a sixty-one-year-old man who had throat cancer, for whom conventional therapies had failed. The man had been given a 10-percent chance of survival.

Simonton's treatment consisted of mental exercises repeated three times a day for seven weeks. First, the patient was to spend several minutes silently repeating the word "Relax," while relaxing the muscles in his throat, jaw, and around his eyes. Next, he was told to visualize something pleasurable for a minute and a half. Then he was to replace that image with a mental picture of how he imagined his tumor looked.

Once he was able to hold a vivid mental picture of the tumor, he was supposed to imagine particles of radiation bombarding it. The last step was to visualize white blood cells clearing away the cells killed by the radiation. At the end of the seven weeks, the tumor's growth had been arrested and the patient was discharged.

Helping Yourself

Dream experts say that you can actually help yourself with your dreams. The first step in using your dreams for healing is to accept that it's possible to induce a dream—any dream. You must believe that before you start. Practice. At first, it will seem impossible, and then, slowly, it will come.

Belief in something is 90 percent of the battle. It's paramount. If you believe that something can happen and trust the world of possibility, you are already on your way to achieving something. Focus and think positively!

Before actually attempting to induce a healing dream, find a quiet spot where you won't be interrupted. A shady spot in your backyard might do, or a secluded place on a beach or in your own bedroom. As you settle down, begin by relaxing your body. One effective relaxation technique is to consciously relax muscles from your head to your toes. Feel the tension drain out through the soles of your feet. Focus on the warmth of the sunlight (outside) or the scent of the air.

Once you're fully relaxed, you're ready for the next step. Concentrate on a clear idea of the dream you want to have. The concentration may be enhanced by the repetition of a relevant word or phrase. If you choose a phrase, be careful how you word it. Keep it positive. Instead of saying "My tumor is gone," for example, say, "I am healed." Use all your positive energy.

Believing Is Key

In *Creative Dreaming*, Patricia Garfield points out another way to induce a dream. She says to "visualize the desired dream as though it's happening." This is actually no different than a visualization of something you want to happen in a fully conscious state. The same principles apply.

Believe, intend, imagine, and charge the visualization with as many positive emotions as you can muster. Keep the visualization in the present rather than in some dim future. Believe philosopher William James, who said that the unconscious manifests any image held in the mind and backed by faith. Or take Judith Orloff's advice: "Allow yourself to believe . . . attend to your dreams . . . When you dream, you merge with a benevolent intelligence that touches you and, in some special circumstances, even heals."

If a healing dream doesn't come to you the first time you try it, keep at it. Share the process with someone you trust—a spouse, sibling, parent, friend, son, or daughter. By sharing, you make it even more real.

Dream Therapists: The Professionals

If you're trying to heal yourself of a serious ailment, you might consider working with a qualified dream therapist. When one of Judith Orloff's patients tried to commit suicide, she was forced to re-evaluate the way she practiced psychiatry. She knew she needed to integrate her psychic abilities into her medical practice, but she didn't know how to do it or where to start.

Perhaps because her need was so great and she was open to synchronicity, she found what she needed: A friend told her about Brugh Joy's two-week retreat. "Working with Brugh," she writes, "I . . . got a firsthand demonstration of how the psychic and the medical could be blended in a positive way."

Orloff's patient was a young woman who had been diagnosed with leukemia three years earlier. Her chemotherapy wasn't working, and her last hope from conventional medicine was a bone marrow transplant. She began Brugh Joy's dream therapy with an exhaustive interview that started with her medical history and finished with her psychological makeup. "Guided by intuition, he uncovered areas in Debbie that might have taken years to emerge in traditional psychotherapy," Orloff writes.

FACT

Max Wertheimer (1880–1943) founded Gestalt psychology. Basically, his theories said that therapy should account for the overall, not the individual parts. If you apply that to dreams, you should note the general meaning and message of a dream, not pick it apart for each clue.

Halfway through the interview, Brugh Joy suddenly asked Debbie if she had ever lost a child. The young woman paled and admitted that, twenty years before, she'd had a stillbirth. The experience was so painful she'd blocked it out. "Brugh saw, in this, the essence of a mind-body link; that there was a strong emotional component to Debbie's illness. Over the next hour, I watched him deftly uncover a lifelong pattern of losses for which she had never grieved . . ."

The therapist's value lies in the objective insight provided. But if you prefer to work on your own or with a spouse or trusted friend, then the interview technique in Chapter 4 will provide an objective base. When you recall a healing dream, especially one that has come to you without induction, you and your interviewer should pay special attention to it. It's the voice of your inner, wiser self clamoring to be heard.

Working It Out

Remember that it's possible to act as your own interviewer. To help you do this successfully, Gayle Delaney suggests that you list particular questions about a dream. For example, what is the location of the dream and your feeling about it? Are there colors in the dream, and if so, what do they mean to you? Are there common objects used for unusual purposes, and if so, what are they? Jot each one of your questions on a cue card. Later, you can use the cards as an interviewer might—to extract the meaning of the dream.

Go back to the beginning of this chapter. Read through the young woman Toni's dream again. Then, acting as though you are the interviewer, create a list of questions for yourself. Compare these questions with those in the following interview with Toni, in which her husband acts as the interviewer:

One of the things missing from this dream is a specific location. Do you recall where the dream took place?

Now that you've brought it up, yes, I think I remember a room. We were in a room with pale pink walls. There was comfortable furniture around, but I was lying on a massage table, my head elevated slightly on a pillow. I don't remember anything else about the room.

Was there a window?

I don't remember one. It's as if I was supposed to focus only on the procedure.

You described the object your friend used as resembling a stick of incense. Can you describe it in more detail?

It was twelve to eighteen inches long. The end that my friend rolled between her fingers was thinner than a pencil, but it gradually thickened, just like a stick of incense does.

Do you know what color it was?

A rich, dark brown, like chocolate.

What does the word "incense" mean to you?

It means . . . oh, good point. I see what you're getting at. I completely overlooked that in my interpretation. What am I incensed about, right? What is it that has made me so angry I don't want to hear about it?

Exactly. It's definitely a metaphor, a play on words.

I don't know what I'm angry about. Maybe it's just things with my parents in general. It infuriates me that two people who have taken such good care of themselves have ended up in a health crisis. I don't understand everything that's behind it.

What significance, if any, do you think there is about this humming occurring in your left ear?

I'm 90 percent deaf in that ear. The humming has made me think a lot about the accident that caused the deafness. It was from a fractured skull, when I was five, and it is supposedly irreversible. But lately I've been wondering if it can be healed.

When your friend began inserting the stick in your ear, how did you feel about it?

Very uneasy. I nearly told her to forget it. But I sensed she knew what she was doing. It struck me later that my unconscious created the ideal figure to act as the healer. If a typical physician in a white lab coat had attempted the procedure, I would have walked out. But I trusted her and associate her with the healing arts and alternative medicine.

You describe a milky liquid that comes out of your ear. Was there any kind of noise associated with this? Anything that indicated a blockage had been punctured?

A soft popping sound. It got my attention.

Was there any pain?

None. Absolutely none.

The liquid was white, like milk. What do you associate with that color?

Understanding. It's the amalgam of all the other colors in the spectrum.

Do you have any idea what time of night you had this dream?

Morning. I woke at seven, realized I didn't have to get up, then remembered I hadn't gotten the dream I'd requested and felt disappointed. Then I went back to sleep and had the dream.

As a result of the interview, Toni remembered more details of the dream. Thus, her insight deepened, and that, really, is the ultimate goal for all dream work. The key is to believe and to ask for healing and guidance before you go to sleep, as Toni did. Toni believed it was possible to heal herself and asked for a healing dream—and it worked!

Chapter 6

Dreams of Death and Sex

Dreaming of death hardly means you or someone you dreamed about is going to die. Likewise, dreaming of having sex with a partner doesn't necessarily mean that you will or even that you truly want to. In this chapter, find out the truth about these two common release dreams.

Don't Be Afraid

You wake up in a sweat. In your dream, you were running from a mugger or robbers or even the devil himself. And you were just about to die. "Thank goodness I woke up!" you think. You wipe your brow and remember that old wives' tale that if you die in your dream, you also die in real life. What blarney! Don't believe it. Sometimes people actually do die in their dreams, dream of their own funerals, or even view themselves dead from above. But every one of these dreamers has lived to tell about it.

FACT

Dreaming about the devil doesn't signify evil. Most of the time, the devil means marriage. If you're married, the devil usually represents your other half. Examine how you feel toward the devil in the dream, and you'll understand how you feel about your partner.

True, in very rare situations, a person could dream of his own death and know it was going to happen. But one thing must be understood. In dreams, there is no time or space. A person can have visits from a departed loved one, for example, who's trying to get him assimilated to the idea of dying. But the person on the other side has no concept of time—death might be five or ten or twenty or thirty years away. Most likely, if it's a prophetic dream—in order and in vivid color—it's not referring to anything that can happen soon.

It's All About You

Only rarely do death dreams portend an actual physical death. In the following dream, which deals with the living and the dead, the dream is more about the woman's future life than her death. Laura, a forty-five-year-old woman, had asked for a dream to confirm that things in her life were "clicking along" as they should be. Laura had the following dream, called "Community Theater":

I'm in a barn-like structure, perhaps a community theater. Both the living and the dead are here, as though this is some sort of meeting place between worlds or dimensions. A woman informs me that by punching in my birth date information, I can find out anything about myself or my life that I need to know.

There are people here who travel about in both the world of the living and the world of the dead. One such woman tells me that one day, the "glass" between the borders of life and death will be so clear that you'll be able to "see" through it.

The dream ends with a fire drill. My former headmistress sticks her head in and orders everyone to get outside.

The dreamer was an amateur astrologer, so the birth date reference made sense to her. She interpreted it as a message to do a progressed astrological chart on herself for the coming year. She also felt this was a clear message from her unconscious that everything she needed to know was available to her in the dream state; all she had to do was ask. It reassured her that her unconscious was always accessible and that she already possessed tools in her waking life to clarify issues and questions.

The akashic record is a hall of records on the Other Side that has every point in history written down. Some experts say that déjà vu is just your soul recognizing life moments you knew were supposed to happen from reading your record beforehand.

When Laura related the dream to her husband, he told her that the birth date reference sounded like a computerized akashic record, the "cosmic" records that seer Edgar Cayce said he accessed during his readings. The dreamer felt that the "glass" that separated the living and the dead was the dream state. The fire drill at the end of the dream was literally a wake-up call, prodding her to consciousness so that she would record the dream.

Death Means Change (Not Death)

Death is the ultimate metamorphosis, the passage from one state of being to another. In the tarot, for example, the Death card doesn't mean death. It means transformation—a major change that hurls you from one way of life to another. In a dream, death usually means the same thing. "Ninety-nine percent of the time, dreams about death are simply metaphors for major changes happening in your relationships, work, or personality," writes Stase Michaels in *The Bedside Guide to Dreams*.

When you have a death dream, you should ask yourself whether an area of your life is undergoing transformation. Are you in the middle of a divorce? About to have a baby? About to get married? Are you considering a career change? Any of these big life decisions can prompt a death dream.

Often, dreams about death involve other symbols. A car, for instance, is a perfect dream metaphor for where you're going in life and how the journey is unfolding. For a sixteen-year-old girl, a death dream involving a car was a result of her family's recent move from the state where she'd been born and raised. For a forty-eight-year-old accountant, a dream about death was caused by a major job transition from a large firm to self-employment.

Relationship Dream

In the next dream, the death symbolism pointed to a young man's changing feelings about his girlfriend. The name of this dream is "Carnival":

Jan and I are at the carnival that's rolled into town. It was her idea to go and she's like a kid, eating cotton candy, running from ride to ride, insistent that I go with her. I don't like carnivals and wish we could leave. She wants to go on the roller coaster; I don't. We argue out there in front of everyone and I'm totally embarrassed. Just to keep her quiet, I relent and go on to the roller coaster with her.

I hate the roller coaster, everyone screaming, Jan clutching my arm and shrieking like a five-year-old. As our car speeds down one of the hills in the track, Jan's seat restraint suddenly snaps open and she's hurled out of the car. I see her shooting like a missile through the air and know it's going to kill her. I feel relieved.

When I woke up, I was shocked at my lack of emotion and couldn't go back to sleep. But the longer I lay there, the clearer it became that she and I no longer enjoyed the same things, that she was immature, and that for me the relationship was already over. Ending it was merely a formality.

Prophetic Dream: A Rare Example

While speaking at the Miami Book Fair one year, author Anne Rice told the heartbreaking story of how she had come to write *Interview with the Vampire*.

She dreamed that her young daughter was dying of a blood disease. Shortly afterward, the girl was diagnosed with leukemia. In the aftermath of her daughter's death, Rice wrote *Interview with the Vampire* in a feverish frenzy in just three weeks, as though it were a kind of purging. It's probably no coincidence that blood is the theme of the book.

In the next dream, a hillside is the setting for a glimpse of a young man's death. This dream is called "The Hillside":

John and I are sitting on a grassy hillside overlooking a valley. I'm not real sure what we're doing here or how we came to be here, but that doesn't seem to matter in the dream. We're talking about people we knew in college and the crazy things we did. Suddenly he turns to me and says, "It's time for me to move on. But don't worry about me. I'll be in touch."

The next morning, I remembered dreaming about him and figured the dream meant he would be showing up any day now. He was nomadic in that sense, taking off when he felt like it, hitching around the country and dropping in on friends, who were always glad to see him. I kept thinking that I should call our mutual friend, Linda, who usually knew where he was. But that evening, Linda called me in tears. John had been killed in a car accident the night before.

Several years later, the woman dreamed that she and John met on the same hillside, talking and laughing again about old times. Then he suddenly turned to her and said he was "moving on to the next level." She hasn't dreamed of him in the more than twenty years since. Apparently, he really was "moving on." There is nothing to analyze in this dream. It should be taken as a real message from John.

If you have a dream about a departed loved one who says she's okay or moving on, chances are that this person really did come to visit you and means just that—she's happy.

In the case of John and the hillside dream, there was nothing the dreamer could do to prevent the death. But some near-death dreams can serve as warnings. You dream, for example, that the plane you're supposed to take tomorrow crashes and because of the dream, you change your flight. Then you hear that something really did happen. Though they are possible, these dreams are extremely rare.

But a dream doesn't have to prophesy death in order for you to benefit from it. You might, for example, oversleep the next morning and miss the doomed plane. Or you might take a route to the airport that plunges you headlong into a traffic jam and, thus, miss your flight. In the latter case, a series of synchronicities would save your life, but the cause would still be the dream you had the night before.

Regarding Family

Dream dictionaries argue that to dream of members of your extended family is not always portentous. To dream of a cousin, the experts sometimes say, indicates you might have disappointment and sadness. Even dreaming of a friendly correspondence with your cousin signifies that there might be a major falling out in the family. If a woman dreams of her aunt, supposedly, she will soon receive severe criticism of choices and actions she makes in life. However, dreams of death and sex involving family members may have very different connotations.

ALERT!

Remember to ask yourself important life questions before you go to sleep. When you recall your dreams the next morning, something in your nighttime visions should give you an answer to your dilemmas.

Death Dreams Involving Family Members

A death or near-death dream involving a family member or relative, like most death dreams, may point to a major upheaval in the dreamer's life. The dream acts as a conduit of information, as in the next example. This dream is called "Apparition":

Aunt Pat, my mother's older sister, appears to me, hovering like a ghost in a corner of the bedroom. In the dream, the image is so clear I can see the lines in her face, the soft gray of her hair, the shape of her mouth. She's speaking to me, but I can't hear the words.

I suddenly associate this kind of apparition with stories I've heard about people who appear to loved ones at the time of their death. I try to scream, but can't, and bolt awake. For seconds it seems that the image of my aunt is actually in a corner of the bedroom, exactly where it was in the dream. Then I blink and the apparition fades. Or maybe it wasn't really there at all; maybe I imagined it. I still don't know.

The next day, I called my parents and asked if my aunt was okay. As far as they knew she was. I forgot about the dream until several days later, when my parents said they'd spoken to my aunt. She had fallen and cracked her hip over the same weekend I had the dream and was planning on moving in with her son.

Despite immediate evidence to the contrary, this dream indicated that the aunt would be or was already undergoing a major life change. Though in the dream she's a sort of ghost—which the dreamer then translated as her aunt being dead and coming to visit her—this isn't the case. Instead, the aunt was about to move in with her son. She was making a drastic life change. This is an example of a precognitive death dream. The dreamer dreamed about the aunt dying or appearing as a ghost; instead, the aunt was actually about to go through a life transition.

Sex Dreams

Sex, dreams, and Freud—the three words seem intricately linked. According to Sigmund Freud, all of our dreams are filled with sexual issues. Freud lived during the Victorian era, when talk of sex was taboo, and his ideas helped free the Western world from the repressive strictures of the time.

However, his view that the sex drive powers virtually all of our dreams is no longer accepted. In fact, some dream researchers now believe that some sex dreams may not have anything to do with sex. Sex dreams can be immensely helpful in recognizing and overcoming inhibitions. If you've had a sex dream, for example, that included the appearance of one or both of your parents, here are some questions you should ask yourself:

- Is there some belief, fear, or expectation you learned from your parents that tends to intrude into your awareness when you make love?
- Is there a sense in which you believe your fulfillment might be disloyal or damaging to your parents?
- Were you more worried about your parents' presence than about your sexual fulfillment? If so, do you worry about their opinions more than is objectively necessary?

You may recognize a familiar theme in some of the following sexual dreams. You and your dreams are unique, so think of these interpretations as starting points, not conclusions. Read the following, and compare them to your dreams:

- **Searching for a place to make love:** You search from house to house, town to town. The dream is more about the search for a place than about the sex itself. Such dreams are a metaphor for a search for intimacy.

- **Making love, but stopping short of climax:** In this dream, you're left unfulfilled. It starts out promising, but just fizzles out, leaving you frustrated and angry. This dream symbolizes a lack of fulfillment and a frustration in life that may have nothing at all to do with your sex life. Look at recent events in your life. What has left you frustrated?

- **Making love in a public place:** Others observe your performance. This dream dramatically calls your attention to a public action in your life. What is it that you recently did in public or are about to do? Take a close look at the event. Look at other aspects of the dream. Who is your partner? How is that person involved in the public event in your waking life? If the person has no connection with the event, what does that person symbolize?

ALERT!

Pay close attention to how you feel about sex! Chances are that if you think something is "dirty" or "wrong," it will come up in your dreams—your mind will liberate what your body won't. Deal with your issues when they come up!

People recovering from illness, depression, surgery, or the grieving process for a broken relationship, for example, may suddenly and inexplicably begin having erotic dreams. Although they may follow physical recovery in some cases, such dreams appear to be associated with an increase in physical vitality and a greater sense of liveliness. The dreamer is often struck with the irony of the situation, considering his or her recent physical challenges. These dreams serve as reminders that, although you've been through hell, you're still very much alive.

Erotica and Desire

Erotic dreams involve heightened physical sensation and are often sexually satisfying. They can be very graphic, like an X-rated movie, and the sexual activity can be the main or only action within the dream plot. These dreams may be the mind's attempt to satisfy the natural sexual appetite, and they can be influenced by outside stimuli, such as erotic novels or movies.

Erotic dreams can be compared with eating rich chocolate without calories; there's no risk, no involvement, and no consequences. They fall into the category of what Freud referred to as wish fulfillment.

Sex with a Star

This dream is titled "In Bed with Paul Newman":

Paul Newman walks into my bedroom. He looks like he did in *Cool Hand Luke.* He smiles—you know that smile. And he knows me. There's nothing awkward about our meeting. In the blink of an eye, we're making passionate love. It seems to go on a long time and he's very intimate, tender, and caring with me. It's a very fulfilling experience.

The dreamer, Elaine, dreamed of Paul Newman after seeing one of his movies. Even though Newman is about twenty-five years older than Elaine, she has admired him since she was a teenager and still considers him sexy. Such sex dreams can fulfill a fantasy or enhance your love life.

To dream of happiness, they say, means happy events will occur in your life. To dream of ecstasy, that feeling of overwhelming, rapturous delight, portends you will have a visit from a long-absent friend.

Dreams in which you are making love to a famous person can also be related to your desire to achieve success in the world in which the famous person has starred. A budding writer may dream of sleeping with a bestselling author, a struggling athlete may dream of marrying a well-known professional athlete, and a beginning television reporter may dream of sleeping with a famous broadcaster. Sexual dreams can also contain clues to important personal needs, desires, fears, and changes.

Ecstasy and Joy Tidbits

Dreaming of joy—a feeling of well-being and good fortune—means that there will be harmony among all your friends. A dream about pleasure—a feeling of gratification—means you will have many financial and personal gains. To dream of being merry, full of gaiety and high spirits, means that pleasant events and affairs will soon prove profitable.

Dreaming about being in a state of delight, in which you feel keen enjoyment, means also that all aspects of your life will go well, and you will be successful. The message is clear. Dream of being happy, and you will be happy!

Sexual Inhibitions

A common dream that deals with sexual inhibitions is one in which one or both of your parents walk in on you while you are making love. In such a dream, your parent may talk to you as if there is nothing unusual about his or her appearance in your bedroom. An important aspect of a dream like this is the identity of your partner. If it's your spouse, consider whether your parents approve of your spouse or whether you feel a need for such approval. But there are also other scenarios, like the one that follows.

The title of this dream is "Parents and Sex Dreams":

In the dream, I'm making love with this attractive guy who works in my office. Everything is going great until I see my mother standing over the bed. I jerk the sheet over my lover, and I demand to know what she's doing in my bedroom. She doesn't answer, but she has a disapproving expression on her face. She simply turns and marches out of the room.

For Julie, the dreamer, this scene was easy to interpret. She found the man attractive and liked being around him. But she also loved her husband and in her waking life wouldn't have gotten involved with another man. Her mother's appearance suggested to her that she felt guilty about her attraction to her coworker.

"If you find yourself enjoying sex in a dream in circumstances your waking mind finds shocking, this is a sure sign that you are imposing a lifestyle on yourself which is at variance with your natural feelings in some way, and your dream is a warning to change it," says Ann Faraday in *The Dream Game.*

ALERT!

Pay attention to others' reactions to your actions in your dream. Though these reactions seem to be coming from other people, they actually signify how you feel about yourself. Change your behavior accordingly, and you'll stop having anxiety dreams of this nature.

Faraday concludes, "The most important thing . . . is to become aware of one's own feelings, thereby avoiding the danger of the repressed impulses seeking expression in some devious way, perhaps by outbursts of anger against one's partner or by 'accidentally' finding oneself in some compromising situation with the dream lover in waking life."

Relationships

Many sexual dreams are a commentary on your past and present relationships. These dreams often feature past lovers. In the most outrageous ones, all of your past lovers show up at the same party or in the same bed. The function of this dream is to help you analyze past involvements that continue to impact current relationships.

Here's a dream with a different plot, but a similar theme. The dreamer, Bill, was a thirty-three-year-old engineer who had never been married. The title of this dream is "The Vanishing Lover":

Everything starts out great. I'm with Sharon, a woman I've known through business for several months. I'm very attracted to her, and now we're in a romantic setting. We both know what we want, and neither of us has any inhibitions. But just as I become fully aroused, Sharon starts to disappear. All of my efforts to keep her from vanishing fail. Sharon simply evaporates.

For Bill, the dream is more about a pattern in his life than a statement about Sharon. He has rarely had a sexual relationship last longer than a few months. Part of Bill's problem, he admits, is that he only likes the exciting early sexual encounters with a new mate. Once the woman starts to become part of his life, his interest fades. Maybe he's not ready for something serious. Or maybe this dream is a big signpost that he needs to work on his issues so that, when the right woman comes along, he'll be ready.

It's important to look for patterns that mark your relationships—especially if you've had a series of unsuccessful relationships or affairs that began filled with promise but ended badly. Until you change the way you handle things, it will keep coming up in your dreams.

You may have had a sex dream that you think concerns your relationship patterns. This exercise will help you understand the meaning of such a dream so that you can get to the bottom of your real feelings and learn from them. Answer these questions honestly to uncover your relationship trends:

- What is the dream telling you about your past or present partner(s)?
- What is the dream telling you about yourself?
- Are you frustrated with difficulties in finding a permanent partner?
- Do you find that your relationships begin in a promising manner and then just fall apart?
- What is the significant pattern that the dream reveals?
- Do you look at your partner through rose-colored glasses until you become close to him or her?

- Do you jump too quickly into relationships?
- Were you too critical of past lovers?
- Does your current lover take advantage of you? Did your past lovers take advantage of you?

Chapter 7

More Classic Dream Themes

Some dream themes seem to be more common than others. It makes sense, since most people have similar experiences over the course of their lives. Sometimes these classic dream themes express fears or anxieties; other times, they express joy or triumph. In all cases, though, they tell you what's on your mind and in your heart. In this chapter, find out more about the most common dreams.

Falling

Dreams of falling may be metaphors for the fallen woman, a fall from grace, or the fall season. The interpretation depends, to a large extent, on what is going on in your life. It can even refer to what happened to you within the twenty-four hours preceding the dream.

One young married woman dreamed she was falling from a building. It later struck her as a metaphor for her affair with a married man from her office. The fall, she said, didn't just represent a fall from grace; it was what would happen to her marriage if her husband discovered the affair.

Quite often such a dream will have that "zing" to it, and you'll immediately know the reference. But other times, its meaning may be as obscure as the solution to a complex mathematical equation. You'll have to take it apart piece by piece, and then you must figure out how to put it all together.

FACT

Classic dream themes such as falling or taking a test don't qualify as archetypal because they're not forces within us. Their genesis usually lies in our daily lives and experiences.

Derek, an actor, dreamed he was in a convertible with his agent, who was driving. While they were speeding along a country road, the car hit a deep hole and the car veered out of control. His agent, a woman, slammed her foot on the brake, but the brakes failed and they plunged over the side of a cliff.

There are many possible interpretations of this dream. But the only one that mattered was the one that made sense to Derek—the one that offered him new insight into his relationship with his agent. He mulled the dream over for a day or two and realized that for quite a while he'd felt as if she had mishandled his career and wasn't able to "apply the brake" to the downward spiral in his relationship with her. He ended their partnership several days later—a split that was, for him, like a plunge over the edge of a cliff into an abyss of the unknown.

Dream therapist Gayle Delaney suggests that you ask yourself how you feel in your dream as you're falling. Do you feel terrified? Helpless? Out of control? Or is the sensation pleasant? If so, how? These responses can be clues to what the falling means for you.

As a sort of exercise, jot down a recurring falling dream you've had. If it was recent, note what was going on in your life at the time of the dream. Had you just reached a crossroads in a relationship? Was an important partnership in the throes of change? Had your children recently left home? Did you, previously, have a drug or an alcohol habit? Interpret the dream. Note if a decision was made as a result of this dream. Let the dream speak to you. Write down:

- The date and time you had the dream
- The action of the dream
- The events immediately preceding the dream
- Your interpretation

Flying

If you find yourself flying in a dream, it could be an astral dream or an out-of-body dream. But flying can also occur in a release dream. Freud connected the action of flying in a release dream with the desire for sex. Alfred Adler associated flying dreams with the will to dominate others. And Carl Jung saw them as the desire to break free of restrictions. Most psychotherapists today tend to favor Jung's interpretation.

Make sure to take note of where you're headed in a flying dream. Your destination can clue you in to where you want to go or where you're afraid of going in your life.

As with other dreams, it's best to look at flying dreams as individual experiences. To that end, ask yourself whether the sensation of flying is pleasurable or stressful. Why are you flying? Are you escaping pursuers? Are you showing off? Do you feel elated? Explore your feelings about the dream and the action that takes place. Does it seem familiar, as if it's somewhere you've been flying before?

Some flying dreams may involve out-of-body travel, a topic that is explored in detail in Chapter 9. Out-of-body experiences have a distinctly different feel to them and often involve "travel" to places both familiar and strange.

In the following dream, Ken, a forty-two-year-old insurance adjuster who is also an avid runner, recalls a flying dream that related to running. In a sense, it was a step beyond running. The title of this dream is "Running to Fly":

I'm running in a field, and my body is getting lighter with each stride. My steps lengthen, and pretty soon I pick up speed. Then I'm airborne, I'm soaring, and it's exhilarating. Then it occurs to me that I've done this before. "It's easy," I think. "Nothing to it." I tell myself I have to remember that I know how to fly. I was excited when I woke from the dream. It took a few minutes before I realized I'd been dreaming and that I couldn't really fly in my waking life.

Ken looked at his flying dream as a symbol of accomplishment. The day of the dream he had placed second in his age bracket and twelfth overall in a local ten-kilometer race with more than 700 contestants. After the race, he felt elevated; that sensation was transferred to his dream.

Test-Taking and Classrooms

Jim, a self-employed contractor, dreamed that he was hurrying to make an 8:00 A.M. class. When he got there, the professor was passing out final exam booklets. He realized that he'd been to the class only a couple of times the entire semester and that he wasn't prepared for the exam.

Although it had been more than twenty years since Jim had graduated from college, he had this dream once or twice a year. The specifics rarely changed. Once he began to record and study his dreams, however, he understood that the dream usually occurred when he was facing a bid on a major project. Even though he spent weeks preparing figures on a prospective project, he rarely felt adequately prepared.

It's interesting to note what age you are in the dream. Are you the age you were when you were in school or the age you are now? If you're the age you are now, the test-taking dream is a metaphor for something you're currently experiencing.

For most of us, the examination dream follows a format similar to Jim's. In *The Dream Game*, Ann Faraday notes that most of these dreams occur when we feel we're being tested or examined by someone, as in a job interview, for example. Everyone feels unprepared at one time or another. The examination dream is often a reflection of an uneasy sensation of not being ready for something coming into your life.

When interpreting this type of dream, make note of whether you have an important deadline or are under extreme pressure in your waking life. If you're not, then ask yourself whether there is something in your life with which you feel unprepared to cope. In your dream journal, don't forget to record the dream in detail.

Learning Curve

When you dream of being in a classroom, examine your surroundings and your reason for being there. Is there a positive feeling about the learning environment? Do you recognize the person teaching the class? What is the subject matter you're learning? Oftentimes, a classroom dream relates to a personal growth period you're going through.

A thirty-three-year-old woman who had recently joined a dream group related the following classroom dream. The dream had occurred eleven years earlier, when she was in college, and it had always puzzled her. She asked if anyone in the dream group had any idea what it could mean. As you read through this dream, take special note of the way the woman describes the lobby and classroom.

Orientation Dream

This dream is entitled "The Next Step":

My friend Tanya and I are sitting in a lobby with perhaps a dozen other people of various ages and races. We aren't sure why we're there. There's nothing about the lobby to tell me exactly where it is. I feel very uneasy about this place. I go up to the information desk and ask the receptionist what we're waiting for.

"For the class to begin," she replies.

"I didn't sign up for a class," I tell her.

"You must have. You're here."

Then she goes back to whatever she was doing, and I return to my seat. Not long afterward, she calls my name and Tanya's. We file into a college-style auditorium. It's crowded with people and brightly lit by a skylight. The color of the sky is odd, a kind of glowing cerulean blue.

The speaker is a well-known literary figure, whose name I forgot when I woke up but whom I had known died some years before. I suddenly realize I am in an afterlife classroom, about to be oriented to dying and to whatever happens next.

FACT

Afterlife dreams can be tricky because nine times out of ten, they're really visits to the Other Side—trips our subconscious refuses to acknowledge as real. These dreams are gifts. Write them down.

Several members of the dream group immediately associated the dream with reports from near-death survivors. The dreamer herself agreed, but she pointed out that no one had died around the time she'd had the dream and that she had never had a near-death experience. In fact, at the time of the dream, Raymond Moody's seminal book on near-death experiences, *Life after Life,* hadn't yet been published.

But the dream confirmed her belief in the survival of consciousness and triggered a lifelong interest in metaphysical topics. The dream recurs periodically, usually when the woman experiences a crisis of faith in her spiritual beliefs. But it always renews her belief in the path she has chosen.

When a teacher has a classroom dream, on the other hand, the meaning might be more practical than symbolic. This was the case in the following dream related by Bharata, the fifty-one-year-old director of the Sivananda Yoga Center in Lake Worth, Florida. He dreamed that he was the only teacher for two classes that were scheduled to meet at the same time, and he had to teach both classes, running back and forth from room to room.

In Bharata's case, the classroom dream was a reflection of his inner concern that he was teaching too many classes. Although he enjoyed teaching, his schedule included two or three classes a day, and he had been considering adding other teachers to lighten his load.

Nudity

In *The Dream Game,* Ann Faraday writes of a young man's dream of being naked in front of a cheering crowd. In the dream, he was exhilarated. What were the circumstances going on in his waking life? Well, he had recently had his first experience of sexual intercourse, and for him the dream meant that he had shed his moral prohibitions. "Had the onlookers in the dream been disapproving, this would have indicated guilt feelings; for in the objective world, his fellow students would certainly have approved," Faraday wrote.

"Breakthrough" dreams are extremely important to watch for. Once your subconscious changes its mind about something, your waking mind follows. This can turn your life around for the better.

Dreams in which you're naked indicate a need to express yourself. Fears, inhibitions, and classic "exposing yourself" issues come up in an instant.

The key is to examine how you feel in the dream about your nudity. Do you feel good? Free? Scared? Nude dreams don't always refer to actually being naked. Sometimes you have problems in which you feel vulnerable, and your fears translate into and liberate themselves as nude dreams.

If you have a nude dream in which you feel silly or scared, ask yourself these questions in your waking life:

- Is there an issue right now you're not facing?
- How do you feel weak?
- To whom do you feel susceptible?
- How can you rectify this problem?

Work toward facing the person and the problem directly, and you'll find that the issue fades away. You'll feel better and more in control of your life. Don't let others treat you without the respect you deserve. Nude dreams in which you feel exposed are often the result of feeling inadequate or insecure about your position in life.

Lost Purse, Wallet, Keys, or Briefcase

Purses and wallets usually contain credit cards, money, and identification—these are important. In fact, they're society's evidence of who you are. Keys open your door, start your car, and allow you entrance to your home and office. Briefcases typically contain papers related to work. In some ways, these things define you. They're your personal possessions—yours, alone. Therefore, says Gayle Delaney, this dream can occur among women whose children have recently left home. Typically, they also occur among men who have retired or who have been fired from their jobs.

FACT

Dreams of lost personal items are frequently reported by people in transition from one way of life or mode of thought to another. This has to do with a shift in perceived identity. Pay close attention to these dreams.

Categorize three of your recurring dreams under broad topic headings like the ones presented in this chapter. Then define what these symbols mean to you in your waking life. Do the definitions fit the dreams?

If these are recent dreams and you've recorded them in your journal, read them over. Note what was going on in your life at the time. Then interpret the dreams. Record the following:

- Broad categories and meanings
- Events in your life at the time of these dreams
- Your interpretation of the dreams

If you're constantly losing things or even being late for appointments, chances are you know full well that you need to get your priorities in order. Sometimes, when we don't want to deal with these things head-on, they come full force into our dreams. Losing personal objects in dreams indicates a lack of dedication to your responsibilities. When you don't feel like you have control over the things that are important, it gets translated—showing up in your dreams as the loss of personal possessions.

Another factor may be that in your waking life, you feel like you're not taking care of your financial obligations. The loss of a purse or a wallet in dreams sometimes indicates how you feel about your monetary situation. Closely examine what you're taking care of and what you're not. Most likely, you'll come up with the solution quickly.

ALERT!

If you're having dreams about losing your wallet, you'd better check your bills! Your subconscious knows that something needs to be paid and is anxious about it.

Finding Money

Another release dream we all have is one in which we find money. Sometimes the money is in the form of coins on or in the ground. In your dream, the deeper you dig, the more coins you may find. Actually, experts say that if you find the coins in the roots of a tree, you should think about how those roots support the tree. The roots are the hidden strength of the tree—without them, the tree dies. This is the foundation of your dream. Think what you're really looking for at the base of that tree. Is it acceptance? Financial gain? Love? What does the money represent to you here? Is it freedom?

Terri, the woman who had the next dream, grew up listening to her father say that money "doesn't grow on trees." It seemed that every time she wanted something, her father replied with that well-worn phrase. Obviously, it stuck. This dream is called "The Money Tree":

I'm digging for something under a large tree. I can feel the dirt under my nails; the scent of the earth fills me. I find one coin, and then several more. The deeper I dig, the more money I find. I feel excited, as though I've just discovered some wonderful secret—that money really does grow on trees!

For Terri, money still doesn't grow on trees, but this dream may suggest that if you dig deep within, you'll find hidden riches. Such dreams don't necessarily refer to money, but rather to the treasures inside: character, strength, self-worth. The inner self roots us to our true nature, and therein lies an abundance of riches, often greater than we realize. Our subconscious, however, knows our true value, and that knowledge sometimes emerges in our dreams. This dream indicates not necessarily that you're digging for money, but that you feel good about yourself!

Traveling

Dreaming of travel could relate to an upcoming trip. But if you have no plans for a journey, your dream sojourn may be a symbolic one. Pay particular attention to details about your trip. Where are you going? Are you traveling alone or with others? Do you have luggage with you? Keep in mind that what happens on your trip might be more important than the destination.

A newspaper reporter named Jerry related the following recurring dream. This dream is called "Missing Connections":

> I'm taking a train in a foreign country and must transfer from one train to another. The problem is that I've lost track of my luggage. I'm looking all over for it, and I know I must hurry or I'll miss the connecting train. Sometimes I'm in a train station without my luggage, which is still on the train I just got off. I usually wake up before I find out what happens.

After discussing the dream with friends, Jerry saw two possible meanings for the dream. In both of them, the journey was his job. Although he didn't travel much, his work relied on making connections with sources for stories. His fear was that he wouldn't make contact with his sources or that, when he reached them, he wouldn't be ready for the interview. His luggage represented his preparation for the interview.

The other interpretation involved the question of his future as a reporter. Jerry was tired of chasing down stories day after day and wanted to make a career change. But he feared that he was not prepared to make the change—that he would miss his connection to a new career.

If in a dream you keep missing your travel connection to meet up with a boyfriend, a girlfriend, or a lover, it indicates anxiety about the relationship. Ask yourself why this might be, and examine the situation.

Losing Teeth: Common Ground

A dream about losing teeth is telling you something about yourself. It could reflect a feeling of being out of control—like your life has no order to it. Because losing teeth or hair is such a natural thing, something that can happen to anyone, your subconscious makes it a very real possibility in your dreams. But it's metaphoric.

Ann Faraday notes that her own tooth-loss dreams "almost always reflect my feeling that I have 'lost face' or 'spoiled my self-image' in some way during the day; usually by giving in to emotions of fear or weakness." Edgar Cayce viewed dreams of losing teeth as metaphors for loose or careless speech. In this case, you might regret gossiping about someone. Women are said to have this sort of dream more than men.

QUESTION?

Why do I keep having the "teeth falling out" dream?
If you keep having this dream, it means you're stuck in a particular pattern because some unresolved issue in your life has gotten out of control. Ask yourself what that may be. Have you been gossiping about someone? Are you not sure which way to go with your career? Do your homework and you'll find the answer.

If the suggested interpretations of the previous dream don't work for you, ask yourself what teeth mean to you. Do they represent power? A nice appearance? Aggressiveness? What is it that makes you feel toothless? Do teeth symbolize something to you? It's important to ask yourself these questions. If you're having some of the other popular release dreams, involving nudity, traveling, losing personal possessions, or taking a test, don't worry. We all have them. What's interesting is that common dream themes, like society itself, undoubtedly change over time. For the children of today, new topics may include UFOs and/or alien abductions, computer system crashes, extreme weather, airplane disasters, or other popular media topics. Still, the same message holds true. These common anxiety dreams will continue until you take control of their sources. Do it today.

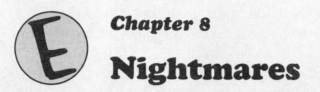

Chapter 8

Nightmares

Most people fear them. Some pray they don't come. You may not want to go back to sleep after you've had one. Nightmares can be frightening and confusing, but it's also possible to use them to your advantage. In this chapter, find out why nightmares happen and how they can actually help you confront your waking fears.

Symbols and Themes

Research suggests that increased levels of anxiety in waking life can increase the frequency and intensity of nightmares. What nightmares really do is invade your dream state to work out problems unresolved in waking life. Some common nightmare symbols include guns, thieves, ghosts, demons, monsters, and the devil. These symbols translate into different meanings for each person. The importance lies in the context of the dream.

The most common theme in nightmares is a chase. Since nightmares are a debilitating fear working itself out, this theme can take many forms. As an adult, you're usually running from yourself. As a child, you might be running from a powerful parent or other authority figure.

Nightmares That Heal

Though many dream experts say it's important to remember your dreams, others say it's equally important to forget them. Francis Crick, a Nobel Prize winner who co-discovered the double helix, studied dreams with Graeme Mitchison. The two determined that dreams and nightmares are the brain's only way of wiping itself clean and preparing for new tasks ahead. In fact, they say, this is when your mind erases and deletes certain obsessive, controlling tendencies.

It's also when incorrect information—ideas that you've changed in your conscious mind to accommodate an idealistic view of things—rights itself. It seems that the brain's neocortex, where memory is stored, must "unload."

If you're obsessing about something in waking life—such as a relationship on its way out—you're probably having nightmares about it. Don't try to overanalyze these dreams. Let it go! Your subconscious can work it out for you.

Recurring Nightmares

Some dream experts say that if you're having the same nightmare over and over again, it could be that your soul recognizes something you've already been through and is still trying to work it out. In other words, this is where reincarnation truly shows itself. A recurring dream, experts say, can simply be made of past-life memories.

As mentioned earlier in this book, dreaming of your own death is almost never prophetic. Usually a dream about death signifies change, transition, or upheaval. Occasionally, however, souls do remember previous deaths, and they replay them in nightmares over and over again until the subconscious accepts it. It's almost like getting stuck in a time warp. Your mind, without your consciousness to filter in who you are now, remembers who it once was. Don't try to analyze these dreams with questions like, "Why do they keep chasing me?" or "Why do I keep waking up when I'm about to die?" Let your subconscious work out the memory, and eventually it will simply go away.

Sometimes it helps to tell a close friend or relative about a recurring nightmare. By acknowledging it, you admit that it's happening. This can help get the burden off your shoulders so you can move on with your waking life.

What They Mean

Ask any three-year-old about her nightmares, and she'll probably tell you about dreams in which she's being pursued by terrifying animals—fire-breathing dragons, ferocious wolves, or dangerous lions.

Quite often, children's nightmares can happen after a scolding or punishment by parents. They also occur when a child is ill or in a transitional phase—during a divorce or a move from one home to another, for example. Sometimes they seem to happen for no apparent external reason, though usually there's something at the core of it. If you gently interview children about their nightmares, you can usually get to their source.

As children near the age of six, their nightmares change. Instead of threats and pursuit by animals, the scary encounter they have might be with a bully in school or a neighbor down the street. These nightmares often deal with real anxieties and fears children have in their waking lives.

In *The Bedside Guide to Dreams*, Stase Michaels outlines three different kinds of nightmares that are common to adults. "In the first kind, you face your actual fears. In the second, you deal with the pain and trauma in yourself and in your life. The third kind is the most common type of dream and is reflected in the saying 'I have met the enemy, and it is I.'" In this last type of nightmare, you encounter a part of yourself you would rather not see. The person or event you're reacting to in your dream strikes an all-too-familiar chord because it reflects some element of yourself that you would rather keep hidden.

Sometimes, these nightmares seem to be literal warnings about something—your health, a personal relationship, or your career. But before you jump to any conclusions about your nightmare being a literal warning, exhaust the other possibilities.

Look for metaphors. Scrutinize the dream for hints that it illuminates some part of your personality you don't want to know about. Be honest. Does it depict one of your actual fears? Does it address a rejected part of you? Consider the following clues:

- **Vividness:** Warning dreams are usually very vivid.
- **Your reaction:** If a dream is a warning, you'll most likely react the same way you would react in waking life.
- **Similar details:** In a warning dream, your house looks like the actual house you live in. Your mother looks like your real mother. There is a literal feel to the dream that is lacking in the other kinds of dreams.

Confronting Fear

If you are often plagued by nightmares, the most important thing to do is confront your fears. Most people don't obsess about the things or situations they fear. They simply react when confronted with the fear. Confronting your fears and emotions will help you to seize control of frightening situations in your dreams. It will also help you to work out your anxieties, which are most likely the root cause of the nightmares. By consciously recognizing what you fear, you take the first step in overcoming it.

In the nightmare that follows, the dreamer was living on the first floor of a condominium complex. Although the complex was safe, the neighborhood outside of it was one of the worst in town. Many people in the complex had security systems in their condos and in their cars. The dreamer didn't. The only thing that stood between her and the outside world were dead bolts.

Dreaming Fear

This dream is called "Dead Bolt":

I'm in the kitchen in the middle of the night, getting something to eat. Only the light over the stove is on. The door, which opens onto the condo courtyard, begins to rattle and I whip around. A horrible paralysis seizes me. I can't move or scream. I can only watch.

A hand reaches inside the door. A man's hand. I can see the dirt under his fingernails. He is trying to reach the chain. I grab the teakettle and slam it against his fingers. His hand vanishes.

I am looking at a broken dead bolt. I kick the door shut and fix a chair in front of it. I awaken in my bedroom, certain the man is out there in the courtyard now, and that he's going to try to break into the condo—my condo.

This dream is literal, with no hidden meaning. The dreamer is being warned about the broken dead bolt on her kitchen door. She admitted that, for some time, the dead bolt had been broken and the entire locking mechanism could easily have been slipped out of the door, providing a peephole to the outside world. Right after she had the dream, she hired a locksmith to come out to the condo and fix the door.

ALERT!

Whether or not you're dreaming of a future event, take warnings in dreams literally! Such dreams don't necessarily mean that something is going to happen, but do yourself a favor and always be prepared.

This dream possessed a vividness the dreamer recognized. It was also quite realistic. Her kitchen was depicted as it actually was. The dead bolt on the kitchen door was definitely broken, and the intruder's hand was rendered in astonishing detail. Two weeks later, a condo three doors down from hers was broken into.

Exercise: Confronting Your Fear

Analyze one of your recurring nightmares. What are the prevalent images? Where does the dream take place? Are there any obvious metaphors or puns that may hold a vital clue to the meaning of the dream? How does the dream end? If you've never confronted your fear in this nightmare, rewrite the ending of the dream so that you do. Record:

- The nightmare
- The setting
- The metaphors
- How you act and react in the dream
- How you would change the dream

Taking Control

The Senoi, a tribe that lives in the mountains of Malaysia, solved all their problems with dreams. Some say they had no fearful, obsessive tendencies or neuroses because they were so psychologically advanced. If they were afraid in their dreams, they would discuss it in depth with each other.

When a Senoi child was frightened in a dream, he was advised to confront the fear. In other words, he was encouraged to call on dream friends to help him. If he was attacked in the dream, he was required to retaliate. Only then, they believed, would his attacker leave him alone.

"To confront and conquer danger," writes Patricia Garfield, "is the most important rule in the Senoi system of dream control." Luckily, some of us stumble on this rule without ever having heard about the Senoi. After one woman was raped, she repeatedly had dreams in which the rapist was chasing her. Finally, in the following dream, she seized control of the situation. This dream is titled "The Rapist":

The scene is the same as in the other dreams, the man chasing me down a dark alley between a pair of brownstone buildings. I'm so terrified, the inside of my mouth is bone dry. I can see the end of the alley just ahead, can see lights, traffic, but I know I'm not going to make it.

So I suddenly stop, turn, and demand that he leave me alone. He looks at me for a long moment, then holds out his hand. I can see something in his palm, but I don't want to approach him to take it. I tell him to drop it on the ground and he does. Then he walks away from me, whistling.

When he's gone, I walk over to where he was standing and find a beautiful, pink shell—the object he dropped. It has my name on it. I've never had the dream since.

The woman interpreted the shell as a womb, which serves as a protective shelter for a fetus. In this case, the shell was a symbol of protection, which the woman had gained for herself. The key here is to take control of your nightmares. With practice, it can be done with great success.

Night Terrors

You've just turned out the light and are settling in for a good night's sleep when a bloodcurdling scream shreds the silence. You leap up and rush into your son's room and find him in a panic, completely disoriented. When you calm him down and question him, he tells you about a single, horrifying image of being crushed or strangled or attacked. And then, five minutes later, he's forgotten about the dream completely. The only thing that's left is his fear.

It isn't a nightmare that woke him, but a night terror. These debilitating dreams are even more intense and more powerful than nightmares. Anyone who's had one will not confuse it with a nightmare. Actually, these are most common in children between the ages of three and eight. Most children either remember nothing about what frightened them or recall only fragmented images, which is characteristic of what happens when you're awakened from the deepest stages of sleep. People who have suffered from post-traumatic stress syndrome, from war or a violent attack, have probably also experienced night terrors.

QUESTION?

What are the symptoms of night terrors?
The person who has had a night terror is almost impossible to calm down and the next day usually doesn't remember the dream images. He may also suffer from a fear of going to sleep, feelings of shame and horror about having night terrors, excessive heart rate, hot sweats, and confusion.

Ernest Hartmann, psychoanalyst and author of *The Nightmare*, says that night terrors sometimes run in families, suggesting the possibility of a genetic susceptibility. They usually last about five to twenty minutes, and they happen in one of the deepest levels of sleep. It's not known why some people don't grow out of night terrors, but, Hartmann adds, "Some adults with night terrors have been noted to have phobic or obsessive personalities." Therefore, it's also possible that night terrors run in families with similar beliefs and thought processes.

Most people who have night terrors are unable or unwilling to notice or express strong feelings in the daytime. This is why those with post-traumatic stress disorder or intense stress have them more frequently. "The night terror episodes may express a kind of outbreak of repressed emotion," Hartmann says.

Your Waking Fears

Lynn, a thirty-year-old mother and photographer, was absolutely petrified of snakes until she got a photography assignment that took her to the Miami Serpentarium. The following is Lynn's description of how she conquered her fear:

> Maybe it was seeing them through the lens of the camera. Maybe it was just that I was ready to deal with the fear. But, suddenly, I recognized their beauty, their incredible diversity. Toward the end of the assignment, one of the snake handlers brought over a boa he had worked with since it was born. I actually mustered the courage to touch it. And from that point on, I was no longer afraid of snakes.

It often helps to recognize and admit your waking fears so you can overcome them in your sleep. Your dreams and nightmares can only do so much. If you have a very real fear of birds, for instance, images of birds or other animals will probably figure in your dreams and nightmares. You may have nightmares of big shadows hovering over you—or even ghosts—and not quite know what this means. But nightmares almost always translate back to very real fears you have in your waking life.

You can start breaking down your fears by performing a simple dream exercise. First, list five of your fears. Have any of these fears shown up in your dreams? Were they disguised as metaphorical images? Make a note of how you dealt with these fears in your dreams. Then outline a plan for conquering these fears in your waking life.

One woman had the following dream, called "Vampires":

Last night I had a dream about girls I knew when I was about thirteen years old. I haven't seen or heard from them since. But even back then, we got along even though I never really was accepted into their clique. They were the "cool" girls, and I wanted to fit in.

In the dream, I noticed that they were all vampires. We were all sitting around and I started feeling very uneasy. Then I eventually saw their fangs and one attacked me and started biting me and drawing blood. After that, I woke up.

FACT

Losing blood in a dream usually refers to a loss of emotion or energy. If you bleed in a dream, you probably feel, in waking life, like you're being emotionally drained in some way. The presence of blood in a dream can also refer to life and matters of the heart.

After further investigation into this woman's feelings about her old friends, it was evident that there was really no hidden meaning here. These friends had been sucking energy from her back then (and she was wasting precious time with them)—hence, the blood-sucking reference. She remembered feeling left out, even though it had happened long ago.

What's important to analyze is not why these friends are coming back into her dreams, or even that she's having nightmares about them as vampires. Instead, she needs to ask herself other questions: Why now? What has reminded me of those isolated feelings? Who am I spending time with who isn't making me feel good about myself? Feelings of rejection constantly come up in nightmares. The important thing is to figure out why and to remove yourself from those people who can do serious harm to you emotionally.

Chapter 9

Out-of-Body Dreams

In out-of-body dreams, the soul actually leaves the body. There is no time, no space—no limits. In your dreams, you can be invincible. You can travel into the past, visit departed loved ones, or fly to a distant planet, if your soul so desires. In this chapter, discover the truth about out-of-body dreams and why they're so important.

Flying Out-of-Body

Some people report that, to fly in a dream, all they have to do is flap their arms. Other people take off at a run, like Superman. Some dreamers can simply lift off the ground and drift on currents of air. Others have only to think of a specific place in order to experience a sensation of tremendous speed and momentum.

Flying dreams vary from one person to another. For some, the experience is joyous and free from the normal confines of the physical body. For others, flying dreams are a means of escaping danger, as in the following dream, called "The Field":

I'm in a field near the town of Coeyman's Hollow in upstate New York, where I lived for a short time after college. It's one of those glorious spring days when everything is in bloom; the air is cool. Bees are buzzing; birds are singing. A kind of bliss sweeps over me and I fall back into the grass and gaze up into the cerulean blue of the sky.

Suddenly, the ground beneath me begins to tremble, then to shake, as if an earthquake is in progress. I don't think about it; I just react. I leap up so fast I'm airborne. I flap my arms and sail across the field, forty or fifty feet above it, and watch as the field breaks apart. As trees topple and a farmhouse caves in, I fly away.

If you've never flown in your dreams, you can learn how. People who fly in their dreams report it as one of their most pleasurable dream activities. Flying in dreams can help you overcome a fear of flying in waking life. It can also release you from waking tensions, empower you, and completely revamp your ideas of what is possible.

Learning to Fly

In *The Dream Workbook*, Jill Morris offers an excellent method for learning to fly in your dreams. She suggests that before you go to sleep, you should think about flying. Visualize what it would be like. As with any visualization, add as many details as you can—feel the wind move through your hair, and imagine how the world looks from above. Tell yourself you're going to fly in your dreams, and repeat your intention out loud. Repeat it again silently to yourself as you begin to drift off. If you wake up during the night, remind yourself of what you want to do.

If you don't succeed the first night, keep at it. Once you do begin to have flying dreams, you can attempt to increase their frequency by giving yourself a specific goal to accomplish in the dream.

Exercise: A Flying Dream Experiment

Using Jill Morris's technique, write out what you would like to experience in a flying dream. Keep it simple, for example: "I want to fly around my bedroom" or "I want to fly into my backyard." Visualize the experience as you're falling asleep, and repeat your written statement several times.

When you wake up, record the results. If you're not successful—and you'll probably know as soon as you're conscious—shut your eyes and try again. Sometimes, in that lazy state just after waking, it's easy to slip back into a dreaming state.

ALERT!

You may not always be able to sustain height in a flying dream or even the flight itself. If you have confidence in yourself, though, and you aren't afraid, you'll make more and more progress with flying dreams. Once you find that flight is possible in a dream, play around with your techniques.

The key with trying to fly within your dreams is to be innovative. Try different types of flight. Fly very low to the ground, for instance, as if gliding along like a bee, and then soar into the sky. Some dreamers start out in a small plane and then bail out and fly on their own, while others find it easier to leap off rooftops or hillsides. One woman found that her flying dreams usually began on the roof of her neighbor's house. Initially, she couldn't lift off the rooftop and into the sky; she could only fly to the ground. She then trained herself to fly to the next rooftop, and then the next and the next, until one night she ran out of rooftops, and there was nowhere to go but up.

Am I Dreaming?

According to Stephen LaBerge in *Exploring the World of Lucid Dreaming,* flying dreams are related to lucid dreams, in which the dreamer is conscious he is dreaming. LaBerge suggests that when you're not sure if you're dreaming, you should try to fly. "The easiest way to do this is to hop into the air and attempt to prolong your time off the ground. If you stay airborne for even a split second longer than normal, you can be sure you're dreaming."

Jane Roberts had numerous out-of-body experiences in her lifetime. During the writing of *The Seth Material,* she decided to see what she could find out about a couple she and her husband knew, who were traveling in Puerto Rico. She laid down, shut her eyes, and gave herself the suggestion that she would find the couple.

QUESTION?

When is the best time for out-of-body travel?
The best time to suggest that it happen is when you've already been dreaming and you wake up. Make sure that you don't fully wake yourself. Try to stay relaxed. Repeat out loud that you're going to have an out-of-body dream. You'll be incredibly surprised by the results!

Suddenly, she descended through the air and landed on a porch surrounded by a low railing. "I knew that my body was in bed, but I lost all contact with it. Regardless of where it [her body] was, I was someplace else entirely." She took in as many details as she could from her surroundings, and then heard her alarm ringing. Her consciousness snapped back into her body. She wanted more information, so she shut her eyes again and told herself she would return to the same location.

"Brief but definite traveling sensations followed. Mountains and skies swept by. Then I found myself hovering in the air above the same motel," she adds. This dreamer had a real out-of-body dream. She dreamed things as they actually were, far away from the comfort of her own bed. The details she gathered were later verified by her friends. She *was* there, in her dream and in real life.

Near-Death Experiences

Near-death experiences are also related to out-of-body travel. The following story about a woman who had two near-death experiences reveals how the phenomenon can lead to very similar experiences in the dream state.

In the early 1960s, a young artist and psychic named Renie had a near-death experience during childbirth. She remembered passing out and then finding herself in the nursery, looking for her daughter, who she knew had been born. She read her daughter's nametag; she counted her fingers and toes to make sure they were all there. Then, suddenly, she found herself somewhere else.

Warning Dream from the Other Side

This dream is called "A Beautiful Place":

It had gardens, trees, flowers, birds, colors, all the things in nature I love. You couldn't paint a place prettier than this. There were people around—no one I knew, but I wasn't afraid. We started talking. They told me I had to go back and give a message to the doctor who delivered my daughter. That the message was important.

The next thing I knew, I was awake, and someone was slapping my face. I was in terrible pain. I grabbed someone's hand and tried to tell the person what had happened. I told the doctor that I had a message for him, but he didn't want to hear it. He told someone to take me into ICU.

An orderly took her into the intensive care unit. He chatted with her, trying to calm her down, assuring her that the doctor she was trying to talk to didn't listen to anyone. By the time she had settled in her room, she'd forgotten the message.

"Four months or so later," Renie said, "I heard the doctor was shipped out to Vietnam. He never came back. I'm sure that the message I was supposed to give him had to do with that, with Vietnam; that he should get his affairs in order."

ALERT!

Little warnings you get in your dreams for you and the people around you are a gift—write them down! It's very rare that you get a glimpse of what's going to happen from the Hall of Records on the Other Side. Take note of these messages, and take them seriously.

Seeing Is Believing

Renie's second near-death experience occurred in 1968, when she seemingly died of pyelonephritis, a total urinary shutdown. She was about to undergo a biopsy in a North Miami Beach hospital when suddenly the pain and fever disappeared. Her dream is called "Another Chance":

I found myself hovering in a corner of the room, up near the ceiling, watching the doctors trying to resuscitate me. I couldn't understand why it wasn't like it is in the movies, with people shouting codes and a team of people pouring into the room. Once they resuscitated me, I told the attending doctor everything that had happened and had been said in the room, while they were trying to bring me back.

The near-death research of pioneers such as Dr. Elizabeth Kübler-Ross and Dr. Raymond Moody cleared the way for other near-death survivors to come forward with their own stories. Bestselling books like *Embraced by the Light* by Betty Eadie indicate a profound hunger in Western culture for this kind of material. But back in the early 1960s, when Renie had her first near-death experience, there was no name for it. One simply didn't talk about such a thing.

Renie, however, seized on her experience and began to explore the topic. She found that she could leave her body with relative ease, sometimes by using a flying dream as a kind of launch pad, and other times by simply willing herself "up and out."

Saying Goodbye

On Halloween of that year, Renie met and fell in love with Mark, a much younger man who had Hodgkin's disease. They were nearly inseparable until his death the following May. A couple of months after Mark's death, Renie lay in bed one night, drifting in a half-sleep, thinking about the young man. She had the following dream, called "Mark's Goodbye":

And suddenly I wasn't in bed anymore. Telephone poles were flying past me. And then I was at this convalescent home, being greeted by this woman in a nurse's uniform. She said she would take me to see Mark, but it would have to be a short visit. She took me to his room. He was wearing a dressing gown and was still confused about the circumstances surrounding his death. He'd been given so many drugs.

FACT

Experts agree that the time varies from when a loved one dies to when you can actually receive a visit from the person in your dreams. Remember, there is no time and space in this realm, so it can be anywhere from an hour to five or ten years. It depends how long it takes a soul to become acquainted with the Other Side.

Renie explained the circumstances about his death, answered his questions, and then the nurse told her she had to leave. "The next thing I knew, I was back in my bedroom, wide awake," Renie recalled. When she dreamed of him again, she saw him on a speedboat, racing across ocean waves. "He looked great. He'd 'recovered' from his death," she said.

Actually, Renie did not receive a visit from Mark. Instead, she was able to astrally travel to him in her dreams. Many people report that they dream about an incident only to find out that it happened at the exact moment they were dreaming it. This often happens within families or with those to whom you're close, but it can also happen with strangers. Read on.

Astral Travel

In astral travel, you can visit distant lands in an instant. People have reported visiting other planets like Mars or Jupiter with no recollection of getting there or back. It's also known that you can visit other times in your astral dreams—the past, for example.

Some people actually see their souls as they were hundreds of years ago and mistake the vision for a future event. Others make astral visits with their spirit guides, who give them advice. Still others see things happening on the other side of the earth. Astral travel is the most intense, enlightening part of dreams. It's a gift, once you recognize it for what it is.

QUESTION?

Why do we sometimes jerk out of sleep?
If you're just waking up and you feel heavy or half-paralyzed, it's an indication that you've been astrally traveling. An American named Sylvan Muldoon coined the term "astral catalepsy" for the feeling that your "cord" is being extended and then pulled back when you wake up from an astral travel dream.

When you experience astral catalepsy, don't panic. The invisible cord that attaches your soul to your body will jerk you back into consciousness, but there is no limit to its length. As mentioned, you can astrally travel to the moon and back. Don't worry when you feel the jerking sensation. Your cord always comes back to you, and it never breaks.

Astral Catalepsy

There are three speeds at which you can astrally travel: normal, intermediate, and supernormal. Normal speed feels like the pace at which you would walk. Intermediate speed can feel a bit scary because everything seems like it's passing by you. Streaks of light are projected off the objects. By the time you get to supernormal speed, though, you're almost completely unaware of traveling. The speed is unfathomable. Within seconds, you can astrally travel to the other end of the universe, into the future, or back to the past.

These are the signs of astral catalepsy:

- Shortness of breath
- Confusion
- Temporary paralysis
- A buzzing vibration
- The feeling of being pinned down
- A sense that there's something evil nearby

A Short Astral Trip

One Sunday afternoon in 1958, Robert Monroe, a Virginia businessman and electrical engineer, lay down on the couch for a short nap. His body began to shake violently, but he couldn't move. Terrified, he finally forced himself to sit upright on the couch. The vibration faded away and he stood up and walked around.

This experience was repeated a number of times during the following months. Monroe thought there was something physically wrong, like epilepsy or a brain tumor, but his family doctor gave him a clean bill of health.

Monroe committed himself to exploring the sensation, which continued to occur over the next few months. Then one night when the vibrations started up, Monroe realized he could move his fingers. His arm was draped over the side of the bed and his fingers were brushing the rug, so he pressed down with his fingertips. His fingers seemed to penetrate the rug, so he pressed down harder and his hand sank into the floor.

He returned to his doctor, who advised him to lose some weight, smoke less, and to look into yoga. Some practitioners of yoga, the doctor said, claimed they could travel out of their bodies at will. The very notion struck Monroe as absurd. The vibrations came and went six more times before he mustered the nerve to explore. Then, one night, with the vibrations in full force, he thought of floating upward, and did.

For Monroe, this was the beginning of a lifelong exploration into astral travel. He wrote three books on his experiences and started the Monroe Institute, a research and educational facility. At the institute, people are taught how to travel out of their bodies and to gather information objectively in these inner realms, using maps and landmarks that Monroe charted during his thousands of out-of-body experiences.

Out-of-body experiences, astral dreams, and flying dreams are quite often related. While flying dreams are often considered from a symbolic perspective, it's also worthwhile to consider their relationship to out-of-body experiences.

Out-of-Body Travel

This section explores how to achieve out-of-body travel while you're asleep. Robert Monroe's technique, gleaned from his more than thirty years of exploration, is not simple by any means. However, it is certainly within the reach of anyone committed to dream work. There are several steps to follow, two of which are described here.

Relaxation

Numerous books are available on how to achieve the total relaxation necessary for an out-of-body experience. Use whatever method feels right to you. The goal is to reach that drowsy state between wakefulness and sleep and to maintain it without falling asleep.

The second stage of relaxation is to maintain the borderland state without concentrating on anything. Just focus on the blackness in front of you. Eliminate any nervousness or unease you might feel.

The third stage involves deepening your consciousness by "letting go of your rigid hold on the borderland sleep edge and drifting deeper little by little." Monroe says that sensory mechanisms begin to shut down. Touch usually goes first, and then smell and taste. Sometimes your vision goes next, while sometimes it's your hearing.

"As you become relaxed and start to drift into sleep," Monroe writes, "hold your mental attention on something, anything, with your eyes closed. Once you can hold the borderland state indefinitely without falling asleep, you have passed the first stage."

Vibrations

This is the critical phase. According to Monroe, the vibrational field that is essential to an out-of-body experience seems to work best when your head is positioned at magnetic north. Also, make sure your room isn't completely dark; you need some light as a point of reference. In addition, don't set a time limit. Make sure you won't be disturbed.

Without weakening your conscious awareness, relax as deeply as you can, then give yourself the suggestion that you'll recall everything you experience that is beneficial to your physical and mental being. Monroe suggests that you repeat this five times, and then begin breathing with your mouth half-opened.

To set up the vibrational waves, he recommends that you imagine two lines extending from the sides of your head and converging about a foot away, in front of your eyes. Think of these lines as charged wires that are joined, or as poles of a magnet that are connected. Once they converge, extend them three feet from your forehead, and then six feet. Now you must move the intersecting lines ninety degrees so they meet over your head. Then reach out toward the point through the top of your head. Keep reaching until you feel a reaction. "It is as if a surging, hissing rhythmically pulsating wave of fiery sparks comes roaring into your head," he writes. "From there it seems to sweep throughout your body, making it rigid and immobile."

Practicing Out-of-Body Dreams

This section describes various techniques of achieving out-of-body experiences. Whether you use Monroe's method, Renie's method, or Tholey's method, there are many ways you can go about making out-of-body dreams happen. Though similar, each technique has its own emphasis. Study all of the theories, and then start to make your wildest dreams real. First, look at Monroe's technique:

1. **Controlling the vibrations:** Monroe stresses that eliminating fear and panic is of utmost importance. The first time the vibrations occur, you'll feel like you're being electrocuted, even though there's no pain involved. "Lie quietly and objectively analyze them until they fade away of their own accord. This usually takes place in about five minutes."

Once you become accustomed to the sensation, you're ready to control it. Monroe suggests that you mentally direct the vibrations into a ring that sweeps around your body, from head to toes and back again. Once you've got the momentum going, let it proceed on its own.

It takes practice to smooth out the vibrations. But once you're able to do it, you should be able to start the vibrations simply on a mental command, thus eliminating some of the other steps. The momentum of the vibration is critical to disassociation from the physical. The faster the vibration, the easier it is to disassociate.

2. **Thought control:** Monroe contends that in the out-of-body state, thought is instantaneously translated into action. Because of this, you have to be focused on a single thought, such as "Float upward." This is also why you have to eliminate fear and panic. If you don't, your fear will instantly manifest itself. It might assume some terrifying shape, or it might propel you right back into your body. Fear, Monroe says, is the biggest obstacle to overcome.

3. **Separation and lifting out:** Monroe recommends that you initially separate just your hand and explore the area in the immediate vicinity. Find an object, identify it, and then wake up and see if you're right. This is a way to build self-confidence.

Once you're comfortable with this partially dissociated state, the easiest way to separate fully from your body is to "lift out." Imagine yourself floating upward. Think about how pleasurable the sensation will be. Imagine yourself getting lighter and lighter. If you hold these thoughts, you'll float upward. You can also rotate your way out—turn over—just as you would if you were trying to get more comfortable in bed. "Start turning by twisting the top of your body, your head, and shoulders—move slowly."

Once you begin this exploration and can summon the vibrational state at will, "you will be committed to the reality of this other existence. How this will affect your personality, your daily life, your future and your philosophies rests entirely with you as an individual."

Renie's Method

Renie's technique, though simpler than Monroe's, involves the same basics:

- **Relaxation:** Renie suggests that you enter a relaxed state using whatever method works best for you. Then, when your entire body is relaxed, visualize the out-of-body experience happening. See it clearly in your mind, and hold the image.
- **Visualization:** Once you're completely relaxed and are focused on leaving your body, visualize yourself shrinking. "For me, this is crucial to getting out. I see myself getting smaller and smaller, until I'm nearly nonexistent," Renie says. "If you can't envision this at first, keep practicing until you can."
- **Vibrational field:** At some point during the shrinking process, a humming may begin in your ears. The humming is comparable to the vibrational field described by Monroe. Remain focused on how small you are, and turn up the volume on the humming.

- **Thought control:** To travel in the out-of-body state, simply think about where you want to go. The clearer your request, the faster you move—and with fewer impediments.

"When I can't possibly shrink anymore without vanishing, and when the humming is very loud, I visualize my astral self floating away from my physical body and say, 'Up and out.' And I'm gone." Practice doing this and it will become second nature to you.

Tholey's Method

Paul Tholey, a German psychologist who has researched OBEs and lucid dreams, offers yet another method of achieving the out-of-body state. Tholey calls his method "body technique." Tholey recommends that, while drifting into sleep, you imagine that your body is somewhere else, doing something other than lying in bed. If you find yourself "elsewhere," you have achieved the out-of-body state.

Alternately, Tholey suggests concentrating on the idea that, as you are falling asleep, you will no longer perceive your body. Then, as soon as you are asleep, it is possible to float freely, at a point of awareness, in "a space which seems to be identical with the room in which one went to sleep."

Other Hints

Keep in mind that with out-of-body travel, there are no guarantees that your experience will be pleasant. The worlds you will visit are not necessarily any better or worse than the physical one in which you exist. Always remember, though, that nothing can harm you and that there is truly no such thing as "evil" in this state—it might just seem that way.

But if you do find yourself in a "lower realm" among disturbed beings, there are ways of effectively dealing with them and moving on. When Jane Roberts encountered undesirable people, or "energy shapes," on her early out-of-body travels, Seth advised her not to panic. If the entity seemed threatening, she was supposed to say, "Peace be with you," and this would dissipate the negative emotion that fueled the entity.

ALERT!

Pay special attention to your ordinary dreams while you're trying to induce out-of-body experiences. If your anxieties and fears are emerging in your dreams, work through whatever causes them. Knowing what you fear is the first step in conquering the fear itself. Once you've conquered the fears, your out-of-body experiences will progress more smoothly.

Chapter 10

Lucid Dreaming

A lucid dream is one in which you're aware that you're dreaming. It may begin as a normal dream, but at some point you wake up inside the dream. Then, depending on your skill, you can manipulate the action in the dream and mold it, second by second. In this chapter, find out more about lucid dreaming and how it can be done.

Awake or Dreaming?

For years, lucid dreaming was primarily the domain of parapsychologists—a critical factor in discouraging mainstream scientists from studying it. But in recent years, lucid dreaming has become a hot topic of study. Stephen LaBerge, a pioneer of lucid dreaming research, attributes this surge of interest, in part, to several landmark books.

In 1968, an English parapsychologist named Celia Green published *Lucid Dreams*. Her book included the most comprehensive overview of the literature available on the subject up to that time. During the 1970s, Ann Faraday, author of *The Dream Game*, and Patricia Garfield, author of *Creative Dreaming*, were instrumental in kindling popular interest in the subject. Even though serious scientific research on lucid dreaming didn't take place until the 1970s, it has been recognized for centuries.

FACT

An eighth-century Tibetan yoga master wrote about lucid dreaming methods in *The Yoga of the Dream State*. A couple of centuries later, another Tibetan master, Atisha, wrote of being simultaneously awake and asleep in *The Seven Points of Mind Training*.

Earlier this century, the Russian philosopher P.D. Uspenskii asked himself, "Was it not possible to preserve consciousness in dreams—to know while dreaming that one is asleep and to think consciously as we think when awake?" Uspenskii decided that it was possible. In *A New Model of the Universe*, he recalled the following lucid dream, which he called a half-dream state.

Half-Dream Means Lucid

This dream is called "Testing":

I remember once seeing myself in a large empty room without windows. Besides myself there was in the room only a small black kitten. "I am dreaming," I say to myself. "How can I know whether I am really asleep or not? Suppose I try it this way. Let this black kitten be transformed into a large white dog. In a waking state it is impossible and if it comes off it will mean that I am asleep." I say this to myself and immediately the black kitten becomes transformed into a large white dog. At the same time the opposite wall disappears, revealing a mountain landscape with a river like a ribbon receding into the distance.

"This is curious," I say to myself. "I did not order this landscape. Where did it come from?" Some faint recollection begins to stir in me, a recollection of having seen this landscape somewhere and of its being somehow connected with the white dog. But I feel that if I let myself go into it I shall forget the most important thing that I have to remember, namely, that I am asleep and am conscious of myself.

Don Juan

Carlos Castaneda is another important person to consider in the discussion of lucid dreams. Like Jane Roberts, his work began in the early 1960s. In his first book, *The Teachings of Don Juan*, Castaneda recounts his apprenticeship with a Yaqui Indian sorcerer named Don Juan. There has been considerable controversy about whether Castaneda's books are colorful fiction or fictionalized versions of true events. Regardless, the fact remains that the dream states Castaneda writes about, in which he explores different worlds, are very similar to lucid dreams.

One of the cues Don Juan taught Castaneda for becoming conscious in a dream is exceptional. In *Journey to Ixtlan*, Don Juan shows him how to find his hand in a dream as a way of stabilizing the dream. Today it is known that the state of your hand is a strong clue as to whether or not you are lucid.

For one science-fiction writer, the vision of his hand in a dream wasn't simply useful. It saved his life.

Life Saving

This dream is titled "Jay's Hand":

My wife and I had a beef dinner that night. I don't remember feeling unusual in any way. We went to bed early and, at some point during the night, I dreamed that I saw my hand. That was it, just my hand. I could see it clearly.

And suddenly I realized I was dreaming and I snapped awake. I could hardly breathe. My chest felt heavy. I thought I was having a heart attack. I woke my wife and she called the paramedics. Since we lived on a farm then, out in the middle of nowhere, it took them a long time to arrive. My wife and my closest friend, who was staying over that night, kept me alive until the paramedics got there.

The upshot was that I'm allergic to red meat and the beef I'd eaten that night caused an adrenaline reaction. If I hadn't dreamed of seeing my hand, I might not have awakened in time to save my life.

There are several different ways to become lucid in your dreams, but the same methods don't work for everyone. One popular approach is to focus on a body part. If you make a point to call attention to a part of your body—something very real—you can make the dream lucid and control how it progresses.

More Than Time-Telling

In the following example, the dreamer was a young woman who had been doing work on lucid dreaming. This dream is called "The Clock":

In the dream, my alarm hadn't gone off, and I knew I would be late for work. I was running around, trying to eat and shower and get dressed, all in the space of a few minutes. At some point, it occurred to me that I didn't really have any idea what time it was and that's when the dream became lucid—when I woke inside the dream. I suddenly realized that if I turned my head ever so slightly, I would be able to see my clock on the nightstand. So that's what I did. The time was 3:07. I opened my eyes, coming fully awake, and the clock read 3:07.

LaBerge's Theories

Stephen LaBerge didn't realize that lucid dreaming was possible until the fall of 1976, when he ran across Celia Green's book and the following quote: "If others had learned to have lucid dreams, then nothing prevented me from doing the same. Just reading about the topic had resulted in several lucid dreams for me." In February of 1977, LaBerge began a dream journal and, over the next seven years, he recorded nearly 900 lucid dreams.

LaBerge used lucid dreaming as the basis for his doctoral thesis and then conducted experiments at the Stanford University Sleep Research Center. At that time, mainstream science still held that lucid dreaming was impossible.

FACT

When LaBerge submitted his preliminary findings on lucid dreaming to the prestigious magazine *Science,* the paper was rejected. The British magazine equivalent, *Nature,* returned his paper without review; the editors didn't think the topic of lucid dreaming was "of sufficient interest" to merit consideration.

Despite resistance by mainstream science, LaBerge persevered, and by the mid-1980s, the scientific attitude toward lucid dreams had begun to change. By then he was well into his exploration and was working regularly with "oneironauts"—a word he coined from Greek roots meaning "explorers of the inner world of dreams." LaBerge taught these oneironauts how to signal when a lucid dream began. He developed certain criteria and techniques for inducing and exploring lucid dreams and believed that anyone could learn to have them.

Your First Lucid Dream

Very often, lucid dreams are first experienced accidentally. Without making any special preparations, you suddenly realize you are awake and still dreaming. If you're lucky, the experience will last for more than a few seconds.

For some, lucidity may arise for the first time from a nightmare. But for most dreamers, LaBerge says, lucidity happens when you recognize some glaring inconsistency or bizarre factor in your dream. Other times, a first-time experience is triggered when you realize your dream is very familiar—that you've dreamed it before. LaBerge calls this entry into a lucid dream "deja reve."

"Reality testing," a reasoning process normally delegated to the waking brain, is one of the elements that distinguish lucid dreams from other kinds of dreams. With practice, you won't even have to ask if you're dreaming. Once you recognize some anomaly or bizarre event in the dream, your realization will be instantaneous.

My House

In the following example, Anita's recurring dream about a Gothic house triggered a lucid dream. This dream is called "Gothic House As Launchpad":

As soon as I stepped into the house this time, I recognized it. I knew it was the Gothic house of my recurring dream, the place I had explored countless times in the past.

With this realization, the dream turned lucid. I found myself in a sunlit living room, an immense and beautifully furnished room that I hadn't been in before. Just to make sure I was actually lucid, I leaped into the air to see if I could fly and I did! My astonishment was so great, I woke up.

Making It Happen

If you have never awakened inside a dream and would like to sample the experience, or if you've spontaneously entered a lucid dream in the past and would like to further explore this region of dreaming, there are methods you can try to induce lucidity. The best times to enter a lucid dream are just as you fall asleep and as you awaken after a night's sleep. If you fall asleep easily and quickly, with practice you can enter a lucid dream within minutes of lying down. LaBerge suggests using a counting method: "One, I'm dreaming. Two, I'm dreaming . . . " Once you reach a certain number, you'll say it aloud and will actually be dreaming.

Alternately, as you are falling asleep, focus on one particular thing—a visualization, your breath or heartbeat, how your body feels, or whatever you choose. "If you keep the mind sufficiently active while the tendency to enter REM sleep is strong," writes LaBerge, "you feel your body fall asleep but you, that is to say, your consciousness, remains awake." You may also find that a lucid state is easier to obtain after you've slept a while.

ALERT!

Since your longest period of REM sleep is toward morning, try not to open your eyes when you wake! Lie quietly and let your dream images surround and flow through you. Afterward, turn over on your side or change positions. The act of moving may allow you to think of yourself as awake as well as dreaming.

Developing a Sleep Routine

The Seth Material and Jane Roberts's own books offer valuable information on dream states. In *The Nature of Personal Reality*, Seth discusses the value of sleeping in four- or six-hour blocks instead of the usual eight-hour block that is customary in Western culture.

By following such a sleep routine, "there are not the great artificial divisions created between the two states of consciousness. The conscious mind is better able to remember and assimilate its dreaming experience, and in the dream the self can use the waking experience more efficiently."

Without ever mentioning the term "lucid dreaming," Seth says that by following this particular sleep routine, it becomes obvious that "the individual sense of identity can be retained in the dream state. When you find yourself as alert, responsive, and intellectual in the dream state as you are in waking life, it becomes impossible to operate within the old framework."

It's interesting to note that Robert Monroe followed a sleep routine similar to what Seth describes. He frequently mentioned sleeping for "two cycles," a reference to two dream cycles of about four hours. Roberts and her husband also followed Seth's suggestions. They slept for six hours a night, with a half-hour nap in the afternoon, as needed.

To develop a sleep routine, first determine how many hours of sleep you need—whether it's seven or eight or even nine. If the answer is seven, for example, try a six-hour block of sleep at night and an hour nap in the afternoon or right before dinner. Try several different combinations, and choose the one that works best for you.

This routine is dependent on a flexible work schedule that lets you nap at some point during the day. If your schedule won't allow it, then try the routine on weekends or vacations, when your time is your own.

By stimulating your mind to focus on the real issues in your life, you can intensify the state of lucid dreaming. There are several exercises that can help you do this, including the following. For this exercise, list five fears or limitations that you would like to overcome. Also list five goals that you would like to achieve in the next three months, in six months, and in the next year. Create a game plan for incorporating these challenges and goals into your lucid dreaming program, and then put them into action. List these things:

- Five fears or limitations you would like to overcome
- Your plan for overcoming these limitations
- Five goals you would like to achieve in the next three months
- Your plan for achieving these goals

- Five goals you would like to achieve in the next six months
- Your plan for achieving these goals

Intent Is Everything

Your intention to explore the world of lucid dreaming is vital in triggering such a dream. When Stephen LaBerge was just beginning his research, he realized that as he clarified his intent to remember, the number of his lucid dreams increased dramatically. "Lucid dreaming rarely occurs without our intending it, which means having the mental set to recognize when we are dreaming; thus, intention forms a part of any deliberate effort to induce lucid dreams."

Malcolm Godwin, author of *The Lucid Dreamer—A Waking Guide for the Traveler Between Worlds*, notes that the method advocated by the tenth-century Tibetan master Atisha creates a similar effect: *Think that all phenomena are like dreams.* "For in continually thinking that everything is a dream during the day, that mind-set begins to appear in your nightly dreams, and suddenly you will start to experience yourself both deeply asleep and yet fully awake at the same moment."

The most important part of inducing a lucid dream is to constantly ask yourself if you are dreaming. Ask yourself this question over and over, even if you are obviously awake. Sometimes our dreams are so incredibly lucid that we think we're awake when we are actually entering a dream state.

LaBerge suggests that you set memory targets during the day as a way of training your mind to wake up during a dream. In this method, you select objects or even sounds as triggers. For example, if you select two targets, the sound of a dog barking and the sight of a red car, you will note that you've found a target whenever you hear a bark or see the appointed vehicle.

You may want to train your waking memory by giving yourself four specific targets each day. Memorize the day's targets. Record your successes. Every time you find one of the targets, write it down, and remember to ask yourself if you're dreaming. Keep track of how many targets you hit each day. If, at the end of the week, you've missed most of the targets, then continue the exercise for another week. Record the following:

- Day One Targets:
- Day One Hits:
- Day Two Targets:
- Day Two Hits:

Continue this exercise for five days and then examine your success. Did you find more targets as time went on? Did you get worse at the exercise? How did your strategy change?

LaBerge's MILD Technique

If you can't remember to do something when you're awake, you probably won't be able to remember to do it when you're asleep. But if you're successful with your target exercise, you should also be able to use LaBerge's MILD technique. Outlined in his book, *Exploring the World of Lucid Dreaming*, MILD stands for "Mnemonic Induction of Lucid Dreaming." There are five basic steps to this technique:

QUESTION?

Why is it so important to have a lucid dream?
Lucid dreams give us so much control over our waking lives. If we learn to recognize our wishes, hopes, and fears, and then how to restructure the "plot" of our dreams, we can effectively steer ourselves toward success on all fronts.

1. **Set up dream recall.** Simply state your intent to wake up through the night and recall your dreams.

2. **Recall your dream.** When you wake from a dream, try to recall as many details as possible. Don't tell yourself you'll remember the dream in the morning; chances are it will be gone by then. Force yourself to write it down in your dream journal right away.

3. **Focus your intent.** While you're falling back to sleep, focus on your intention to recognize that you're dreaming. Mean what you say. Stay centered on this one thought. Remember, intention is everything!

4. **Visualize yourself becoming lucid.** The best way to do this is to see yourself back in the dream from which you've just awakened. This time, however, recognize that it's a dream. Look for something to tip you off that you're dreaming. For example, as you relive the dream, decide that you're going to fly. See yourself doing it, see yourself realizing that you're dreaming, and then continue reliving the dream.

5. **Repeat.** LaBerge recommends repeating steps 3 and 4 just to fix your intent in your mind.

Mirror, Mirror on the Wall

No matter what method you use to reach the world of lucid dreams, once you become successful, the benefits are enormous. You can overcome your fears by directly confronting them in your lucid dreams. You can increase your self-knowledge, which expands your awareness. By consciously facing danger in your dreams, you develop self-confidence, which spills into your everyday life. And you can solve problems in the dream state that will benefit your waking life. Try as many methods as it takes—mastering the art of lucid dreaming can greatly improve your life.

Malcolm Godwin offers another method of entering a lucid dream that is a variation on an Eastern technique known as *tratak*. Before going to sleep, sit comfortably in front of a mirror for about half an hour. Place a lighted candle nearby to illuminate your face, and stare steadily at your reflected image without blinking for as long as you can. The face in the mirror will start changing quite dramatically, like a series of wavering masks. Godwin notes that many practitioners believe these masks are images of our past lives.

As you continue to gaze into the mirror, *intend* to dream that night. Watch the changing faces for a while longer, and then ask to see your real face. "Meditators claim that in waking life the image in the mirror disappears altogether," Godwin says. "In lucid dreams prepare to be even more surprised."

Chapter 11

 Shamanism and Power Dreaming

The ancient practice of shamanism is alive today, not only in the remnants of primitive cultures but also through a new age of shamans. Many of them were raised and educated in the Western world. No longer called witch doctors or medicine men, these modern shamans are students of elders who were once part of a primitive culture or who still have strong links to one. In this chapter, discover the magic of shamanism and power dreaming.

Myths in History

"Shamanism is not a religion," explains Alberto Villoldo, Ph.D., a medical anthropologist and an Inca shaman. "There is no Christ figure, no Buddha, no guru; nobody who says, 'Follow my footsteps.' Shamanism demands that you take your own steps with courage, compassion, and vision. It requires that you learn from nature. It teaches you to meet power directly, embrace it, and claim it."

Villoldo's own sojourn into shamanism began in 1973, when he met Antonio Morales Baca, a philosophy professor at the Universidad Nacional de San Antonio Abad in Cuzco. At the time, he was the only Indian on the university's staff. With Morales as his guide, Villoldo set out on a trek along the Urubamba River in the *altiplano* in search of a *kurac akullec,* a master shaman named Don Jicaram.

FACT

Ultimately, and quite by chance, Villoldo realized that Morales and Don Jicaram were one and the same. From there, he began the fourteen-year apprenticeship described in his books, *Dance of the Four Winds* and *Island of the Sun*.

In *Island of the Sun,* Villoldo tells of a waking dream sequence that revealed itself to be dreams within dreams. It began after Villoldo arrived at Machu Picchu on a solo trek of the Inca Trail. He stole into the ruins as darkness fell and found a secluded alcove. Unable to sleep, he crossed the central plaza under a full moon and moved to a meadow that edged the ruins near the Pachamama Stone, an upright slab twenty feet wide and ten feet high.

Villoldo's experience began with a meditation that led to his vision of an ancient Inca ceremony in which several colorfully garbed participants were dancing and chanting around the fire near the Pachamama Stone. He joined the dancers and then followed one of them—a young girl with plaited hair woven with ribbons—away from the fire and along a trail leading up Huayna Picchu, a steep mountain peak near the ruins. The girl disappeared among the rocks, and Villoldo came to a cavern where he met an old woman who seemed to be waiting for him. The woman, who was busy making candles from animal lard, spoke rudely to him.

> My first thought was that I was dreaming; it was a fact that I was dreaming. I was *aware* that I was dreaming. And then the room collapsed . . . and in the dream I see myself, sitting before the Pachamama Stone, and the dancers are moving in the soft rain and the orange light of the fire. I knew that somewhere I was in my body and dreaming about myself watching the dancers down there. That is a dream. And this?

He found himself back in the cavern with the old woman. He described her in detail, from the bone pipe she was smoking to her woven wool dress, but he couldn't hear what she was saying to him. He followed her out of the cavern and over to a pair of huge condors, who taught him how to project himself into an animal. He did so, merging with the consciousness of one of the condors and soaring through the night. When he returned to the cavern, the old woman told him to leave.

He tried to go back to his dream so he could then awake: "And when I see myself sleeping in the meadow before the Pachamama Stone, I struggle to wake myself. The dancers have gone and dawn is threatening to break and I am asleep on the grass. It is only when I see myself stir and watch my eyes open that I realize that I am dreaming of myself waking in the meadow."

QUESTION?

What does Villoldo do now?
Villoldo is a shaman associated with the Q'ero Indians of the Andes, who are considered direct descendants of the ancient Incas. For more than twenty years, Villoldo has led workshops and shamanic journeys. He still teaches at the Learning Annex and other learning facilities.

It was that dream, of watching himself wake up and inspect the ground where the dancers had trod, from which he truly and fully awoke.

He found that he was not in the meadow at all, but in a cavern in the side of Huayna Picchu, a mountain adjacent to Machu Picchu.

Obtaining a Power Dream

To make a power dream happen, you don't necessarily need a shaman to guide you or even a power object from an ancient lineage of shamans. You may have a power object in your own possession without even realizing it. Such an object might be a family heirloom that has been passed down from generation to generation. Perhaps it's your grandmother's wedding ring, which once belonged to her mother or grandmother. The idea is that such an object has stored memories or messages that can be accessed through shamanic-like dreaming.

To prepare for your power dream, hold the object in your hand before going to bed. Quiet your mind. It's okay if you don't know the history of the object. Note any thoughts that seem to come to your mind from elsewhere after you've quieted your thoughts. If any of them appear to be warnings, heed them and don't go any further.

ALERT!

Even if the power object you select has been in your family for a century, make sure you know the identity of its previous owners. Don't knowingly select an object that could have belonged to an unkind person or a criminal. The result could be a distressing nightmare!

After your meditation, place the object under your pillow or someplace in close proximity to your body. As you fall asleep, concentrate on your desire to receive a dream of power from someone once associated with the object. Tell yourself that only a positive experience will result and that your life will be enhanced by the dream.

Power Objects

Rachel, a mother of three who joined Villoldo on one of his treks to the canyon lands of the Southwest, recalls a dream of power that she experienced. The following dream is called "The Black Panther":

One evening, Alberto unwrapped his *mesa*, a bundle of hand-woven cloth that contained ancient power objects—carved stone figures, metal pieces, bead necklaces, crystals, and cloth bags containing things that rattled. All the power objects had been handed down from Inca shaman to Inca shaman and finally to Villoldo. Some of them were hundreds of years old.

The objects were passed around the circle in the dimly lit tent. Rather than looking at them, we felt them. We were to select one that appealed to us, and then quickly pass on the others. That night we were to sleep with the power object we had selected.

My dream began by seeing mountains around me. Somehow, I knew I was in South America. I didn't understand why I was seeing another place, since we were in the Southwest. Then I saw the black panther. It came right into my forehead through a physical opening. Everything opened up then and I had a sense of being in a primordial lost paradise of the Native Americans. I sensed the people and the earth.

If you don't have a power object from a past generation of your own family, you can select something you feel gives off good energy. Old pieces usually work well, but almost anything can be used, as long as it speaks to you personally. Indian reservations usually have wonderful new and older artifacts and healing objects that are perfect for this purpose.

Rachel's power object was a small, smooth stone wrapped in a rough piece of cloth. Villoldo told her he wasn't surprised that she'd seen South American mountains and experienced the panther entering her forehead. The stone had been given to Villoldo by the high shaman of the Q'eros—the Incan equivalent of the Dalai Lama.

That night, Charles, who was also on the same journey, selected a smooth, three-pronged stone as his power object. He recalled, "I dreamed of seeing myself dressed and packed for a journey. I was on a train and directly above me was a woman, who was also me. Then there was my dreaming self who was observing the other two."

After Charles told of the dream, Villoldo explained to him that the three-pronged stone was associated with the three worlds of the Incas: the *Kaypacha,* the physical world; the *Ukhupacha,* the inner world or dreaming world; and *Hanaqpacha,* the higher world. "We all have multiple selves living simultaneously in each of these worlds," Villoldo stated.

Power Dreaming Exercise

Record your experience with power dreaming. List the following:

- The date
- Your power object
- How it makes you feel
- Thoughts about the object before going to sleep
- Results

Do this every night for two weeks. Write down everything you remember about your dreams. If you're not having positive results, and you start to feel less and less confident and happy about your choice of article, place the object in a closed stone or metal box and put it away. Find another object to use. You should feel very comfortable with your power object.

Big (Important) Dreams

"A shaman is a man or woman who enters an altered state of consciousness—at will—to contact and utilize an ordinarily hidden reality in order to acquire knowledge, power, and to help other persons," says Michael Harner, an anthropologist who has practiced shamanism for more than a quarter of a century.

Harner says that from the shaman's perspective, there are ordinary dreams and "big" dreams. The shaman's interest is in the latter. Big dreams involve communication with a guardian spirit or a power animal. "A big dream is one that is repeated several times in the same basic way on different nights, or it is a one-time dream that is so vivid that it is like being awake."

The difference between a shamanic dream, or big dream, and a lucid dream is that the former deals with spirit or guardian contact and/or the intent of gaining power or knowledge. A lucid dream is typically an adventure or journey that is not necessarily connected with any spiritual tradition or related goal.

Director of the Foundation of Shamanic Studies, Michael Harner has held numerous workshops on shamanism, teaching skills that have been handed down over millennia. "In my shamanic workshops, these new practitioners are not 'playing Indian,' but going to the same revelatory spiritual sources that tribal shamans have traveled to from time immemorial. Their experiences are genuine and, when described, are essentially interchangeable with the accounts of shamans from non-literate tribal cultures."

Big dreams are often literal. If you dream of being in a car accident, the dream may not be symbolic, but a warning of an actual accident. Harner says that in such a case you may not be able to prevent it, but you can enact it symbolically and thereby minimize its impact. In other words, you can begin to accept an event before you even know if it really happened. This way, if the dream turns out to be true, you will be better prepared to receive the news.

In his book, *The Way of the Shaman*, Harner describes a big dream recounted by a woman who had attended one of his workshops. In the dream, she was in a car accident in which she hit metal twice but wasn't seriously injured. This dream is called "Big Warning Dream":

> While waiting for the car to stop its 180-degree spin, I was aware of being pinned against my son within the car by the momentum of the spin, and being outside and slightly over the car watching the entire 'dream' taking place—again. During the entire episode I was aware of a feeling of deep peace and the awareness that my guardian spirit was right there with me and shielding me from danger.

Even though she knew about symbolically enacting such a dream, she didn't do it. About a month later, she was driving with her son when a car veered in front of her. She struck the car, was spun around, and struck it again. Just as in her dream, she struck metal twice and was not seriously injured.

The difference between a shamanic dream, or big dream, and a lucid dream is that the former deals with spirit or guardian contact and/or the intent of gaining power or knowledge. A lucid dream is typically an adventure or journey that is not necessarily connected with any spiritual tradition or related goal.

Enacting a Big Dream

You don't have to be a shaman or even a shaman's apprentice to enact a big dream. The technique can be carried out whenever you have a particularly vivid dream, whether it's ominous or providential. First, ask yourself what the message is, and then decide whether it is literal or symbolic. You can enact the dream either way. Gary's experience, which follows, is an example of how to do it.

When Gary had a brief, but vivid, dream, its contents were so startling that he bolted out of his sleep and sat up gasping for breath. In the dream, he had taken a gun, put it to his head and fired. Bright red blood spurted from the wound and he knew he had just killed himself. Gary was puzzled by the dream because he wasn't suicidal and had never thought about killing himself. However, he had recently left his wife and was starting out on a new life. He realized that the dream image was symbolic of killing his old self. He would never be the same person again.

QUESTION?

Does dreaming that I kill myself in a dream mean I secretly want to do it?

No! Remember that death in dreams usually refers to transformation or ending an old way of life to start a new one. Dreaming of death or suicide usually means that you're ready to shed your old skin and begin anew. Though it may seem very negative in the dream, it could be a good sign for your real life.

Gary enacted the dream by beginning divorce proceedings, even though his wife wanted to wait to see if matters could be patched up. He felt that there was no going back to the old ways and that the dream was a confirmation. It was a difficult, highly emotional situation, but he felt he was taking the right action.

He also made a symbolic gesture to move ahead into his new life by visualizing a frayed rope connecting him and his wife. In the visualization, he took a pair of scissors and cut the remaining threads. Sometimes it helps to visualize such things.

Visualization can have profound effects on your psyche, your energy, and the world around you. Decide first what you truly want before you picture it in your mind. Always ask for the highest answer you can receive. For example, don't ask for the return of an ex-boyfriend or ex-girlfriend. Ask that the right person for you come along.

Dream Control

Undoubtedly the most famous practitioner of shamanism—or sorcery, as he calls it—is Carlos Castaneda (also mentioned in Chapter 10). His Native American teacher, Don Juan, stressed the importance of dream voyages: "Dreams are, if not a door, a hatch into other worlds." According to Don Juan, what we call reality is only a description of the world in which we are currently engaged, and that description can be altered through dreaming.

Setting Up Dreams

To begin his instruction in dreaming, Don Juan taught Castaneda to set up dreams as a means of controlling them. This process engages your "dreaming attention" in order to shift your perceptions to new worlds or new ways of seeing this world.

"To set up dreaming means to have a precise and practical command over the general situation of a dream," Don Juan says in Castaneda's *The Art of Dreaming*. "For example, you may dream that you are in your classroom. You don't let the dream slip into something else. You don't jump from the classroom to the mountains, for instance. In other words, you control the view of the classroom and don't let it go until you want to."

But to reach a state of control takes practice. The first step for Castaneda was to be able to find his hands in his dreams, which helped him realize he was dreaming. Once you achieve this state of awareness, you can stop the action within a dream and closely examine your surroundings.

When you can control your dreams, you will have passed through the "first gate" of dreams. "The most astonishing thing that happens to dreamers is that, on reaching the first gate, they also reach the energy body." According to Don Juan, the energy body "can transport itself in one instant to the ends of the universe."

Finding Your Hands

The following procedure can help you find your hands during a dream and take control of your dreaming. It's derived from a technique practiced by George Gurdjieff, a nineteenth-century Russian mystic and teacher.

First, close your eyes and visualize your hands. As you prepare for sleep, remind yourself of what you've been doing during the day, and visualize your hands again. Take this image with you into sleep. Tell yourself that you will be dreaming when you see your hands again, and you will become awake in your dream.

Once you have succeeded in finding your hands, go on to the second part of the procedure: stopping your dream. It may take many attempts before you are able to do this. Before going to sleep, tell yourself that you will find your hands in a dream, and then you will be able to stop the dream and carefully examine your surroundings.

Keep in mind that it may take weeks or even months before you see your hands in a dream, but with practice and consistency, it's likely that you'll succeed. It took Castaneda several months before he saw his hands, and Gurdjieff's disciples reported results in three to six months.

For Gurdjieff, the practice of visualizing your hands during the day undermines your certainty that you are awake. It was his belief that everyone is asleep and that when people finally awaken, they will realize that what they thought of as consciousness was actually a dream.

What Dreams Can Teach You

The Australian Aborigines, whose shamanic traditions are said to reach back forty thousand years, regard dreaming, or Dreamtime, as the foundation of the world. "Dreams continue to connect the Aboriginal people with what they call 'Dreamtime,' a primal state which embraces the creation of the world at the very dawn of time," writes Malcolm Godwin in *The Lucid*

Dreamer. "Dreamtime is the realm of the mythical beings who first breathed life into the universe."

Another disciple of the new shamans, John Perkins, emphasizes that the dream that created this world is only one version of the world; we can create new versions and new worlds. Perkins describes a shaman as "a man or woman who journeys into Dreamtime or parallel worlds and uses the subconscious, along with physical reality, to effect change."

FACT

John Perkins first encountered shamans when he worked in the Peace Corps in the Amazon rain forest in the late 1960s. His later training came from indigenous Ecuadorian shamans. Today, he teaches workshops on shamanism and leads ecologically oriented tours of the Amazon and the Shuar.

Dreaming is at the heart of the world of the Shuar, Perkins explains in *The World Is as You Dream It: Shamanic Teachings from the Amazon and Andes.* In fact, this title summarizes the Shuar philosophy that the world is created through dreams. When he writes of the Shuar's dreaming, Perkins refers to the collective dream of a people—the dream of how we perceive the world. "If the world is as we dream it, then every reality is a matter of perception," he explains. "When we give our energy to a different world, the world is transformed." But to create a new world, we must first create a new dream.

Chapter 12

ESP in Dreams

Extrasensory perception, or ESP, dreams can be telepathic (involving mind-to-mind communication) or precognitive (involving events in the future). These types of dreams may be about you or your family, friends or acquaintances, strangers or public figures, or private or public events and situations. Basically, they can be about anything! In this chapter, you'll discover the mystery behind ESP in dreams.

Telepathy in Sleep

In his research during the 1960s and 1970s, psychiatrist Montague Ullman noted that more women than men reported telepathic dreams. Today more people are aware of the value of dreams, and this difference may no longer apply. His book, *Dream Studies and Telepathy*, written with psychologist Stanley Krippner, has become a monumentally important work in dream study.

ESP dream research was once the exclusive domain of scientists in dream laboratories. Ullman, however, formed dream groups of participants with one thing in common—their interest in dreams. In many of these groups, no professional dream researchers were involved. Dream experiments in telepathy since have even been conducted among strangers communicating through online services.

In one online experiment called "The Dream Game," the group was divided into senders, receivers, and observers, all of whom were miles apart. The sender selected an object and visualized its image going out to the receivers. The sender described the object to the observers, including details like shape, color, texture, history, location, and other pertinent details. The receivers would then expound on the resulting dreams to the sender and observer, and would check the accuracy of the experiment.

QUESTION?

Are you a sender or a receiver in life?
Well, if it's common for you to think of someone and then have them call, you're a sender. You're calling them to you. On the other hand, if you know who's on the phone before you pick it up, you're a receiver. It's also possible to be both.

Gary Joy, the man who started this sender/receiver game on Prodigy, recalls the first time he played. He sent out an image of his dog, Skip, that had recently been put to sleep. None of the people involved knew about the dog or his death. "Out of the ten people, nine had dreams of being separated from something or someone they loved. And eight of the dreams recorded were about an animal that had died."

In other words the people involved actually received the message he was sending out without being told. The importance of such nonscientific experiments is obvious. We are all explorers of the dreamscape. You don't need to be a scientist or a dream researcher. The anecdotal information we glean from these explorations is also as important, on a personal level, as anything proven in a lab. Telepathy exists. It's still in the exploratory stages, but it does happen.

Family and Friends Connecting

In his book *Parent-Child Telepathy,* psychiatrist Berthold Schwartz recorded over a hundred instances of telepathy within his own family. Many of the episodes involved trivial but fascinating incidents from daily life, which led Schwartz to believe that telepathy is the missing link in communication between parents and their children.

Sisters

In the following dream, the close emotional connection between two sisters aptly illustrates how telepathy functions in dreams. This dream is called "Sister":

When my younger sister was a freshman in college, I was in graduate school at the same university. We saw a lot of each other and were close friends during this time.

One Friday night, I dreamed that I was staying at her place off campus, but it looked different than the actual apartment. The hall was long and narrow and the floor buckled in the middle. There were many closed doors off the hallway, and I didn't seem to know which one to open to find whatever I was looking for. I was afraid of opening the wrong one.

I finally stopped in front of a heavy wooden door; I touched the knob. The door wasn't locked, so I pushed it open and stepped inside.

It was completely dark and I heard my sister shouting my name. She sounded frightened. I woke with a start, and for seconds afterward, her voice seemed to echo in my bedroom. It spooked me.

The next day, I found out that her car had broken down as she and her roommate were on their way back to their place from a party. It had happened about the same time I'd had the dream.

FACT

The dream "Sister" is a clairvoyant dream, in which the dreamer senses what is going on while it's happening. You can also have a telepathic dream (communication between two dreamers), a mutual dream (two dreamers with the same dream), or a precognitive dream (dream of the future).

Sensing

The following dream may be a case of telepathy as well as precognition. A woman dreamed of another woman she barely knew. But in the dream the two seemed to know each other well. This soon proved to be the case. This dream is called "Teardrop":

When my daughter was in preschool, she was friendly with a girl whose mother I met and liked. Sue and I agreed to meet for lunch one day, and I decided to squeeze in a nap before I left.

I dreamed that while Sue and I were talking great waves of sadness washed over me; a single teardrop rolled down her cheek. That's all I recall of the dream. But I remember thinking it was a totally bizarre dream because she seemed so vivacious, so full of life and optimism.

When we got together that day, we talked for a long time, like old friends. I realized how accurate my dream was. She and her husband were on the verge of divorce. Since then, we've become close friends and see each other more often than our daughters even do.

ESP Dreams

"ESP dreams," writes Stase Michaels in *The Bedside Guide to Dreams*, "show us that the psyche is capable of a wide range of psychic dynamics." Judith Orloff, author of *Second Sight*, says, "Dreams are my compass and my truth; they guide me and link me to the divine." Both authors are regarded as experts in the field of dreams and ESP.

Many ESP dreams involve the people who are closest to you. Yet, in these dreams, the familiar people you encounter there may be completely different than they are in waking life. Watch for clues. Sometimes a "stranger" you're dreaming of really refers to yourself or to someone who's very close to you.

For instance, psi researcher Alan Vaughan recalls a dream he had two nights after watching one of his favorite writers, Kurt Vonnegut Jr., on a television talk show. In the dream, recorded on March 13, 1970, he and Vonnegut were in a house full of children. The novelist was planning to leave on a trip, and it was there and then that he mentioned he was moving to an island called Jerome.

Vaughan wrote Vonnegut about the dream. Two weeks later he received this reply: "Not bad. On the night of your dream, I had dinner with Jerome B., and we talked about a trip I made three days later to an island named England." It can be tough to recognize what's real and what's imagined, but when your dreams start coming close to reality, you'll have that *feeling* that they are. Test them and find out.

The Inner Senses

In the course of a lifetime, you may recall a single telepathic or precognitive dream, or you may recall hundreds. It depends on how actively you explore your personal dreamscapes and how deeply you penetrate the layers of yourself. "When you look into yourself, the very effort involved extends the limitations of your consciousness, expands it, and allows the egotistical self to use abilities that it often does not realize it possesses," says Seth in *The Seth Material.*

Seth calls these abilities the Inner Senses. They often manifest in common dreams about public situations. In the following example, a woman named Jan dreamed about the collapse of a major airline more than a decade before it happened.

A Precognitive Trip

This dream is called "Eastern Airlines":

I'm hurrying through a crowded airport, making my way to the Eastern counter with my ticket. When I get there, the counter is deserted. Panicked, I run over to the information booth to find out what's going on. The woman behind the booth, a prissy type with horn-rim glasses, looks at me like I've just asked a ridiculous question.

"They've gone under," she says.

"Under? What do you mean by under?"

"They declared bankruptcy, then disbanded. It was in all the papers."

She then whips out a newspaper and shows me the lead story on Eastern's collapse. I try to read the date, but it's too blurred. I had this dream in late 1974."

Jan was able to access an inner sense that jumped ahead in time. "According to Seth," writes Jane Roberts, "these Inner Senses are used by the whole self constantly. Since past, present, and future have no basic reality, this (particular) sense allows us to see through the apparent time barriers. We are seeing things as they really are. Any precognitive experience would entail use of this Inner Sense."

Destiny: How It Works

Even though Jan's dream happened years before Eastern Airlines' actual demise, it doesn't mean that the future is predetermined. The dream depicted one possible version of the future, based on the patterns that were prevalent at that time for the airline. In truth, things could have gone a different way.

Usually destiny is set up with gateways. A person, a company, or even society can choose either to go through a particular gateway or to pass right by. This is what alters fate. In this sense, precognitive dreams seem to operate on the same principle as divination. Your dreams may reveal to you one possible destination.

As many researchers emphasize, you don't have to be a prophet to have prophetic dreams. These dreams happen all the time to ordinary people. In fact, some psychics claim that they only see visions in their waking hours. Dream prophecies, many times, happen to non-psychic people.

Prophetic Dreams

In 1865, Abraham Lincoln dreamed that he heard strange sounds coming from the East Room of the White House. When he investigated, he saw a corpse resting on a catafalque, a funeral platform. He saw soldiers standing around the body, guarding it, while a throng of people looked on. The face was covered, so Lincoln asked one of the guards who had died. "The president," the guard replied. A week later, Lincoln was assassinated.

ALERT!

Once again, remember that there is no time or space on the Other Side. If you're receiving any information about the future from a departed loved one (though this is rare), be sure to record it. But remember that something that seems as if it could happen tomorrow might actually happen twenty years from now. Keep this in mind!

Careers have been built on predictions like these. One such prophecy was reported in the May 13, 1956, issue of *Parade* magazine: "As for the 1960 election, Mrs. (Jeane) Dixon thinks it will be dominated by labor and won by a Democrat. But he will be assassinated or die in office, though not necessarily in his first term." Jeane Dixon was, of course, talking about John Kennedy. Even though Dixon was wrong about other things, this prediction tended to stick in people's minds. She won acclaim and credibility from it.

Nostradamus's reputation as a seer was already established by the time he predicted the death of King Henry II in a jousting tournament. Depending on which interpretation of his writings you read, he also correctly predicted the death of John Kennedy, the fall of the Berlin Wall and of Communism, the alliance between the Soviets and the Americans, the AIDS plague, and the explosion of the *Challenger.*

FACT

History's most famous prophet is Nostradamus (1503–1566). By focusing on a bowl of water, he was able to enter a dreamlike state in which visions appeared to him. Divination by use of a crystal ball, water, or other reflective surface is called scrying.

Nostradamus, like Edgar Cayce and other psychics, also predicted a pole shift in which Earth would tilt on its axis, hurling the planet into utter chaos and destruction. Nostradamus even gave a date: May 5, 2000. Cayce didn't give a specific date, but he did predict geological changes of massive magnitude. Cayce said that the western part of North America would break up, with California falling into the sea as a result of "the big one." Florida would become a series of islands and "the greater portion of Japan must go into the sea."

Dreams Stories That Link

It's possible to have connecting dreams that may be separated by periods of up to many years. Rose, a nurse, dreamed the next two dreams about fifteen years apart. In the first dream, the global situation influences her life directly; in the second dream, it impacts her daughter's life. The basic theme is the same.

This first dream is called "The Bahamas":

I'm panicky. Water is everywhere. It's flooding my backyard and is beginning to seep into my living room. It's raining very hard outside, but I understand the flood isn't caused by just the rains; it has something to do with the rising oceans.

In the next scene, I'm running around outside, sloshing through all this water, trying to find a rowboat that I can take to the Bahamas. I know the Bahamas are safe, that the land is rising there. I apparently find a rowboat, because in the final scene I'm headed through a raging sea toward the Bahamas. I bolt out of this dream so fast I nearly roll out of bed.

Dreams about the state of the world are rare. Usually, the references are symbolic and not literal or specific. Dreamers who dreamed about big events such as the sinking of the *Titanic* or the attack on the World Trade Center blame themselves. Unfortunately, though, it's difficult to use prophetic dreams to prevent disaster. Dreams don't offer time and place for the incidents.

The following is the second dream Rose had, about fifteen years after the first. This dream is titled "The Night After":

The night after my daughter was born, I was in a ward with three other women. It was late, nearly two o'clock in the morning, and the nurse had just left with my daughter, after her feeding. I was falling asleep and heard someone call my name. I thought it was one of the women in the ward and snapped upright, but everyone was asleep.

I remember that the door was cracked open, so light seeped into the ward from the hall. I could hear a phone ring and the soft hiss of the cool air coming through the ceiling vents. I lay back down and fell asleep again. I heard my name called a second time, a loud, piercing shout, and realized it was an internal voice. So I kept my eyes shut, not entirely sure whether I was dreaming or not, and opened myself to the experience.

I had a painfully clear mental image of my daughter—who was absolutely beautiful—about thirty years in the future. She was intent on her task. I understood that she was in the midst of a hypnotic regression or its equivalent and tried to communicate my willingness to cooperate in whatever she was trying to find out. Mentally, she asked me to verify her birth data. Where were we living when she was born? What time was she born? At what hospital . . . questions like that.

During the exchange, I had the distinct impression that I was no longer alive. I felt she was speaking to me from a future in which the world was vastly different. The world as I knew it no longer existed. Massive geological changes had happened. I sensed that pockets of humanity had survived and these people were struggling to come to terms with what had happened. They possessed knowledge about the true nature of time and space. They were capable, in some sense, of manipulating time and space. I'm not sure what that means. At any rate, I gave her the information she requested and told her that I loved her. She thanked me, and the dream or experience or whatever it was ended.

Rose's take on her two dreams is that the futures predicted by Nostradamus and Cayce are two distinct possibilities. But the Earth changes seem to happen at a later date than predicted.

"In the first dream, which I had in the early seventies, my sense was that the destruction would occur within the next ten or fifteen years, sometime during the early or late 1980s. In the second dream, which I had on September 1, 1989, the destruction seemed more distant. Since my daughter was about thirty, that would put her in the year 2019 or thereabouts and she was already living in this profoundly changed world. It's as if these two dreams depicted two different timelines, two different probabilities, linked because both involved geologically changed worlds."

The Greek letter psi refers to any paranormal activity such as ESP, telepathy, or psychokinesis. The nineteenth century saw significant progress in the study of dreams. However, it wasn't until the 1960s that Montague Ullman and dream expert Robert Van de Castle began dream study with everyday people.

Although Rose thinks the dreams represent a pattern for the future, she believes what she saw is only one possibility. "I have to believe that the future is not written in stone, that it's possible to avoid some of the catastrophes—at least the manmade ones." As you become more proficient at interpreting your dreams, telepathic and precognitive dreams will be easier to spot. You may want to keep these kinds of dreams in a special section in your journal or record them using a different organization technique. These dreams are your most intimate link to your own future.

Chapter 13

Past Lives and Dreams

As you've already learned, there are no limits of time, space, or even distance you can travel in the dream world. Many people revisit their past lives in dreams without knowing they've done it. Whether or not you believe in reincarnation, dreams of past lives can feel startlingly real—and they may just be! In this chapter, find out how to recognize a past-life dream and the ways you can learn from one.

Reincarnation

About two-thirds of the world's population believe that the soul or some other aspect of the human personality not only survives but is reborn time and time again. Reincarnation is intrinsic to Eastern religions. It is also found among Shiite Muslims and certain African tribal groups. In the Western world, however, the interest in past lives is often associated with New Age concepts.

Although there is nothing new about reincarnation, the interest in exploring past lives through hypnotic regression and through dreams is opening new doors for more and more spiritual adventurers. Dr. Brian Weiss explores past-life regression with patients in *Through Time into Healing*. He says about Freud, "Not all dreams are Freudian dreams with symbols, distortions, and wish metaphors. Some dreams convey literal past-life memories."

FACT

In the 1970 movie *On a Clear Day You Can See Forever,* actress Barbra Streisand is accidentally hypnotized by a psychiatrist (Yves Montand) and discovers her past lives through regression. Watch this film to get a better handle on this phenomenon.

"Perhaps the ninety percent of the brain that is rarely put to use holds memories not only of what's happening now, but of what happened in the past—the past of past lifetimes," explains Stase Michaels, author of *The Bedside Guide to Dreams*. "And because dreams draw images from your unconscious, it would not be surprising if every now and then a dream accidentally touched a vivid memory from a past life and replayed it for you, just like the discovery of old photographs in an attic."

Dreaming of Past Lives

Dream experts say that dreaming of past lives is even more common than dreaming of the future. Sometimes we don't realize we're dreaming of ourselves in another body doing something that truly happened a long time ago. Recurrent dreams often indicate that our souls are trying to get over the past. For example, if you keep dreaming of a woman who falls down a flight of steps—and you wake up right before she dies in the dream—dream experts say this could have been you in a past life. Your soul still remembers the loss.

Past-Life Decisions

Some past-life dreams are simply brief hypnogogic images that sometimes deal with death. In the following dream, Michael glimpsed a past life during a relaxation session at the end of a yoga class. This dream is called "Revolutionary War":

Dream experts say that choices and fears we had In past lives can, in fact, carry over into this one. Someone who has a fear of water, for example, could very well have died in a previous life by drowning. Pay close attention to your dreams. When you're looking for these clues, you will find them.

I was drifting off to sleep when I saw myself as a soldier with several other soldiers. We were all carrying rifles. The uniforms were from another time. I sensed it was the American Revolution. I'd no sooner glimpsed the image than an explosion of some sort ripped me apart. I watched the scenario dispassionately, even though I knew it was "me" who was killed. It was really vivid, a movie of the mind, and it ended with my death.

In Michael's case, the dream of being a soldier was startling, because in his current life he had refused to serve in the Vietnam War and had even been tried and convicted for his belief that the war was immoral. "Maybe my war experience in that other life affected my decision to avoid involvement in war in this life," he says.

Another Life

Bernard, a librarian residing in South Florida, recorded the following past-life dream. It provides a brief glimpse of another time and place. Pay attention to the detail. This dream ends with a provocative scenario regarding access to reincarnation dreams. Bernard's dream is called "A Trip to Nineteenth-Century London":

In the dream, I found myself on a street with horse-drawn carriages moving past me and sewers running down the edge of a road made of stone. The road was bordered by sooty brick buildings. I was dressed in heavy dark clothing of another era and wore a brimmed hat. I was definitely in another time and place and sensed it was mid-nineteenth-century London.

The dream faded, but I didn't wake up. Instead, I found myself in front of a panel with a horizontal row of red buttons. Although there was no writing, no instructions, I knew that each button represented a life in a different time. When I held my hand near one of the buttons, I knew instantly when and where the life took place. One was in ancient Egypt and another in Rome at the time of Christ. Still another took place in France during the Renaissance. All I had to do was push a button and I'd be there. I grew excited by the possibilities and that was when I woke up.

Bernard was skeptical about reincarnation and thought his dream might relate to his own interests. He maintains a strong interest in world history. Yet, when it was pointed out to him that his interest in history could be related to his past lives, he admitted that was a possibility. Bernard remains on the fence about the reality of past lives, but he is looking forward to dreaming again of the control panel and pushing the buttons.

Bernard's skepticism isn't surprising. Reincarnation has not been widely accepted in the West, despite a growing interest in the concept. The reason is at least partially related to the prevalent Judeo-Christian heritage. There is passing mention of reincarnation in the Old Testament and more references in the New Testament.

FACT

The turning point in Christianity's relationship to reincarnation appears to have taken place in the Second Council of Constantinople (the Fifth Ecumenical Council of the Church) in A.D. 553. One of the Council's fourteen anathemas, or denunciations, stated: "If anyone asserts the fabulous pre-existence of souls, and shall assert the monstrous restoration which follows it, let him be anathema."

A devout Christian who popularized reincarnation in the United States in the early twentieth century through his clairvoyant readings, Edgar Cayce refused to debate whether the New Testament endorses or rejects the belief. As he put it, "I can read reincarnation into the Bible and you can read it right out."

Famous Past-Life Experts

The resurgence of interest in past lives in recent decades can be attributed in part to writers such as Helen Wamback, Frederick Lenz, Ian Stevenson, Brian Weiss, and others. Their individual opinions and testimonies brought substantial focus back to this important subject.

Weiss's *Many Lives, Many Masters* spent months on the *New York Times* bestseller list. Here, after all, was a medical doctor and psychiatrist talking about a topic that had been largely relegated to the land of the weird and the strange. His books gave the topic credence. He was willing to go on the record and say, "Yes, I'm a doctor. But this exists. It's real."

In *Through Time into Healing*, Weiss describes a dream in which he was chained to a wall in a dungeon somewhere in Europe during the Middle

Ages. He was tortured to death for teaching about reincarnation. While still in a hypnogogic state following the dream, he recalled another life in which he was a powerful priest at a ziggurat in the ancient Near East. He had abused his position for material gratification. Then he heard a voice speaking to him in a gentle, loving tone:

> When you had the chance to teach, you didn't. Then, when you didn't have the chance, you did. In that lifetime, you died for this belief when you didn't need to. You could have just as easily and successfully taught about love. At that moment, it wasn't right to force the issue. This time, get it right.

Weiss, however, is hardly the first Westerner to study reincarnation. In 1960, Dr. Ian Stevenson published a paper called *The Evidence for Survival from Claimed Memories of Former Incarnations*. It consisted of forty-four cases that Stevenson had investigated personally, in which children identified enough details of their previous lives to identify the deceased persons who were supposedly reincarnated. Stevenson has spent most of the last three decades investigating the subject.

QUESTION?

What is a good argument for the existence of reincarnation?
Child prodigies. How could Mozart compose a symphony at the age of nine that was as good as or better than something written by a person who had studied music all his or her life? Was it just the luck of the draw, a random collision of the right genes? Or was it because his musical ability had been refined through many lives of practice?

In early 1973, bestselling author Taylor Caldwell was questioned about her thoughts on reincarnation during an appearance at a book fair in Jacksonville, Florida. There was a great deal of interest in her visit—not only because of who she was, but also because of who she might have been. Jess Stearn's *The Search for a Soul: Taylor Caldwell's Psychic Lives* had been published recently and many of those who attended Caldwell's talk had read it.

When Caldwell asked for questions from the audience, the first one was whether or not she believed in reincarnation. She admitted that before she underwent the hypnotic regressions that constituted the background for Stearn's book, she'd been a die-hard skeptic. "Now I'm less skeptical," she said.

And yet, she had no way of explaining how she'd written so authentically of medical practices in ancient times, as she had in *Dear and Glorious Physician* and *Testimony of Two Men*. In *Physician*, for instance, one surgery scene was written with such breathtaking authenticity that Caldwell received letters from physicians all over the world asking where she'd gotten her information.

Nothing discussed in this book actually proves that souls are born again. Ultimately, you have to settle that question for yourself. But it's interesting to consider this possibility. When you imagine that you are made up of many lives of different experiences, you may feel more confident about yourself as a person.

Fantasy Versus Being There

It's possible to dream of past events, places, or things that you realistically shouldn't know about. There have been many documented cases of children who, when questioned, talked with surprising detail about things in their dreams that they couldn't possibly have seen or read about. Who can explain this? How could a five-year-old from New Jersey who's never been out of the country, for example, talk about an event that really happened hundreds of years ago in another part of the world?

What Is Real?

In late 1974, one young woman, Christina, who was twenty-five years old at the time, began having a series of dreams that took place in Scotland. She'd never been there, but was planning a trip in the summer of 1975 with a woman coworker. This sequence is called "The Scotland Dreams":

These dreams were unlike any I'd ever had. They were vivid, in living Technicolor. They would often begin in the mountains that surround Caracas, Venezuela, where I was born—mountains that are so green the air there smells green. I would be running through all this green, racing toward the edge of a mountain, and then I would plunge over the edge and wildly flap my arms until I took to the skies. When I landed, I would be in Scotland. I don't recall specific people or specific places in these dreams. But always, I awoke with the feeling that Scotland was as familiar to me as the rooms in my apartment.

As the real trip to Scotland neared, Christina's dreams increased in frequency and detail. They became more like real memories than dream visions. When the trip finally arrived, she found some shocking connections between her dreams and reality.

My friend and I spent six weeks in Europe and had set aside two weeks at the end just for Scotland. The day we boarded a bus for Edinburgh, I felt as though I was finally going home. As soon as I saw the city, I knew I'd lived there before. It was the only city I've ever been in where I could walk down a particular street and know what I would find if I turned the corner. Most of the time, I was right. I remember sitting in a meadow of heather one night in early August, when the sky never got completely dark, and knowing with utter certainty that I'd often sat in a field of heather near here in another life. This wasn't fantasy to me; it was a clear, absolute knowing.

Before leaving Scotland, however, I felt that I had missed an opportunity—there was something I was supposed to do or someone I was supposed to meet and somehow this event, whatever it was, hadn't happened. The feeling puzzled me, since the trip had surpassed my expectations.

Resolution

Six years later, Christina was teaching English to Cuban refugees under a federal program to help them integrate into American life. A local reporter, Peter, visited the teaching center to find out how the program was going. Within five minutes of meeting him, Christina knew she'd met the man she would marry. During the next year that they dated, Christina and Peter compared the parallels in their lives and travels. It turned out that Peter had been in Edinburgh during the same week in July 1975 that Christina had. Christina felt sure that her "missed opportunity" in Scotland was meeting Peter. They were married in July 1983, eight years after they missed meeting in Scotland.

ALERT!

"Destiny dictates the meeting of soulmates," writes Brian Weiss. "We *will* meet them. But what we decide to do after that meeting falls in the province of choice or free will. A wrong choice or a missed chance can lead to incredible loneliness and suffering. A right choice, an opportunity realized, can bring us to profound bliss and happiness."

Children's Past Lives: Coping

A fascinating new area of research involves the past lives of children. Author Carol Bowman, in her book *Children's Past Lives*, cites distinct characteristics of dreams that may be related to a child's past lives:

- **Vivid and coherent:** This type of dream is often like a memory—clear and sharp in detail, with a fluid story line.
- **Recurring:** Past-life dreams are often repetitive. "They usually start and stop in the same place in the story, like a video cued up to play the same segment over and over," writes Bowman.
- **An image:** Sometimes, these dreams revolve around a single image that the dreamer dreams in exactly the same way each time. Again, this image is like a memory. Other times, the dream progresses through a story line, then stops just short of a crisis point. Quite often, the crisis point is imminent death.
- **Different personae:** These are dreams in which the dreamer sees herself as another person in another time and place. "If that person

is of a different sex or greatly different age, the dreamer, upon awakening, knows that this dream was 'not like any dream I've ever had,'" Bowman writes.

- **Nightmares:** Kids have nightmares that aren't past-life memories, of course, but Bowman feels that some nightmares are "past-life memories screaming to be healed." These are the kind of nightmares from which a child awakens screaming night after night. Usually, the child heads for the parents' bed, crying for protection.

Only a Dream

Even if a parent doesn't believe in reincarnation, Bowman says, a child's nightmare shouldn't be brushed off as "only a dream." The child should be allowed to talk about it, and the parent should listen with an open mind. "Unlike waking past-life memories—which are already conscious—past-life nightmares remain unconscious until your child talks about them while awake."

Don't worry that talking about a nightmare will make your child have it again. Studies have shown that once children talk about and unload their fears, the problem is challenged and acknowledged—and it usually goes away. Discussing a nightmare can only help, and it will not hurt your child!

Dream experts say to never tell your children, "Don't worry; go back to sleep" after they've had a nightmare. Once again, encourage them to talk about it. They'll feel safer when they know a parent cares about how they're feeling. If a child is having problems such as socializing with other children at school, this may be the closest a parent will get to really understanding the inner workings of a child's mind. It's truly a golden opportunity that should be seized.

Exercise: My Child's Past-Life Dreams

Ask your child about his dreams and write them down. Did the dreams take place in other time periods? Ask him what the people were wearing, what the landscape looked like—the mood of the dream. Was he frightened? Happy? Scared? Ask him about the action of the dream. What was going on? What were people doing? How did they react toward him? Did these dreams have a different feel to them than other dreams he's had? If so, how? Ask for as much description as possible.

Remember to approach your child and question her gently immediately after she wakes up. Children often forget their dreams even faster than adults do because adults will make a conscious effort to remember dreams. Children usually will not make that effort, as they are unaware of the value of their dreams.

Programming to Remember

Once you're able to consistently recall your dreams and are familiar with their symbols and language, you may find that some of your dreams or fragments of your dreams involve scenes from times preceding your own birth. Brian Weiss believes these types of dreams are past-life memories.

In *Lifetimes: True Accounts of Reincarnation*, author Frederick Lenz isolates four ways in which dreams of past lives differ from ordinary dreams. According to Lenz, past-life dreams usually do the following:

- Entail sensations completely unlike those you experience in ordinary dreams.
- Involve your awareness that you're seeing one or more of your past lives.
- Have something in them that makes you remember these dreams long after ordinary dreams have faded from your memory.
- Tend to change your attitudes toward death and dying.

Sometimes, as with Christina's dreams of Scotland, past-life dreams may precede a trip to a particular place and may intensify once you're in that place. Other times, such dreams may happen spontaneously, during periods of personal tension or anxiety. Once you become proficient at recalling these dreams, you can program yourself to dream about your other lives.

This is similar to requesting an answer in a dream to a problem in your waking life, but in this case you request dreams of past lives.

Dream Answers

The next reincarnation dream began with dream incubation. Before going to sleep, Anne asked herself why she and her husband were going through such a rocky period in their marriage. The answer was hardly what she had expected. This dream is called "Prison":

I'm in a damp, musty-smelling room. The walls are stone, the floor is stone, and the air is dank. Very little light spills through the tiny window way up there near the ceiling. I realize I'm in prison. But this isn't any contemporary prison. This is like something out of another century. I'm wearing a long dress that is tattered and soiled. I'm very young, maybe eighteen or nineteen, and I'm terrified.

One of the prison guards is nice to me. He brings me extra food. He talks to me. He consoles me with stories about the outside world. But sometimes, he's cold to me; he seems to feel guilty that he likes me. He says mean things to me, indifferent things. But then he'll try to make up for it with another gesture of kindness. I realize I'm going to die in this place and wake up with a choked, dry feeling in my throat.

Problem-solving techniques can work with past-life dreams. Before you go to sleep, ask out loud for answers to specific questions about past lives. Ask if you now know certain people from whatever life you had "back then." If you do this every night, the answer should come to you.

The dream "clicked" for Anne. She knew the prison guard was her husband in this life and that she was the inmate. What struck her most about the dream was the vividness of the time period; it felt like the Middle Ages somewhere in England. Anne believed the dream was the vestige of a memory of a former life.

This certainly wasn't the kind of answer she'd asked for when she'd gone to sleep. But the dream explained facets of her marriage, and it deepened her interest in reincarnation. Anne felt it also explained the acute discomfort she experienced when she traveled through England years before—a kind of choking gloom that clung to her until she left.

Her husband, not unexpectedly, remarked that the roles were reversed in this life. Although they joked about the dream, their relationship improved in the aftermath. "It was as if we became more aware of how we treated each other," Anne said.

Working with Past-Life Dreams

Michael Talbot, in *Your Past Lives*, recommends that you express your request in a clear, concise statement. Always tell your unconscious mind that you don't want to uncover any past-life memories that are too painful or traumatic to deal with. Talbot says he once forgot to add the qualifier when he'd requested a dream on a past-life injury. He was inundated with vivid nightmarish images and sensations about his death in a twelfth-century Persian war.

Talbot suggests using a pendulum to find out if your request is safe to dream about. This entails nothing more than tying a small, weighted object like a ring to a piece of thread about ten inches long. With your elbow resting firmly on a flat surface, pinch the top of the thread between your thumb and forefinger and ask a question that has a yes/no answer. This establishes the direction the object will move when the answer is yes; the opposite direction means no. If the pendulum swings in a circle or moves diagonally, then rephrase the question. If you still can't obtain a clear answer, then it's best to leave that particular request alone for the time being.

As you're falling asleep, Talbot says, repeat your request several times. As with all dream recall, note your impressions of dreams the next morning, as soon as you awaken. A past-life dream, like any other dream, may be a literal visual experience or couched in symbolic terms.

Look up symbols in a dream dictionary, and then ask yourself what these symbols mean to you. If the dream or the dream symbols don't make sense, leave it alone for a while. Later, try the interviewing technique. Be alert for thoughts that may drift through your mind during the day. If the dream still hasn't made sense to you by that night, repeat your request, but change the wording. Be specific, but make sure your wording covers what you want to know.

Dreaming the Past

When dreams feel especially real, it often means that they once were—in a past life. Ask yourself how this past life you're dreaming about could pertain to your present situation. Teresa, who was pregnant with her first child at the time, requested a message about her current life from a past one. This dream is called "Iceland":

Before I went to sleep, I specifically asked for a dream that would tell me which life was the most important connection now for my husband and me and our unborn daughter. I dreamed I was in the early stages of labor and standing around in a giant warehouse, waiting for someone to help me. But the warehouse was empty of people and of furniture. There wasn't any place to lie down or even to sit.

The baby started to come out and I delivered her myself as I stood there. I remember holding her in my arms, astonished that the delivery had been so easy. She opened her eyes and said, in a very plain, clear voice, "Iceland."

When I woke up, I realized this was the exact answer to the request I had made. I'd asked which life, not for details of that life, and that's what I got. Iceland—a life in Iceland. I knew, in fact, that we still had some connection to Iceland. We were supposed to go there and our trip had been canceled. Obviously it was a trip we needed to take.

What is the best thing about discovering a past life in dreams?
Without a doubt, the best things you can discover from a past life are your strengths. If you learn that you did a certain thing well in a past life, chances are you have similar talents in this life you're not aware of.

Colliding Lives

Paula, an elementary school teacher, began to have vivid dreams about being an artist five years into her teaching career. This dream of hers is called "The Artist":

As I approached the age of thirty, I began to feel restless and unfulfilled as a teacher. I felt like I spent most of my time trying to maintain discipline in my classes. I was worn out by the time I left school every day and dreaded getting up in the morning because the whole cycle would start all over again. I wanted desperately to change careers, but didn't know what I would do.

In the midst of all this, I had a sequence of dreams in which I attended art classes. I learned how to draw, then to paint, and then to sculpt. These dreams refreshed me, so that when I got up in the morning, I was ready to deal with whatever happened at school. I was less uptight and conditions improved. But I realized I had to get out of teaching. So I enrolled in art classes.

Everything felt right about art. It was easy for me to learn, and I loved doing it. Sculpture became my passion. When school was out, I attended an art institute for the summer. My sculptures began to sell—to family and friends, then by word of mouth to other people.

Two years later, I quit teaching for good and became a full-time sculptor. Throughout this time, the dreams continued and evolved; they became more detailed. I realized these were period dreams, set in France around the time of Van Gogh.

A few years later, I visited Arles, France, where Van Gogh lived, and I felt a real kinship with the town. I don't think I was Van Gogh, by any means, but I might have been a contemporary, and maybe a friend of his, another artist. Somehow, that artist life came to my aid when I needed it most.

FACT

Sometimes you may have a flash of inspiration or an inexplicable hunch to do something that is totally out of character, but you do it because the intuition, the "click," is strong. In a sense, you have slipped into the state of mind that Australian Aborigines call Dreamtime—what dream experts call imagination.

Paula's case is fairly dramatic in that her dreams resulted in a career and total life change. More typical, perhaps, are the ways that the abilities and strengths of past selves manifest themselves ordinarily. One thing is for sure, though: You should always pay attention to dreams of a past life. You won't necessarily recognize or understand their messages right away, but when you do, it can make all the difference in the world to the life you lead right now.

Chapter 14

Coincidence or Truth

Dreams and waking life are not so different. Dreams come from your subconscious, a part of you. Therefore, you can take the signs and coincidences from your dreams and apply them to your life. If you watch for prophecy and heed your guides (spiritual, animal, and otherwise), you can change the way things are going and plan for your future. That's what dream interpretation is all about.

Signs and Symbols

When stuck in traffic one afternoon, your mind wanders back to a friend you knew in college, whom you haven't seen or heard from in years. That night, out of the blue, he calls.

A couple go to the beach together but soon get into a heated argument. At the peak of the argument, a bolt of lightning zigzags across the sky, followed quickly by a crack of thunder—effectively ending their fight. Before they can get away, a storm blows in and drenches them. They laugh, realizing their debate was ridiculous.

Coincidences? Not according to Carl Jung, one of the first to seriously study the seemingly random coinciding of events. In the Richard Wilhelm edition of *The I Ching*, Jung writes, "Synchronicity takes the coincidence of events in space and time as meaning something more than mere chance, namely a peculiar interdependence of objective events among themselves as well as with the subjective (psychic) states of the observer or observers."

In essence, synchronicity is when universal forces become perfectly aligned with your mind or perception. Perhaps you think of a person and she calls, or you know something is about to happen and it does. Synchronicity usually involves a feeling that something was destined.

The intent of this chapter is to look at everyday life from a new perspective—the dream perspective. Synchronicity is one reminder that a subtle dreamlike quality underlies your waking life. In fact, synchronicities are like road signs of the unconscious that point out certain patterns to you. As you become aware of them, you begin to notice them more and more. You can eventually learn to read these signs and understand what William Brugh Joy calls "the pattern level of reality."

Matter and Mind

There were many instances of synchronicity in Jung's life, but one of the most vivid involved a beetle. As Jung was listening to a patient relate a dream in which she was given a golden scarab, he heard a tapping at the window and saw an insect fluttering against the glass. He opened the window and caught the insect. It was a scarabaeid beetle, the closest thing in his part of the world to a scarab. The scarab is a symbol of rebirth, and Jung interpreted this incident to mean the woman would now be helped by therapy.

Jung believed that synchronicity is inexorably linked to activation of energy deep within the psyche. "It is as if the formation of patterns within the unconscious mind is accompanied by physical patterns in the outer world," writes F. David Peat in *Synchronicity: The Bridge Between Matter and Mind*.

The most dramatic synchronicities seem to happen when people are undergoing a transition in their lives that leads to transformation—birth, falling in love, marriage, divorce, creative work, a career change, or a spiritual awakening. Sometimes long-distance journeys can evoke these seemingly impossible coincidences, as is the case in the following example provided by Jeffrey, an advertising executive.

You're Not Alone

Jeffrey's dream is called "On the Bus in Morocco":

It was the mid-1970s and I was traveling in Europe by myself. I only knew one person who was traveling in Europe at the time, but Frank was in Sweden, as far as I knew, and I was heading south. As I journeyed through France and Spain, I kept running into an Australian named Maurey, who was also traveling alone. Every time we met, we would greet each other, exchange a few words, and head on our individual ways, only to meet again.

One day, I decided to venture into Morocco and took a ferry from Gibraltar to Ceuta, a Moroccan border town. The scene was chaotic at the border and I was in a cultural shock—the Arabic language and writing, the style of dress, and even the music were all foreign and left me dazzled and confused.

But finally, I managed to get on a bus headed for a mountain village. As I found a seat I noticed a couple of other Westerners two rows in front of me. One of them turned and to my surprise, it was Maurey. Then I saw the other man's face. It was Frank, who I thought was in Sweden.

FACT

The movie *Sleepless in Seattle,* with Meg Ryan and Tom Hanks, is based on a series of synchronicities: They seem destined to meet and finally do at the end of the movie. In real life, this actually happens more than you can imagine. If it happens to you, don't question it. Seize the day!

For Jeffrey, the series of synchronicities was important. He realized not only that there are hidden patterns in life but also that they're meaningful. He took the meaning of these synchronicities to be a message that no matter how isolated he felt, he was never alone.

Waking Life as a Dream

If you can step back from the dramas in your life and think of them as dreams, then you can interpret them the same way. By doing so, you can gain a new perspective on your life.

For Jim, a reporter for a local television station in Iowa City, and his wife, a teacher, a broken garage door was initially merely an annoyance. Jim was attempting to get a new job with a station in a large metropolitan market and was frustrated by continual rejections. He knew he was ready to move on to a more prominent station, but the competition was enormous for those higher-paying, prestigious positions.

Jim paid a repairman to put the garage door back on its track and thought nothing more about it. But three weeks later, the door struck a ladder and was knocked off-track again. That same day, a notice about a recall on the family minivan arrived in the mail. The bold lettering read, "VERY

IMPORTANT INFORMATION," and the letter went on to say that the lift-gate latch should be repaired.

That was when Jim noticed the symbolism. Doors. Big doors. Big openings. Problems with big openings. The minor annoyances reflected his life. But they were also easily repaired. It took only ten minutes for a repairman to fix the door, and an hour at the dealer to replace the latch. But how was he going to fix his career?

Three weeks after the second garage-door incident, Jim heard about an opening at a station in Philadelphia. It turned out the station manager was from Iowa City and was familiar with his work. Jim got the job. After all the frustration, it was as easy as getting the garage door repaired.

Animals as Guides

While it might be easy to overlook the significance of a minor repair, the incident is harder to ignore when a wild animal is involved, and the symbolism can be dramatic. Animals you encounter in your dreams can be symbolic or actual guides. Psychic Sylvia Browne calls them totems. She says that before a soul is reborn into this world again, it picks its protectors: a spirit guide, a totem (or animal guide), and angels who will help it through both dreams and waking life.

Browne also says that if you have an extreme affinity for one particular animal, chances are that this is your animal guide. Animal symbolism can be very strong and meaningful. This was the case when Anne, a Florida commercial artist, encountered a snake in her house.

Translating Real Life as a Dream

Anne's real-life experience is called "Snake in the Den":

I was at the computer, updating my files. The sliding door to the atrium off the den was open because I'd just let my cat outside. Suddenly, I heard bushes rustling and my cat flew through the open door, chasing a snake.

It happened so fast, that for seconds I just sat there in a kind of paralysis. The only thing I could think of was that I was barefoot and the snake was under my desk. Then I leaped up, grabbed my cat, and ran out of the den, shouting for my husband. He came running in with the broom. We didn't want to hurt the snake, but we didn't want the snake in the house, either.

We finally coaxed it near the door, but it darted between the glass door and the screen door and got trapped. It took us half an hour to get it out of the space between the doors and into the atrium. Several days later, I found that it had shed its skin in the atrium.

Anne works with symbols and thinks in symbolic terms, so she immediately wondered what the snake experience meant. To figure it out, she turned to her medicine cards. These are divination cards that are based on Native American beliefs about the role of nature and animals in human lives. Although it wasn't a dream, the event transpired very much like a dream, and that was how she chose to interpret it.

FACT

The shedding of skin represents the life/death/rebirth cycle—"the energy of wholeness." When snakes play a prominent role in an experience or dream, or if you choose the snake card for yourself in a medicine card reading, it means that "there is a need within you to transmute some thought, action, or desire so that wholeness may be achieved."

According to the medicine cards and certain Native American teachings, snakes represent transmutation. The idea of transmutation "clicked" for Anne. At the time, she was dealing with the aging of her parents. Her mother had developed a short-term memory problem and it was a tremendous strain on her father. Two days after the experience with the snake, her father was rushed to the hospital with a high fever and abdominal pain that was diagnosed as diverticulitis. Her mother was so disoriented by his absence that Anne didn't want to leave her alone. This was when she realized the extent of her mother's memory loss.

Anne believed the snake symbolized the transmutation that had to occur in her own thoughts concerning her parents. She had to accept the reality that they were aging and weren't going to live forever.

Remember that snakes do not always have a negative connotation; they also symbolize healing. A snake coiled around a staff is a symbol of health and medical practitioners. Because many symbols have a few different meanings, it's important to consider them all before making a final interpretation. Analyze your dream and what's going on in your life, and then see what makes sense for you.

Further Translation

You can create additional entries in your personal dream dictionary by adding other common objects that appear in your dreams. You might also focus on specific types of symbols, such as animals. To one person, a frog might represent luck; to another, the creature might represent transformation. Rabbits played a key symbolic role to Edith, a French-Canadian massage therapist who was feeling depressed when she had the following dream, called "Black Rabbits":

I'm in a school gymnasium, but there are no bleachers. It's a large, open room with lots of cages. I go over to the cages and see that they are filled with black rabbits. There are hundreds of them, but they are all dead.

I'm horrified at what I see. Then I notice an older man nearby. When I tell him that the rabbits are dead, he doesn't seem concerned. He says he can redo them for me. It won't be a problem. When I look again, I'm surprised to see that the cages are filled with black rabbits, more than before, and they're moving about and very much alive.

The events in Edith's life at the time of the dream are important in its interpretation. She had recently ended a bad relationship and was feeling depressed when she called her father one night. She told him that she felt dead inside, that no matter how hard she tried to keep a positive attitude, it wasn't working.

Her father, also a massage therapist, is known in Quebec for his healing touch. He asked her if her third vertebra was sore and she said that it was. He told her that he would work on it in the astral plane while she slept, and that she would feel much better.

The next morning Edith didn't notice much change. Although she felt somewhat better during the day, she went to bed again feeling empty and dead inside. Then she had the black rabbit dream. The following morning she felt much better and wondered why she had been feeling so burdened and depressed.

She interpreted the black rabbits as a symbol of magic and good luck. The fact that they were alive, for Edith, meant that the magic in her unconscious mind had been revived. She felt elated and called her father. He said he'd worked on her spine in the astral plane on the same night she'd had the rabbit dream.

Animals that appear in dreams can be frightening, charming, or puzzling. But they can also be revealing. The meaning is related to your own thoughts about the particular creature. Do some free association with the animal you dream about. It will clue you into whether or not that animal is your totem.

The problem with a static outlook on interpreting dreams is that the meanings of the symbols change as you change. What makes a seven-year-old happy probably doesn't thrill a twenty-one-year-old. Likewise, the joys or fears of a person at forty may be different from what pleases or concerns someone at seventy-five. So, periodically update your personal dictionary—delete and add as necessary.

Dreams impart guidance even when you don't remember them. But once you have a fairly strong grasp of what certain symbols mean to you, you can become more than a passive observer in your dreams. You can request guidance from dreams, and receive answers.

Past Beliefs and Religions

In many primitive cultures, the distinction between dreams and waking life was much less defined than it is today in the Western world. The dream life and the waking life were closely related and even flowed together. The Naskapi are an example of one such culture, which still lives on.

The Naskapi Indians, a tribe of about 300, inhabit an inhospitable region in northeastern Canada. They have no government or institutions and no organized religion. Their life is centered on hunting caribou and bear and on the tribe's rich spiritual environment.

"Central to the life of the Naskapi," writes F. David Peat in *Synchronicity,* "is the Big Dream, in which the hunter goes on the trail, meets friends and locates herds of caribou." Once the hunter wakes from the dream, he will quite often start drumming and chanting to communicate the dream to those around him. In this way, the spirits of the animals in the bush are alerted to the dream.

FACT

According to the beliefs of the Naskapi, a hunter's dreams will become clearer and more powerful if he respects the animals and other members of his tribe. If instead he violates this code of respect, his dreams will desert him.

In conjunction with dreams, the Naskapi also use various forms of divination, including a bone oracle. The greatest diviners in the tribe are those who are in deepest harmony with the Manitou, or spirit of the animals. After tossing a bone into a fire, they study the cracks and dark spots for information on everything from trails to the location of herds.

The survival of the tribe depends on each hunter's ability "to recognize patterns and flux of nature and to live in harmony with them," Peat notes. Through the bone oracle and dreams, the hunter maintains contact with the Manitou. "The Naskapi live in a world of meaningful pattern in which no distinction exists between what we have come to call mind and matter," Peat notes.

For the Naskapi people, the recognition and understanding of patterns is a way of life. Think about the events in your current life. Try to think of your life as a dream, and interpret the events in it using the same techniques you've learned in the earlier chapters. You might interview yourself to uncover the meaning of the events. Be alert for symbols or significant images or words.

Consider recurring real-life events similar to recurring dreams. Write them down and analyze them. If you're single, do your relationships tend to follow the same path? If you're married, do the same issues keep coming up again and again? Do your kids consistently do well in school, or do they get into trouble? Is money flowing into your life, or are you facing recurring financial problems? Is your career flourishing, or are you unsatisfied?

Patterns are basically the internal made manifest. In other words, your thought processes create what happens in your life. By learning to recognize, interpret, and work with the patterns that operate, you can become better able to control and shape your destiny.

If in cataloging your recurring experiences you wrote, "My money goes out as fast as it comes in," you might rewrite it as: "Money flows into my life." In doing this, you're creating an affirmation—a positive statement about a condition that doesn't exist yet, but which you would like to manifest in your life. You can also practice working with these new statements, these new patterns, in your dreams by suggesting them to yourself before going to sleep.

Knowing the Future

It's impossible to know the future instantly, without work. Dreams are good indications of what *can* happen, but they don't always reveal what *will* happen. It's up to you to interpret them and then shape your future. That's the surest way of obtaining results. Of course, you can wait for a prophetic or precognitive dream, but those are rare. The best way of knowing your future is asking for guidance in your dreams and getting answers. It's simpler than you think. With practice, signs and guideposts will be easier to recognize.

This dream of Rick's, a forty-year-old man, is called "Riding the Wave":

> I'm standing onshore, beneath a purple sky, watching huge ocean waves rolling in and crashing on the beach. Suddenly, the ocean rises and flows into the streets and I'm surfing on top of a tremendous wave. I feel exhilarated by the experience. Then the wave lowers me gently to the street.
>
> When I glance around, I find myself in a winding corridor, which gets progressively narrower. I turn around and head the other way. A woman is moving in my direction, and I ask her if she knows where I can find University Avenue. She says she doesn't know, but suggests I send a telegraph.

When Rick woke up, the word "telegraph" stuck in his mind and allowed him to recall the dream in detail. When striking messages or images occur in dreams, they often do so to grab your attention.

Rick deliberated over the meaning of the dream. Riding the waves gave him a sense of being on top of things, of going with the flow, enjoying it. But what about the corridor, and why did he want to find University Avenue?

He realized that the corridor symbolized the unconscious and he was there seeking knowledge, symbolized by University Avenue. When the woman told him to send a telegraph, she was telling him that he could ask his dreaming self for an answer to any of his questions. Thus, the dream was offering guidance, and the guidance was to ask for a dream.

Guidance

You are constantly guided by your dreams, whether you remember them or not. But once you begin to recall dreams with ease, it's possible to request dreams that will guide you. Your dreams can even give you hints of future events on particular issues or dilemmas—a relationship issue, a health matter, a career question, or something else. Or you may simply request a dream that you will remember. The act of asking for a dream, for whatever purpose, is called dream incubation.

A Future Career

In the next example, the dreamer, a published novelist, asked about her future with her publisher. She had a number of successful titles in print, but her editor had died the year before, and she felt her books weren't being promoted as aggressively as they had been in the past. This dream is titled "Dinner":

> I'm having dinner with the editor-in-chief of a publishing house and several other corporate people from that company. My editor, who worked for the house, is also there, even though he had been dead about a year at the time of the dream. I don't seem surprised to see him, though. Even though everyone is pleasant, I feel uncomfortable, like I'm not fully aware of everything that's happening under the surface.
>
> We're eating on an outside terrace suspended high above a city. It's night; I can see the lights below. A wind is blowing and the terrace begins to tremble, and then shake. Someone at the table laughs nervously and jokes that an earthquake is in progress. Someone else replies that it can't be an earthquake; we're not in California.
>
> My books, paperback originals, are stacked in the center of the table and they slide around as the terrace trembles. No one but me seems to notice. Or maybe the others don't care that the books are sliding all over the place. At any rate, I'm the only one who reaches out to straighten them.
>
> Just then, a waiter hurries over with a tray. There are only two things on it—a hardback book and an envelope, which he hands to me. I open it. Inside is a card, like an invitation, with one word on it: Hyperborean.

The novelist interpreted the shaking terrace in the dream to mean that she was on "shaky ground" with her current publisher and had been since her editor's death. The peculiar word on the invitation was actually similar to the name of another publisher and seemed to be an indirect response to her question.

"On shaky ground" is a perfect example of a metaphor in a dream relating to your life. "Hope springs eternal," an example from an earlier chapter, is another. Turbulent water and problems hearing another person on the phone, by the way, usually translate as trouble in a relationship.

Several weeks later, the writer mentioned the dream to a friend, an editor at another house. He told her that the day before, the head of her publishing house had been fired and rumor had it that more resignations were on the way. The shaking terrace apparently applied to more than just the author's standing with the publisher. Four months after this dream, the author signed a contract with Hyperion Books—a name close to Hyperborean and related to Greek myth. This dream not only offered guidance, it provided a peek at the future as well.

Creative Vision

In a South Florida writers' group, several writers reported that when they were really plugged in to a novel, they often dreamed about the scenes they were going to write the next day. "I usually find myself in a library, where my book is on a shelf—finished, published, and distributed," said one woman. "I open it up and page through it until I find where I left off that day, then read the next fifteen or twenty pages. I never remember what the pages say when I wake up, but whenever this happens, the words just flow out of me the next day."

A science fiction writer in the same group said that whenever he gets blocked, he takes a nap. Even though he usually doesn't request a dream to help him past his block, that's invariably what happens because he's been so focused on it. "Quite a few times, I dream that I'm working on the book, literally typing away on the computer. Then, when I wake up, whole chunks of the story have fallen into place."

Some creative dreaming was a hallmark of the works of Robert Louis Stevenson. He considered his work a collaboration between his dreams and waking state and claimed that he could dream scenes in sequence, picking up a story where it left off the night before. *The Strange Case of Dr. Jekyll and Mr. Hyde* came to Stevenson in a dream when he was in need of a story. In his waking life, Stevenson had been toying with the idea of man as a double being. In a dream, he saw Hyde ingesting a powder and undergoing a metamorphosis in the presence of his pursuers. But it's important to keep in mind that dream interpretation doesn't only benefit writers, psychics, and the other specialists mentioned throughout this book. Everyone can learn to use their dreams to enhance their lives. Creative dreaming, animal guides, destiny, and all of the other symbols and phenomena mentioned in this book play specific roles in your dreams and help move you toward your future. Pay attention to your dreams, and learn how to interpret them. Do this consistently and you can discover (and reroute) your path in life. Knowledge is power, so use it wisely.

Chapter 15

Dream Glossary

Dream symbols are incredibly help-ful in interpreting your dreams, so use this dream glossary any way you like. As mentioned, symbols can mean different things to different people. The key to using this glossary is to read the given interpreta-tions and then decide if the meanings make sense to you.

Using the Glossary

Through the various exercises in this book, you may already have built an impressive glossary of personal definitions. If there are still symbols that puzzle you, however, this glossary may trigger ideas that "click." Use it as much or as little as you deem necessary.

When you begin interpreting symbols and themes in your dreams, work with your own dream symbols first. Take note of details in your dreams—colors, vividness, action—and anything unusual that stands out. If you dream of a particular animal, for instance, you should first associate it with situations and people in your life, and then decide whether or not this animal is your totem—one of your dream guides.

When it comes to dreams, keep in mind as you interpret your dream symbols that there are no universal rules or meanings. Have fun with your dreams. Explore them thoroughly, and learn from them. Enjoy!

A

abandonment
Dreams of being abandoned by a lover, a friend, or a family member suggest that this is something you fear in waking life. It also often refers to a difficult financial situation—you're scared you won't be able to carry your burden. Remaining childhood feelings of being left out often translate into abandonment dreams. In this case, the dreamer needs to work on self-esteem.

abdomen
Seeing your abdomen in a dream suggests the gestation or digestion of a new idea or phase of your life. If your abdomen is swollen, the birth of a new project may be imminent. If you have pain in your abdomen in the dream, consider going to a physician and getting a checkup. Sometimes a warning in a dream deserves attention.

abduction
If you're abducted or kidnapped in your dream, it means you're feeling pressured to do or say something you don't believe in and don't want to do in waking life. Abduction dreams often stem from guilt over things you've done or are about to do that aren't typically in your character. If you witness someone else being abducted, it means you're not acting on the opportunities you've been given.

abnormality

If strangely formed things appear in your dream—a crooked mirror, a misshapen arm—it's a good omen. This just means that your mind is open to new and unusual things.

abortion

Dreaming of abortion is not usually literal. Many times, an abortion dream reflects the guilt you feel about doing something you shouldn't. The abortion in the dream is a warning to "abort" your actions and stop. If the dreamer is female, she could be worried about her choice of a partner and whether she truly trusts him.

abroad

Dreaming of going abroad predicts positive new situations you'll soon encounter. It also foretells luck in business and the opportunity to meet wonderful new people.

abuse

If you dream of being abused, it's a sign that you feel you're being emotionally taken advantage of in your waking life. If the dreamer is female, it signifies that she feels out of control with her emotions or with her love life. Something hurting her needs to be turned around.

abyss

Dreaming of falling into an abyss signifies that some part of your life is out of control. It could be that you're not working hard enough or not taking care of yourself. Maybe you're due for a move—career or otherwise. Looking into an abyss means you'll soon be challenged but that you'll come out of it victorious.

accelerator

This could be a release out-of-control dream. If the accelerator on your car is pushed down and you can't stop it, it denotes that you feel things have taken a turn for the worse and you don't know how to bring them around for the better.

accent

Hearing or speaking with a foreign accent indicates that you'll soon be around foreigners who will give you insight into an irksome problem. It may also signify that you should travel soon—it would be a great getaway.

accident

A car crash is usually a literal warning—be careful in the following weeks or months. A skiing accident or crash while going very fast is an out-of-control release dream. You need to take hold of your life before things get more complicated. A plane crash usually indicates worry about business or financial situations. Accidents at sea signify problems in or worry about a love relationship.

accordion

Accordion music signifies a longing for the past. There will be joy in the future mixed with a little sadness and melancholy for things long gone. This is an indication that you should march forward, and things will turn out well.

accusation

Accusations in a dream may be literal. Do you feel you've done something wrong? If you're accused, you may feel that you're being judged. The one judging you in these dreams is usually you.

ace

An ace in your dream is always a good omen of things to come. Aces and the number one stand for positive beginnings. Perhaps there's a new business opportunity coming your way, or a new friendship or love interest.

ache

Aches or pains in your dreams can be literal warnings. Is it time to get a checkup? If you actually feel the pain in the dream, you're probably half-lucid and feel the pain in waking life, as well. If the ache is imaginary, it could mean that you should beware of what people think of your public image.

acid

To dream of acid being poured on you signifies that your anxiety levels are high right now. It may be time to take a break. If you dream of drinking acid, the dream is a metaphor that something is "eating you up." Figure out what's bothering you and fix it.

acorn

A dream about an acorn is usually an abundance dream—you want something you can't have. It can also mean financial success and improved mental and physical health. An acorn may also refer to sexual desire, a sexual event that may be taboo or morally prohibited.

acrobatics

Performing acrobatics in your dream is a good sign that you feel vital and healthy. It could also mean you're able to overcome emotional difficulties now because luck is on your side.

actor or actress

Perhaps you're only seeing your own or someone else's persona—the side that person wants to show to the world. Seeing yourself as an actor in the spotlight suggests a desire for publicity or a more public life. Such a dream can also suggest that you're acting out a role or putting on an act for someone.

admiration

If someone is admiring you in the dream, it's a sure sign that you're feeling good about yourself. If you're admiring someone else in the dream, it signifies that your insecurities may be your downfall with your current problem.

adoption

If you dream of adopting a child, it could be a literal dream; perhaps you'd like to do so in the future. This dream can also be a sign that you have a lot of extra love to give and need an outlet to express it.

adultery

If you're committing adultery in a dream, it means you worry that you could fall into it or that you're contemplating doing it. If you dream your partner is committing adultery, chances are that you worry he *could*. But it doesn't necessarily mean that he *is*. In this case, use the dream as a jumping-off point to explore possible problems in the relationship.

affliction

Dreaming that you have an affliction of some kind actually means the opposite. It's a good sign of things to come and indicates worry over nothing—you're in good physical health.

afternoon

Dreams that take place in the afternoon suggest clarity and lengthiness. Are you with friends in the afternoon? If so, then positive and lasting associations may soon be formed. If it's a sunny day, good news is soon to come.

airplane

You may be soaring to new heights in some facet of your life or taking a metaphorical journey into the unconscious. An airplane dream can also mean career advancement or refer to an upcoming journey. A flying dream can be used as a launching pad to a lucid dream. If you miss your airplane, it refers to a missed opportunity you need to look into.

age

To dream of old people—strangers—indicates a fear of aging, but it can also signify a hint of reason or wisdom coming from you or your unconscious. Do the old people give you advice? Take it. This is your inner sage telling you what to do. This is also true if you dream of yourself as an aged person. If you dream of an older relative who has already passed on, it could be that you're receiving a visit from the Other Side.

aggression

Aggression in a dream signifies that you feel someone has control over you. You're feeling weak and vulnerable. If you're the one who's aggressive, it signifies that you have harbored resentment against yourself or the person you're attacking.

alarm

If you dream of an alarm ringing in warning, it indicates you have worries about some aspect of your life. Try to figure out what the problem is, and do something about it. On the other hand, an alarm in a dream may be literal. It's time for you to wake up.

alien

To dream of space aliens or one alien signifies that you'll soon have strange occurrences in your life that may help you toward a better future. If you're kind to the aliens, positive influences are entering your life.

alligator

This symbol may suggest that you're being thick-skinned or insensitive to someone else. It may also signify danger. An alligator that guides you or talks to you may just be your totem.

altitude

In your dream, you're looking down from great heights. What are you standing on? Is it something steady or something moving? If it's a big mountain, for example, you probably fear the future and need to make plans to ensure financial stability.

ambulance

Being in an ambulance signifies excessive worry over things that are out of your control. If you have a medical problem in the dream, though, it might be time to get a checkup. If you see someone else in an ambulance, you may have some hidden guilt about treating that person badly.

amusement park

Dreaming of an amusement park may suggest that you are in need of a vacation from your concerns over a troubling issue. To dream of being on a ride denotes enjoyment of life and feelings of being uninhibited.

ancestor

To see an ancestor in your dream could indicate worry over your marriage or future marriage. You could be looking to the past for answers. What do they tell you in the dream? Do not take this as advice. Normally, this is you releasing your worries in a dream.

anchor

An anchor grounds you—acts as your foundation. It also holds you in place, which can be either beneficial or detrimental. If there's a situation you need to let go of, do it now. Otherwise, if you've been contemplating making some kind of commitment, it's a good time to do so. An anchor also predicts stability and luck. If you dream of having problems with the anchor, however, it means that there is a difficult situation you're currently dealing with that needs to be resolved.

angels

Angels represent help from your higher self or from a guardian. The appearance of an angel may suggest a growing spiritual awareness. If you encounter an angel with a human face, this is most likely your personal spirit guide. Listen to what he or she has to say.

animals

Animals can relate to various sides of your animal nature—a guardian spirit, wisdom, innocence, predatory tendencies, or sexuality, depending on the perceived nature of the animal. An animal can also represent the physical body, or appear as a metaphor for an illness within the physical body. If you're not scared of the animal in your dream—if you're intrigued by it—this may be your totem, or personal animal guide.

anniversary

To dream of an anniversary signifies current and future happiness and many festive occasions. It also indicates good health to those who dream about it. Also, take note of your feeling about the anniversary. Are you happy? Envious? Then interpret the meaning as it applies to you.

ant(s)

This signifies difficulties that can be overcome with a little bit of work. Normally, they're small problems that you may be making into a big deal. Look within yourself to find the source of the negativity. Ants suggest restlessness ("feeling antsy"). They also signify small annoyances and irritations. Alternately, they may represent feelings of insignificance. Consider the number of ants in the dream. Is it a single ant? A colony? A huge, swollen anthill? One ant suggests loneliness. Many ants suggest trivial problems.

anxiety

Anxiety is very common in a dream. Normally, your anxieties in your waking life translate into your dreams in very strange ways. Anxiety dreams are best forgotten, not analyzed. Let your subconscious work it out for you while you sleep on it.

ape

Dreaming of an ape signifies that you should beware of the people around you. Are they trustworthy? If the ape is smiling in your dream, it means that you're unsure of the intentions of others.

apparition

An apparition can signify a message or warning. It can be seen as communication with the dead. Alternately, you might feel that another person in a relationship is like an apparition—someone who is there, but not truly present.

applause

Applause in dreams signifies a search for a reward for genuine efforts. This is a healthy dream that means you feel good about what you've done and you're looking for the respect and appreciation you deserve.

apples

Apples stand for wholeness and for knowledge. Ripe apples on a tree may mean that your hope and hard work have borne fruit. Apples also stand for long life and achievement. To dream of eating an apple suggests that you're currently in good physical health. An apple in a dream is a good sign.

appointment

A missed appointment signifies the same thing as a missed train, bus, or airplane. You know there's an opportunity you've missed or will miss if you don't act soon. Figure out what that opportunity is, and put your best foot forward.

April

As April showers lead to May flowers, a dream of this month suggests that much pleasure and fortune may be heading your way. If the weather is bad in the dream, it may suggest the passing of bad luck.

arch

Passing under an arch in a dream may symbolize a transition in your life—a move from one phase or stage to another. If you avoid walking under the arch, the indication is that you are resisting transition or change. Note the shape of the arch, whether it's adorned in any way, and whether other people are also using it. This will flesh out the symbol for you.

argument

If you have a dream in which you're arguing with someone, it could be that you fear intimacy with this person in waking life. On the other hand,

it may also be that you've had an argument or feel an argument is soon to come. If you see two people arguing in your dream, it indicates that you feel there is too much confusion around you right now. Lighten your load.

arm

Arms allow you to manipulate things in your environment. The same might be true in a dream. Seeing an arm suggests that you can maneuver or manipulate things in your dream environment. If you flap your arms in your dream, it may indicate a desire to fly.

arrow

An arrow can signify bad news in love, but it depends where the arrow is pointed. If you're defending yourself from a foe, it means that you'll have the strength to triumph in whatever situation you're soon to face.

artist

To dream of yourself as an artist suggests a great need to express your emotions and creativity on a bigger scale. It doesn't necessarily mean you want to paint. Try to integrate some of your more creative ideas into your work or love life.

ashes

Are they the ashes of a person or just from a fire? If the ashes are from someone you know who is alive, you may fear losing that person. If the ashes are from someone who has passed away, maybe that person is actually giving you a message from the Other Side. If the ashes are from a fire, you may fear financial ruin.

atlas

Dreaming of an atlas suggests that you are considering moving or taking a trip, or that you should.

attack

If you're being attacked in a dream, physically or otherwise, you feel that you are under emotional attack in real life. Chances are, you're feeling very vulnerable. Who's attacking you? If you dream you're attacking another person, it means you have very strong feelings of resentment toward someone.

attic

If you dream of entering an attic, you may be exploring the realm of the higher self or seeking knowledge there. An attic can also suggest a place where things from the past are hidden or stored. The suggestion might be that you take some part of you out of hiding or that you should dispose of the things you are clinging to from your past.

August

Dreams of August may suggest unfortunate dealings in business and love. A young woman's dream of a wedding in this month can mean an omen of sorrow in her early married life.

authority

A dream that you're in a position of authority can be a release dream or a wish dream. Usually, you work out responsibilities from waking life in your dreams. This is simply a matter of figuring things out during the nighttime, when your choices make you less vulnerable than they would in real life.

avalanche

This dream is a prediction dream and a warning. It means that something big and a little scary is coming your way and, deep down, you know it. It is also a message that you should proceed with caution and everything will turn out just fine.

award

If you've won an award in your dream, it means you secretly desire more recognition for your achievements. It also signifies that luck is on your side right now. Create some momentum, and ask for that job promotion you've been hoping for.

ax

How is the ax used in your dream? If you're wielding it, it means that news is soon to come and that you'll be able to overcome impending difficulties. If the ax is aimed at you, it refers to fear you may feel of being at the mercy of others.

B

baby

A baby in a dream may represent an idea that is gestating or growing. It could also relate to the pending birth of a child or a desire for a family. Alternatively, a baby could indicate dependent behavior or infantile longings. A baby walking alone indicates independence. A bright, clean baby represents requited love and many warm friends.

bachelor

A dream of being a bachelor indicates unwillingness to give up single life and a fear of being weighed down with responsibilities. For an older person to dream of being a bachelor, it actually means the opposite—fear of being left alone.

back

To see your back in a dream indicates worry about getting old. It can also warn you of a health condition. If you see someone else's back, it could indicate that you feel this person has turned away from you or that you're afraid he or she might.

baker

To dream of seeing a baker signifies happy and joyous times to come. If the baker is sad, it may indicate an unwillingness to accept the luck fate brings you. A baker also signifies warmth and security in family life.

baking

A dream of baking could be literal—you're thinking about upcoming events. It also signifies that you crave more family-oriented activities. Baking in a dream is good luck and an indicator of happy times soon to come.

balcony

Consider the condition of the balcony. If it's clean and polished, the dream indicates that others hold you in high regard. If it's a crumbling, tarnished balcony, it may suggest that you need to repair your public image.

baldness

For a woman to dream of being bald indicates her fear of getting older or losing her femininity and appeal. For a man to dream that he is bald signifies his fear of financial problems or ruin.

ball

A ball may signify ups and downs—good times and bad. You need to let go of the trivial matters and take the good ones to heart. Ironically enough, a ball can also signify that you need to be stronger in a certain matter.

balloon

Seeing a balloon in the air indicates a wish to fulfill some desire or fantasy. You'd like to be more creative and rise to new heights. It also may refer to a longing for childhood. If your child is carrying a balloon in a dream, it signifies your sadness over the fact that he's growing up quickly.

bank

Generally, a bank is a symbol of security and power—a foundation—but the meaning depends on what you're doing in the bank. If you are receiving or depositing money, it's usually an auspicious sign, an indication that you are financially secure. If you are waiting in line, it literally may mean waiting for a check or money to arrive. Likewise, if you're holding up a bank, it may symbolize that money you're expecting is being "held up" or delayed.

bankruptcy

You may have a dream about being bankrupt even if you have no financial problems. Though the dream could be literal, more often it has to do with feeling that you've missed an opportunity that was foolish to pass up.

basement

Dreaming of being in a basement could indicate that you are connecting with the subconscious mind. You could be unearthing something hidden in your past that you need to examine (see **underground**).

bath

To take a bath in a dream usually means that there is something you feel guilty about that you need to be cleansed of. If the scene in your dream is sexual, however, this is merely wish fulfillment. If you see others bathing, you wonder in waking life, whether these people are sincere with you.

bathroom

Dreaming of being in a bathroom could simply mean that your bladder is full. It could also symbolize a place of privacy. If the bathroom is crowded, the dream could mean that you lack privacy. If you find yourself in a bathroom for the opposite sex, it may suggest that you are crossing boundaries. A bathroom dream may also relate to the elimination of something in your life.

beach

To dream of being on a beach is, most likely, a wish or release dream. You'd like to find some time in your life to take off, go on vacation, and leave your responsibilities behind. If you're on the beach with someone, notice what he or she is doing and examine the symbolism behind it.

bear

A bear, in your dreams, can signify transition; it can refer to change of address. However, if your bear is leading you along, he can be your totem, your animal spirit guide.

beating

Taking a beating, Freudians would say, refers to masturbation or sexual longing. Giving a beating, on the other hand, indicates repressed aggression and resentment toward the other person in the dream.

beggar

If you dream of a beggar, take note of how you treat this person. This is how you feel about your weak side. Are you kind to him? If so, it most likely means you are good to yourself. If you're nasty to him, you need to be less hard on yourself.

beheading

If you dream about a beheading, notice who the victim is. If it's you, it means you feel you're not putting enough time into your emotional relationships. If it's another person, you somehow feel your career is at stake. Beheading dreams can also be past-life dreams.

bell

Unexpected good news is on its way. If you're ringing a bell, it means you may soon need to call upon trusted friends. They'll help you in your current situation. Dreaming of bells tolling means a distant friend may be very sick. If you dream of a joyous bell ringing, however, expect success in all aspects of your life soon.

birds

The appearance of a bird in a dream could relate to a wish to be free, to fly away, or to flee from something. A bird is a good omen. Birds can also be spiritual symbols. Among certain Native American tribes, an eagle symbolizes spiritual knowledge. If a woman dreams of birds with beautiful feathers, it means she will soon find a good partner in love.

birthday

Birthday dreams can have contrary meanings depending on the context. To dream of receiving birthday presents may mean happy surprises are coming or advancement is in order. For an older person to dream of a birthday may signify long hardship and sorrow; to the young, it may be a symbol of poverty.

black

The color black in a dream may indicate transformation and canceling-out of negative energy. It can be a good sign, depending on how you felt toward the black object. The color black can also signify boredom, but the former translation is usually correct.

bleeding

Blood is vital to life, and to dream of bleeding suggests a loss of power or a change in matters of the heart. If you dream of having your blood sucked by a vampire or other entity, it refers to a partner or friend emotionally draining you. End contact with this person.

boat(s)

If you're on a boat on calm water, it signifies tranquil and peaceful times ahead. Rough water indicates trouble with a significant other. Boats appearing in the distance can mean freedom and protection from harm. Boats with no one on them signify loneliness, and boats holding many people indicate an impending unexpected visit.

bones

Bones, in a dream, signify the bottom line—bones are the raw material of a dream. Are the bones scattered? Maybe you're torn in waking life over a decision you have to make. Notice the condition of the bones. That's how you feel about a current nagging issue.

book

A book in your dream can signify new beginnings or a new chapter in your life. It also signifies inherent wisdom and listening to your gut. An old or worn book means that you should leave the past behind you and look happily toward your future.

bottle

Translation depends what kind of bottle it is. If it's a water or liquor bottle, it means you'll encounter jealousy from work colleagues. A baby's bottle signifies a greater need for trust and intimacy with those involved in your dream.

breakdown

To dream of having a mental breakdown indicates that you feel completely overwhelmed and out of control in waking life. This is a serious sign for you to seek out some help with your problems. Talk to a professional.

break-in

Dreaming of someone breaking into your house means you fear people changing your ideals or getting involved where they shouldn't. It could also be a literal dream. Is the security for your home adequate? You'd better check it out.

breasts

Women's breasts may relate to sexual desire. They can also symbolize nurturing, motherhood, or a concern about exposure. Are the breasts exposed? Are they diseased or injured? This can be an indication of how you feel personally.

bride

To dream of a bride, whether it's you or another person, is good luck and can mean financial prosperity or inheritance. If a man kisses a bride in your dream, it indicates happy times ahead for family and friends. To dream of an elopement, though, may indicate unfavorable events happening soon.

bridge

Since a bridge connects one place to another, in dreaming it may represent a crossing from one state of mind to another. Consider the other elements in the dream. Are you crossing dangerous waters? What's waiting for you on the other side of the bridge? What did you leave behind?

bubble

Bubbles, in dreams, stand for rebirth or a completely different way of looking at things. If the bubbles are in the air, it stands for excessively lofty ideas. You need to be more practical about the situation at hand.

bugs

Seeing bugs in a dream can actually signify peace and family security. But it depends what the bugs are doing. It can also mean the opposite—you fear for your family security and peaceful home life.

bull

A bull signifies impending victory over the difficult situations you're soon to encounter. Be patient. Luck is on your side. Stick to your morals.

bus

A bus can be a vehicle for moving ahead to one's goal. If you're traveling with others, you could be on a collective journey. Notice other aspects of the dream, such as the luggage you're carrying, your destination, and what you're leaving behind.

butterfly

Butterflies are peaceful, tranquil creatures. To dream of them signifies upcoming happiness, but be careful of fickleness among friends and coworkers.

buttons

Buttons in a dream signify social change and how the public perceives you. Are the buttons fancy? Do you have problems buttoning? If they're very tight, it could mean you are being too rigid in your ideals.

buzzard

If you dream of a buzzard, watch out! An old scandal may resurface and injure your reputation. If you dream of a buzzard sitting on a railroad, you might experience an accident or loss in the near future. Should the buzzard in your dream fly away, all your current troubles will be resolved.

C

cabbage

Cabbage represents simple and inexpensive food that everyone has access to. When you dream of cabbage, it may signify a heaviness of the heart or a longing for simpler, easier times.

cafeteria

A cafeteria in a dream can signify social times in your life without real connection. You may yearn for more emotional nourishment. Is the cafeteria nice and clean or dirty and depressing? This is how you feel about your social life.

cage

A cage represents possession or control, and what you see in the cage is the key to interpreting this sign. A cage full of birds may signify great wealth and many children, while a single bird may represent a successful marriage or mate. An empty cage may mean the loss of a family member, while a cage full of wild animals may signify that you have control over a particular aspect of your life and that you will triumph over misfortune.

cake

A cake may symbolize that a celebration is at hand. It can also indicate that perhaps there's something to celebrate that has been overlooked. Maybe you should push for that promotion at work.

camp

Dreaming of camp depends on how you feel there. If you're having fun, it signifies longing for youth, fun, and freedom and a release from the constraints of everyday life. If you're not, it means that you feel like someone is trying to steal your thunder and take away your simple pleasures.

canal

Canals suggest a journey through the unconscious. Pay attention to other details in the dream. Is the water muddy or clear? Are you traveling with friends or family? A dirty canal suggests that you have hidden issues with love or family you need to work out as soon as possible.

cancer

Dreaming of cancer doesn't mean you have it or are going to get it. To be successfully treated for cancer in a dream signals a change for the better. Dreaming of cancer may symbolize a desperate or foreboding situation or a draining of resources.

candles

Usually the appearance of candles indicates spirituality. A candle provides light in the dark, or guidance through dark matters or the unknown. If a candle burns down to nothingness, it might indicate a fear or concern about death or impotence. A candle being put out could indicate a feeling of being overworked. A steadily burning candle may signify a steadfast character and constancy in friends and family.

cannibalism

To dream of cannibalism shows that your unconscious feels a need to consume someone else's energy. Are you emotionally draining the people around you? If you dream of someone eating you, be careful of the people you surround yourself with. They're not good for your self-esteem.

canoe

Canoes suggest a short journey that requires some effort but that is often pleasantly tranquil. Pay attention to other elements in the dream, such as the state of the water and how hard you are paddling. A dream of paddling on a calm stream symbolizes confidence in your own abilities. If the river is shallow and quick, the dream may indicate concern over a hasty decision in a recent matter. To dream of paddling with your lover may indicate an imminent and lasting marriage; but if the waters are rough, then some effort is required before marriage.

car

A moving car may mean you are headed toward a goal or moving ahead. If you're in the driver's seat, a car can symbolize taking charge of your life. Is there a backseat driver in the vehicle? Or are you taking the backseat in some situation in your life? Being a passenger indicates that someone else might be controlling a situation. A stolen or lost car could indicate that you are losing control of your life. Cars sometimes represent the physical body, so take note of the car's condition.

carousel

To dream of riding a carousel suggests that you are going around in circles and not making any progress in your endeavors. Seeing others ride a carousel symbolizes unfulfilled ambitions.

carrot

Carrots, in dreams, could mean you're hoping to express yourself in a more creative way. They also stand for earthy passions and standing your ground. You need to be true to yourself.

castle

Seeing one of these majestic structures in a dream might suggest power and strength, security and protection. Castles in the sky are fantasies and illusions—wishes to escape from one's present circumstances. Help will come soon if you need it.

castration

Dreaming of castration refers to feelings of inadequacy or impotence in life. You fear the unknown. It can also signify a fear of getting older and losing things and people in your life you hold dear.

cat

Cats can have both positive and negative attributes, depending on your association with cats and the surrounding circumstances in the dream. Cats can mean prosperity; kittens can mean new ideas. Kittens in a basement could be ideas arising from the unconscious mind. Cats can represent independence, the feminine spirit, or sexual prowess. They can also stand for evil or bad luck, or a catty or cunning person (see **leopard**).

cattle

To dream of healthy, content cattle grazing in a green pasture suggests prosperity and happiness. Conversely, dreaming of weak, poorly fed cattle suggests you are wasting your energy on the wrong things. Stampeding cattle implies that something in your life is out of control.

cave

A cave represents the hidden you—who you truly are. How did you feel inside the cave? Were you frightened? Was it cozy? Caves also refer to rebirth and a changing of old ideas.

cedar

Cedar represents strength of conviction and health. It can also signify earthiness. Do you need to get back to basics? Cedar chips can signify scattered thoughts. Get your ideas together and focus your priorities.

celebrities

Celebrities in your dreams can signify a yearning to be more in the social scene. It also signifies a part of you that craves recognition for past efforts. Dreams about having sex with celebrities are merely wish fulfillment.

ceremony

Dreams about ceremonies indicate that you're entering a new phase of your life. Do you feel comfortable with the changes? Are you enjoying the ceremony in your dream? Dreaming about a ceremony is a positive sign of good things to come.

chain

Seeing a chain predicts good news in matters of the heart. If the chain is shiny and sparkling, it can also predict a wedding engagement.

chair

A chair in a dream usually indicates that you should expect a guest soon. If you're thrown off the chair, expect problems at work. If this chair is a throne, be careful signing contracts. A business deal may be too good to be true.

chanting

Hearing chanting in your dream can refer to two things. If the chanting is loud, it means there is a problem in your life that you're ignoring. If the chanting is soft and meditative, it means that there is too much confusion around you and your unconscious is telling you to slow down and take a break.

chariot

Riding in a chariot in a dream suggests positive news or success in a matter. It also signifies upcoming travel that is destined.

cheese

Dreaming of cheese can indicate some sorrow ahead. However, Swiss cheese in a dream means that you will come into substantial money soon and that your health will be very good.

chemistry

The mixing of potions in a dream refers to intensity of life and purification. What things do you need to simplify in your life in order to make it work? Are you balancing your life well? This is also an indication that you need to take responsibility for your actions.

cherry

A cherry can signify lust, female desire, and forbidden fruit. It also represents wholeness, as a circle does. Who is eating the cherries? Are they in a bowl? Are they beyond your grasp?

childbearing

Dreaming of childbearing signifies that the dreamer is giving birth to new ideas. If the childbirth is difficult, it means you'll have some serious struggles along the way, but it will eventually come to fruition.

children

By dreaming of children, you possibly may yearn to return to a simpler, less complicated life. Such dreams might also relate to a desire to return to the past to recapture good times or to satisfy unfulfilled hopes.

chimney

To dream of a chimney signifies a spiritual ascension and approach to life. Your dreams are becoming more defined, and you need to follow your instincts. This is a positive dream.

chocolate

Chocolate suggests a need or a desire to indulge in something. It can also indicate a need to limit your indulgences.

cigarette

This may be a warning telling you to concentrate more on important issues rather than foolish pursuits. If you are a smoker, this dream could be a literal warning to quit.

circle

A circle in Jungian terms represents the Self and wholeness. It can also relate to a symbol of protection or social connections, as in a circle of friends. If you're "circling around something," caution is indicated. Finally, the Freudian interpretation is that the circle represents the vagina and sexual desire. A circle may also indicate gifts or money coming your way. If a woman is engaged or about to get married, a circle is an excellent omen of good things to come.

circling

Circling around and around can mean that you literally feel that you're going in circles without getting anywhere. Pick and choose your battles. Analyze your goals.

city

Cities represent challenges, fun, and new enterprises. Are you starting something that can directly affect your financial situation? If so, examine how you feel about being in the city. That's how you feel about which way the tides are turning in terms of your career.

climbing

Climbing up in dreams represents a longing for more knowledge. It can also signify that you want more challenges, yet emotionally you may feel drained. You're searching for a belief system for your ideals.

cloak

A cloak hides your true intentions. It protects your secrets. Are you feeling guilty about something you've done? If someone else is wearing the cloak, chances are you're feeling left out of the loop.

clock

A clock is a sign of good health. It can also refer to a past event you wish you could change. Don't be so hard on yourself.

closet

Closets are places where things are stored or hidden. If you are hiding something in your life, your dream may indicate that it is time to release this secret.

clothing

The clothing you wear in your dreams represents how you currently feel about yourself and your accomplishments. Is your clothing regal and expensive? Or is it tattered and torn? The clothing refers directly to your self-esteem.

clouds

Dark, stormy clouds rolling in at a low altitude and flashing lightning may represent your anger regarding a situation. A slate-gray cloudy sky might indicate that your views are clouded on a subject. What is it in your life that needs clarity? Dreaming of white, billowing clouds floating in a blue sky suggests that matters are clearing up.

clover

This is a good sign that happiness is soon coming your way. A clover always signifies luck. If the clover is any color but green, it means that it will take a bit of perseverance on your part before the good things start to happen.

clown

Clowns can represent fear of the unknown and the dark, insecure side you feel within. If your reaction toward the clown is one of happiness and joy, it can also mean that you long for happier, simpler times.

club

A club in your dream represents hidden aggression from your past. Because clubs were used long, long ago, it can refer to an old hurt that something current has unearthed. If someone is shaking the club, it represents a warning to deal with current emotional issues.

cockroach

Dreaming of a cockroach can be a literal dream—you saw one while you were awake and it filtered into your dreams. It can also stand for dirt and shame. Were the cockroaches in your house? Since a house represents you, figure out what you may feel dirty or ashamed about.

cocoon

A cocoon represents safety, warmth, and protection—with family and friends. It also signifies rebirth and a new stage in your life soon to come or one that has already begun. This dream means you need to accept the new factors in your life. This is a positive change.

coffee

If you dream of drinking coffee, it means that your friends disapprove or will disapprove of your current or upcoming marriage partner. If you are already married and dream of drinking coffee, be prepared for little disagreements and quarrels. If you dream of roasting coffee, you will soon meet a new love. To dream of ground coffee signifies you will be soon be successful in overcoming adversity.

coffeehouse

Whether you are a man or woman, a dream of visiting a coffeehouse denotes that women are conspiring against you and your possessions. Beware of false gossip among coworkers.

coffin

A coffin may symbolize a feeling of confinement. Coffins also relate to death, so ask yourself what might be causing you to feel "dead."

coin

A coin in a dream indicates a change of fate. Many coins signify money and prosperity. If the coin is heads-up, it means things are going in your favor. Tails-up on a coin indicates that tides are about to turn.

collar

A collar refers to possessiveness. Who is wearing the collar in your dream? Are you looking for your dog's collar? Many people dream of a dog's collar if the dog is sick or after the dog has passed away. It indicates true love and affection for your animal. If you dream that you're wearing the collar, it signifies oppression you feel from others.

college

College represents distinction and the attainment of your hopes through hard work. To dream of a college may suggest that you will advance to a long-sought position. Dreaming that you are back in college suggests that distinction will follow a period of hard work.

columns

To dream of a building with columns suggests higher wisdom, intelligence, and authority. Are you standing near the columns? If you are, it means you long for more mental stimulation. Columns also stand for sexual prowess and virility. Incidentally, the akashic records—on the Other Side, where your soul's purpose is written down—are located in a building with huge columns.

contamination

This dream can be a warning about your health. If you feel that you're contaminated in the dream, it may be that your body senses something is not right. This dream can also refer to obsessive tendencies.

contract

Seeing a contract in a dream means that you have some financial worries in your life. If you sign the contract, it means all should turn out well. If you don't sign the contract, this could be a warning against making bad career decisions.

corn

Corn refers to fertility, health, and rebirth. When a woman dreams of corn, it means that she can get pregnant very soon. Her body and mind are prepared for new life. Corn, in a dream, is a positive sign of good things to come.

corpse

To dream of yourself as a corpse or to experience your death is not necessarily a prediction of your demise. It could signify a major change in your life, such as a divorce or the ending of a long-held job. If you dream of killing yourself, it could mean that you are going through a traumatic personal transformation and want to leave your old life behind.

costume

Notice the costume in the dream. Are you wearing the costume? If so, this is how you may see yourself. A costume represents the disguise you wear and show to others. Is someone else wearing the costume? This may be how you see this person.

couch

A couch, in dreams, represents analysis of the Self. Are you comfortable on the couch? If so, you're probably comfortable with the way things are going in your life. Is the couch tattered or torn? If so, then it's time to reorganize your priorities.

court

To dream of going to court can be literal. Is there a pending legal matter in your life? Dreaming of being in court also indicates a fear of being judged. Who is the presiding judge in your dream, and why do you feel he or she disapproves of you?

courtyard

A courtyard, in a dream, represents tranquil, peaceful times. It can also refer to family. What are you doing in the courtyard? If there is a lot of green, it can be a positive omen of prosperous financial times ahead.

cow

A cow can represent fertility, sustenance, or even prosperity. A cow might also signify a desire for sexual intercourse or a fear of being unable to resist sex.

coyote

A coyote is considered a sleek, sly creature. Is there someone in your life who you feel is sneaky or taking advantage of you? Are you scared of the coyote? If you're not, the coyote could simply be your totem.

crab

Dreaming of a crab indicates unstable mood swings and emotional upheaval. It can also indicate pesky annoyances and fear of being brought down by trivial matters. If you get bitten by a crab, it means that your emotions are getting the best of you.

cradle

A cradle can be literal if you already have a baby. It can also symbolize yearning for one. Cradles signify protection and comfort. Who is in the cradle? Is the cradle secure? If the cradle is faulty, you might feel you're not providing a stable-enough life for a loved one.

creek

A creek represents a short journey or a new experience. Are you exploring a creek with a friend? Is the creek muddy? Note the other aspects of the dream.

crevice

A crevice, in a dream, signifies the unknown. Be wary of upcoming situations you may be placed in. Is there something inside the crevice, or is it simply dark? This also refers to hidden desires in your unconscious.

crocodile

If the crocodile in your dream is immersed in water, it means that you may be looking for the key to hidden emotions. Something is blocking you. If the crocodile is on land, it may signify that you're not being truthful with yourself.

crow

A crow can signify financial problems or rough times ahead. It can be a warning to be careful about whom you trust and where you're investing your money. On rare occasions, the crow signifies what you deem evil inside you.

crowd

Being lost in a crowd can signify a loss of individuality. You may feel the need to stand out from others. It can also mean confusion around you, or even boredom. Maybe it's time to travel.

crown

The obvious definition is wealth, position, power, and authority. But is the crown something desired or feared in the dream? Is it within reach or escaping your grasp? A crown may also indicate good advice from an older person or mentor.

crutches

If you have a dream about crutches, you may feel that you're relying too heavily on something or someone. It also signifies fear of being more independent and venturing out on your own.

crying

To dream of crying indicates repressed sadness, usually referring to problems of the heart. It can also signify a release from problems. Try not to analyze this dream. Let your unconscious work it out for you.

cup

Notice the other influences in the dream. A cup indicates that your answer to a current situation is right under your nose. Is the cup full or empty?

cursing

If you dream that someone is shouting curses at you, it could mean you're in for rough times. If you're cursing in the dream, it means you're picking up bad habits from unsavory friends.

cypress

A cypress tree indicates travel to a Mediterranean destination. It also signifies wholeness and immortality. Cypress trees can indicate security and wisdom as well.

D

dagger

Beware of betrayal by friends and those close to you. Also, be meticulous in your wording. A misunderstanding could get you into big trouble.

daisy

A daisy indicates that there is a possibility for new love with someone you already know.

dancing

A dream about dance evokes movement, freedom, joy, and a time of happiness. It also indicates liberation from constraints and deep connection with your current emotional state.

darkness

Darkness is a symbol of the unconscious, the hidden and the unknown. Darkness can also stand for evil, death, and fear. To dream of being overtaken by darkness suggests fear or trepidation about a matter at hand. To dream that you lose a friend or child in the darkness symbolizes that you may be provoked from many different sources.

dawn

Dawn signifies rebirth and a new transitional state. Translation of this symbol depends how you feel about the dawn. If you're afraid, it could be the turmoil you feel within about moving forward with new projects.

daybreak

Daybreak symbolizes that the outlook on a matter is brightening. A gloomy or cloudy day suggests bad luck in a new enterprise.

dead

The appearance of the dead in a dream typically signifies a warning of some kind. To see the dead active and happy represents an influence that may be affecting your life. If you dream of a loved one who has passed away, this person may actually be visiting you.

death

A death dream usually isn't a premonition of death, but it may indicate a death. If there's no sense of fear in the death, the dream can mean you're letting go of something. On the other hand, a corpse can indicate a lifeless routine.

decapitation

A dream about decapitation can happen when the dreamer feels a certain distancing from the body. It can happen in a period of illness or when the mind of the dreamer is unwilling to accept a new physical limitation, such as age.

decay

Decay, in a dream, can indicate that the dreamer is ready to get rid of the old to make room for the new. It can also signify neglect of body or of mind. What is decaying in your dream?

December

A time of gift giving and receiving, to dream of this month can suggest the accumulation of wealth and fortune.

deer

A deer in a dream may symbolize hunting. Deer are also graceful and gentle creatures that are easily frightened. In folklore, deer are the messengers of fairies and therefore could be messengers of the unconscious.

dentist

Going to the dentist in a dream can signify a few things. It could be literal. Do you have an upcoming appointment or a need for one? If not, dentists in dreams can refer to pain or an authority figure. Dreaming of a dentist also alludes to your level of trust with the people around you.

desert

A desert is usually thought of as a barren place, where little grows. It can be symbolic of a fear of death, or of being infertile. But a desert can also symbolize hidden beauty and hidden life that is camouflaged by ordinary perceptions.

dessert

Desserts represent forbidden pleasures and hidden guilt. How do you feel about eating the dessert?

devil

The devil means karma—something that is meant to happen—and impending change. It can also signify a marriage that is meant to be. Are you scared of the devil in your dream? If you're married, the devil can represent your partner. Pay close attention to how you feel toward him.

dew

Suggestive of tiny treasures or small pleasures, to dream of sparkling dew may represent coming wealth and achievement. For a single person, perhaps a fortunate marriage is imminent.

diamond

A diamond symbolizes love, as in a diamond ring, and money. A lost diamond, especially a ring, may symbolize a concern about a love relationship. A gift of a diamond depends on who is giving it and other circumstances. A diamond from a parent or relative could refer to an inheritance; one from a friend might indicate a wish to obtain the person's love.

digestion

Digestion could be a literal dream alluding to what you ate earlier. It can also signify spiritual nourishment—becoming more emotionally committed to your personal relationships.

digging

What are you digging for? If it's something lost, you may be attempting to retrieve a part of your past. If it's a treasure, you may be delving into the unconscious—a treasure chest of knowledge. However, if you are burying something, it indicates a wish to cover up an act, hide your feelings, or hide the facts of the matter.

dirty

Dirty surroundings can pertain to your feelings of impure thoughts. Is there something you fear about your sexuality? It can also refer to feelings of being unorganized or disorderly.

disappearance

This is a common dream, in which the dreamer is searching for someone who is missing. If it's an object, you're merely coping with a trivial loss. If it's a person who is nowhere to be found, it means you long for a connection with this person or you want to make up, but your unconscious knows this may be impossible.

discipline

Being disciplined in your dreams could refer to how you feel about yourself or how you feel about others. Are you getting things done the way you should? If not, you could feel you need to punish yourself.

disinfectant

Disinfectant in your dreams can refer to cleaning up your own life. Do you feel dirty about particular emotions you're experiencing? Are you comfortable with your own sexuality? Disinfectant is also the way you might deal with bad situations.

dismemberment

Dismemberment, in a dream, refers to breaking apart before putting things back together. It has to do with joining the pieces of your own life puzzle.

disobedience

A dream about being disobedient signifies that you're feeling too many restrictions in your life right now.

diving

To dream of diving into a body of water may indicate that you are about to dive into something related to your waking life. On a deeper level, a diving dream may symbolize an exploration of the unconscious. From a Freudian perspective, such a dream suggests the dreamer is diving into a new sexual relationship.

doctor

A doctor can indicate healing or a healing guide. For some people, a doctor in a dream might symbolize mainstream thinking as opposed to alternative health options. Dreaming of a doctor may also signify that you need to visit one but are afraid to.

dog

Dreaming of a dog can mean that you're seeking companionship, affection, or loyalty. If the dog bites, it might indicate a feeling of disloyalty. To hear dogs barking suggests a message or a warning from your unconscious. On another side, a dog sometimes represents your mother. Pay attention to how you feel about the dog.

doll

Dreaming of a doll refers to childhood thoughts and memories. Is the doll in good condition? If so, it means you're feeling good about your past. If it's in poor shape, it's a sign that you need to heal certain issues from your past.

dolphins

A dolphin may be considered a messenger of the unconscious, since it resides in the sea. The dolphin is a guide to the unconscious realms, which may suggest that you are diving into your unconscious. What do you fear? What do you hope for?

door

A common dream symbol, doors can indicate an opening or a new opportunity at hand. A closed door suggests that something is inaccessible or hidden. If a door is broken, there may be something hindering you from taking a new opportunity. The condition of the door, the material it's made of, and any markings that appear on it often provide clues about what lies behind it or about your perception of reality.

doorbell

If you dream you hear a doorbell ringing, expect to be called away to visit a friend or relative in need.

dove

A dove in a dream is always a lucky symbol meaning peace, affection, love, and prosperity. Take notice of where the dove goes. Is this your heart's true desire?

dragon

Dragons refer to intuition and psychic ability. You may know that something is about to happen but you don't want to admit it. Dragons also represent authority and power. How do you feel about the dragon in your dream?

drawer

A dream of a drawer or putting something into a drawer is about putting aside foolish pursuits and dealing with the current situation. You may dream of drawers when there is a part of yourself you'd like to keep hidden from the rest of the world. If you take something out of a drawer, analyze the object to determine what part of yourself you're now ready to share with people.

dream

To have a dream that you're dreaming usually indicates that you're having a lucid dream. These dreams are excellent to have because you can learn how to control the outcome and steer things toward positive results.

drinking

Symbolically, water is related to the unconscious and emotions. Drinking may suggest you are being nourished or have a thirst for emotional involvement. As a metaphor, the drinking of spirits may suggest a search for spiritual sustenance. For an alcoholic or someone close to an alcoholic, a dream of drinking alcohol may be a warning.

driving

Driving signifies a need to take the wheel and gain control of your life. If you're driving and the car swerves out of control or the accelerator is stuck in one place, it's possible that your unconscious knows that you need to buckle down in life.

drought

Generally an unfavorable omen in a dream, droughts represent the absence of life or the drying up of your emotions. Are you with someone in the dream? Maybe there is an unresolved issue between you and someone you are close to that is leading to a quarrel or separation.

drowning

Drowning in a dream signifies deep-rooted fear of delving into your unconscious mind. Is the water rocky or smooth? Drowning in rocky water indicates fear of being deserted by loved ones.

drugs

Many times, dreams about drugs are literal—you're under their influence. But being offered drugs in a dream usually refers to negative influences around you. Who is the person offering you the drugs?

drum

Dreaming of a drum or drumbeats may relate to a primitive urge. Alternately, a drum possibly symbolizes communication, magic, or even an entrepreneurial spirit, as in drumming up business.

drunk

You often dream of being drunk when you've had too much to drink in real life. If you dream of seeing a drunk, it could refer to your feeling that you're being foolish and indulgent in a current situation.

dusk

Dusk denotes the end of the day, the end of happiness or clarity on an issue, or a dark outlook on a matter at hand.

dwarf

Dwarves are traditionally associated with magical powers. Dreaming of a dwarf could be an extremely fortuitous sign. On the other hand, a dwarf can symbolize a stunted condition. If growth is limited, alternate paths must be pursued.

dying

Dreams of dying represent the end of an emotional state or situation at hand. To dream that you are going to die suggests an inattention to a particular aspect of your life. Seeing animals in the throes of death means bad influences are a threat.

dynamite

If you dream of dynamite in your dream, you fear a potentially explosive situation. Is it your repressed emotions? Or are you treating an important person badly? Examine the dream to determine where the problem lies.

E

eagle

The eagle, soaring through the sky, can symbolize a spiritual quest. It can also stand for combat, pride, courage, and ferocity. Eagles are traditionally associated with nobility. They also can symbolize a father figure or the sun.

earrings

Earrings can represent joyous times ahead. They can also refer to fickleness and time wasted. Pay attention to the type of earrings they are. Are they demure, like pearls, or fun and large, like gypsy earrings? If they're more conservative, it may be that you're longing to change the way people see you. If they're more outrageous, it may be that you're worried about the way people see you.

ears

A dream of human ears can be a warning to watch what you say. Ears can also call attention to something. You need to listen carefully to what's going on around you.

earth

To dream of the earth signifies an awareness of spiritual things. It also signifies your need to be more grounded and stable in your relationships and financial matters. Dreaming of the earth is a positive, healthy sign.

earthquake

Dreaming of an earthquake might suggest that personal, financial, or business matters are unstable. Is something upsetting taking place in your life? Earthquakes can also have sexual connotations, such as the desire for sexual release. If there are others in the dream, does one of them make the earth move for you?

eating

A dream of eating might suggest a craving for love or power. It can mean you are enjoying life or indulging in its pleasures. If you are the one being eaten in the dream, ask yourself if something is eating at you. Do you feel as if you are being eaten alive?

echo

To hear an echo in your dreams means two things—that you feel nobody is really listening to you or hearing what you're trying to say, or that your feelings of loneliness are becoming a huge burden.

eclipse

An eclipse suggests a disruption of the normal. When something is eclipsed, it means a period of activity has ended. Also, an eclipse can mean that cosmic forces may be at work in your life.

eel

An eel can be a phallic symbol. Its movement through waters indicates sexual overtones. Take your cues from what the eel is doing.

egg

In the Freudian interpretation, eggs can symbolize the male testicles and stand for virility. In the Jungian view, eggs represent wholeness, fertility, and new life. Eggs can also represent ideas that have not yet hatched. Finding a nest of eggs might indicate a waiting period, or that ideas are gestating. Or financially, eggs can allude to your nest egg. What is the context of the dream? Is someone egging you on?

election

To dream of running for office means you'd like to have more authority and power with others. It can also mean that you don't feel you've been rewarded enough for your efforts. If you win an election in your dream, it symbolizes that wonderful new changes in your life are on their way.

electricity

Dreaming of electricity signifies drive and spontaneity—new life. It refers to the need to be more active. If you see something being electrified, it means that you're aware of the inner battle you're currently having with issues of growing older and, possibly, financial stability.

electrocuted

To dream of being electrocuted signifies two things. First, it means that you may be shocked by the happenings around you. It also signifies a fear you have of losing power in a close relationship or in your career.

elephant

The appearance of these large, solid animals may portend the possession of wealth, honor, and a steadfast character. As the elephants rule in the wild, their appearance in your dream may suggest that you reign supreme in business and at home. How many elephants are you seeing? A herd of elephants may suggest great wealth, while a single elephant may represent a small but solid fortune. An elephant with its trunk held up is a symbol of excellent luck soon to come.

elevator

Rising in an elevator may symbolize a rise in status, such as a promotion, or a heightening of consciousness. Is the ascent rapid? Are you frightened? Exhilarated? A descent in an elevator might indicate a lowering in status or position, or a journey into the unconscious. A stuck elevator might suggest that some aspect of your life is presently being delayed. A plunging elevator could indicate a rapid descent into the unconscious, and your fear of losing control in life.

elopement

If you have a dream of eloping, it's very possible you're unhappy with your current love situation. If you're happy in the dream, it could also mean that you're anxious for more stability with your emotions and in love. If you watch two people eloping, it could mean that you don't approve of the actions of others around you now.

embarrassment

If you dream of being embarrassed in a dream, it indicates that you're unsure of what to do next. It also signifies a general lack of overall confidence. Issues from the past that used to bother you have probably resurfaced in your life. Resolve them, and you'll stop having this type of dream.

embrace

To dream of embracing someone in a dream simply means that you have a new kind of affection for this person. If you're forced to embrace someone, it means that you feel you're being harshly judged or criticized—not necessarily by them, but by someone close to you.

embroidery

Embroidery, in a dream, can refer to departed loved ones or unfulfilled dreams of the past. Do you feel as if you've missed an emotional opportunity? Was there a relationship you broke away from that you're thinking about? This also refers to the little details in your life.

embryo

To dream of an embryo signifies beginnings and kernels of ideas you need to develop. It can also, of course, refer to birth, rebirth, and pregnancy. For a man to dream of an embryo signifies that he'd like to have more emotional contact with the women in his life.

empty

An empty room, cup, container, or object is a metaphor for the way you feel about yourself currently. You'd like to find the object full, simply because you're ready for things to go your way. It also refers to boredom and loneliness.

enema

An enema, in a dream, refers to something emotionally draining you. It could also stand for people in your life who depend on you financially. What is it that you feel is pulling you under?

enemy

Dreaming of an enemy signifies that you long for peace with this person but believe it is not possible. To dream of an enemy you do not know usually refers to yourself—you are the enemy. Are you running from the enemy in your dream or facing him?

engagement

To dream of an engagement is usually a release or wish-fulfillment dream. Perhaps you long to have more security in your love life so you can plan for the future. This is also a good omen for positive social experiences to come.

engine

If you dream of putting together the engine of a car, it means that your unconscious knows it needs to get down to bare basics—start over and rebuild things from the ground up. This may refer to a business or to your insecurities and doubts about current relationships.

entrance

An entrance in a dream refers to the choices you need to make. Do you walk through the entrance? Are you scared to go in? You may often have a dream about an entrance when you're at a turning point in your life. To dream of making a big entrance signifies your need to be more socially proactive.

eruption

An eruption, in a dream, means that you're holding back in your waking life. You need to release some angst and start things fresh. If the eruption occurs with a volcano, it can also refer to repressed sexual desire.

escalator

Dreaming of an escalator refers to slowly climbing the ranks in either business or spirituality. Who is at the top of the escalator? Can he or she help you with your pursuit? Does this person have authority over you?

escaping

If you dream of making an escape, consider whether you are avoiding or need to get away from something in your life. Examine who the people are in your dream. Are you trying to get away from them? Have they done something that you need to confront them about?

eunuch

Whether you have this dream about yourself or about another person, it refers to you and harbored feelings of inadequacy. It could also signify guilt over how you've acted toward others around you.

Europe

To dream of traveling to Europe is good news. It indicates that taking a journey right now will benefit you financially somehow. It could relate to work, inheritance, or new opportunities.

evening

A dream that takes place in the evening suggests uncertain or unrealized hopes. To dream of stars shining suggests present troubles followed by brighter times. A dream of lovers walking in the evening may symbolize separation or a sense of loss.

evergreen

A dream of an evergreen—especially the word itself—may be a metaphor. To be "ever green" indicates wealth or at least financial stability. An evergreen or pine tree might also indicate hope or even immortality. A decorated evergreen or Christmas tree suggests giving or receiving gifts.

examination

If you dream of taking an exam, it might indicate a concern about failure. A stack of tests could suggest you feel you are being tested too often. You feel that someone is judging you. Look at the surrounding elements in the dream. If you forget to go to class in your dream, it suggests that you are worried about being unprepared.

exchange

To dream of exchanging one thing for another indicates a recent change in your way of thinking or even your style—the way you present yourself to others. What is it you're exchanging? Notice the people around you in the dream and how they're acting toward you.

excrement

A dream of excrement can be a good omen. First of all, it can nourish new ideas and beginnings. It also signifies ridding yourself of what you no longer need to start out anew. In rare cases, it can refer to feelings of being dirty (see **dirty**).

execution

If you're about to be executed or about to witness an execution in your dream, it refers to the current sadness and heaviness of heart you feel. If you're depressed, seek professional help. In rare cases, execution can also refer to the end of the old and a new start, in terms of a way of life.

executive

Dreaming of being an executive in your dream is usually quite literal. You may long for more power and authority in your career. In some cases, this also refers to having more stability in your home and family life.

exhaustion

More times than not, this is a literal dream referring to your current physical health. It may be time for you to take a break or go on vacation. Also, it can refer to feelings of being overly emotionally drained.

exhibitionism

Exhibitionism, in a dream, is very healthy. It signifies a willingness to take things on with open arms and to show the world your vulnerability. In some cases, exhibitionism also refers to an affinity for more sexual adventures. It also refers to feeling free without the constraints of society or age.

exile

To dream of being in exile represents three things. You could feel that you're being left out or punished by a social circle or relationship you long for. It can also mean you feel judged or criticized. Another possibility is that you just feel alone right now.

expedition

To set out on an expedition signifies an openness and willingness to have new adventures—both with travel and in your relationships. It's a good sign for positive experiences soon to come.

explosion

A dream of an explosion could be an attempt by your unconscious to get your attention on a matter of concern. An explosion could suggest a release or an outburst of repressed anger, or an upheaval in your life.

eye

To dream of one eye or two intense eyes signifies that someone from your past is currently thinking about you and may soon be in touch.

eyeglasses

Eyeglasses, in a dream, refer to seeing the world more clearly. Your unconscious is trying to tell you to take a good look around. If eyeglasses are handed to you in the dream, it signifies that this person is trying to tell you something important. You need to take notice of issues around you now.

eyes

If you dream of brown eyes, it denotes that there may be deceit or treachery in your life—watch out! To dream of blue eyes means you may be weak right now and need to carry out your intentions. Dreaming of gray eyes means you crave flattery.

F

face

Whose face is it? If you dream of seeing your own face, you may need to re-evaluate where your life is going. If the face is attached to an angel, pay close attention to what he or she says—this could be your spirit guide (also true if it's just a face with no body). Seeing a face also means that you need to better define your goals.

facelift

To dream of having a facelift signifies that you'd like people to see you in a different light. What is it you're imagining they feel toward you? On rare occasions, dreaming of a facelift can be a literal dream—you fear becoming and looking old.

fairy

This indicates that someone is looking out for you. On this planet or on the Other Side, a spirit guide or mentor wants to help.

falcon

Dreaming of a falcon represents spiritual awareness and rising to new heights. It also indicates freedom from the burdens of society. On another note, a falcon can signify news soon to come.

falling

Falling is a common dream symbol and usually an expression of concern about failure. The dream could be a metaphor for falling down on the job. In most falling dreams, the dreamer never lands. If you do hit the ground, it could mean that you've struck bottom in a matter. If you are unharmed, the dream may be suggesting that you won't be hurt by something that you perceive as a failure.

famous

To dream of being famous signifies that you long to be in the public eye and to be rewarded for your previous efforts. This dream can be a release dream or a wish-fulfillment dream.

famous people

If you're friends with famous people in your dream, it's usually a wish-fulfillment dream. Deep down, you wish some of their success and recognition would rub off on you.

fan

Fans represent spiritual guidance and the key to a nagging situation. Fans in dreams symbolize your need to go with the flow now and take things as they come. You may struggle a bit, but you'll come out on top in the end.

fat

A dream of being fat might be a concern about your diet, but it could also be a metaphor either for wealth and abundance or for overindulgence.

father

The appearance of your father can have many connotations, depending on the context of the dream and your relationship with him. Typically it represents a need for advice in a troubling situation.

father figure

To dream of a father figure in your dream represents the need for more stability in your life. It could also be your unconscious telling you to be wary of the current situation you're facing. If you have bad feelings about this father figure, it may be that you doubt your place within your own family. Are those around you treating you with respect?

father-in-law

To dream of your father-in-law suggests that you are worried about being unprepared. This may refer to work or to an upcoming social or family event.

feather

To dream of a feather floating through the air bodes well. Your burdens will be light and easily mastered. To dream of an eagle feather implies that your aspirations will be met.

February

A dream of this short winter month suggests continued ill health and melancholy. To dream of a sunshiny day in this month may suggest an unexpected change in fortune and outlook.

feet

Dreaming of feet means that you could be overworking yourself. Take a break when you need it. Bare feet symbolize freedom and a need to be more spontaneous in life and with meeting new people. A cut on your foot means that you feel a bit trapped in your current social situation.

fence

A dream of a fence can indicate that you feel "fenced in." A fence can block you or it can protect you. If you are "on the fence," the dream might suggest that you are undecided about something.

fever

To dream that you are suffering from a fever suggests a needless worry over a small affair. Be patient, and it will work itself out.

field

To dream of green fields, ripe with corn or grain, indicates you will have great abundance. If you dream of plowed fields, you will have wealth and prestige at a young age. Of course, if you dream of a field full of dead corn, expect some hard times to come before the good ones. If you dream of a freshly plowed pasture ready for planting, a long struggle will soon be resolved and you will have great success.

fig

A dream about figs refers to all things erotic—desire, sex, sexual need, and longing. Who is eating the fig in your dream? A fig also signifies hidden pleasures you should take advantage of. They're waiting for you.

fight

To fight in a dream may represent a conflict or the need to resolve an issue. Pay attention to other details in the dream so that you may interpret it better. Are you winning or losing a fight? Are you fighting with a loved one?

filing

To dream of filing signifies a hidden need you feel to separate your feelings and emotions from a potentially difficult situation. It could also refer to a need to better organize your life.

fingers

Fingers, in a dream, refer to touch, emotion, accusation, warmth, and communication. In order to determine the meaning of the dream, take note of what you're doing with your fingers or how the other person is using them. Translate this literally, and then look for other symbols in the dream.

fire

Fire is generally a favorable symbol to the dreamer, as long as he or she is not burned. It represents continued prosperity and fortune. If you're on fire, it's probably a metaphor for passion—perhaps you're burning with desire. Alternately, fire can symbolize destruction, purification, illumination, and a spiritual awakening. Look for other metaphors. What are you getting fired up about? Are you (or another figure in the dream) concerned about being fired or getting burned?

fire engine

A symbol of distress and ultimately of protection, a fire engine indicates worry over an important matter at hand that will soon be resolved.

firefighting

To dream of fighting flames suggests that hard work is required before success is achieved. To dream of a firefighter may suggest solid friendships. To dream of an injured firefighter indicates that a close friend may be in danger.

fireplace

Fireplaces signify warmth, comfort, financial stability, home life stability, and a longing to increase social status. Examine the aspects of the dream to determine which meaning fits for you. Sitting in front of a fireplace with a friend or loved one means that you'd like to be closer, emotionally, to this person.

fireworks

A dream of fireworks suggests a celebration, a joyous explosion, or a release of repressed feelings.

fish

Fish swimming symbolize exploration of the unconscious or something that lies below the surface. In the Freudian interpretation, fish are phallic symbols and dreaming of fish is related to sexual desires. The Jungian interpretation is that fish symbolize a spiritual quest. Fish in dreams also represent good intuition, so trust your gut.

fishing

To dream of fishing signifies your need to examine your emotions and to delve deeper into your unconscious. Because fish also refer to your intuition, you might be fishing for a solution to a problem you already know how to solve.

fit

Dreaming of being physically fit is a good indication that you're feeling psychologically good about yourself. This can also be a wish-fulfillment dream—you'd literally like to look better and be more fit.

flag

Your unconscious is aware of social issues around you. Are there political issues that are festering for you? Or it may be that you long for less confusion and more cohesiveness in a partnership.

flames

To see flames in a dream represents the need for purity and purification of thoughts and deeds. Take note of what is on fire, and then look up that symbol in this glossary. Flames can also refer to hidden passion or a crush you prefer not to admit to.

flint

Striking flint can mean fickleness or a little devil in you waiting to get out. It can also refer to love and marriage or a spark between you and another.

flirting

If you're flirting in your dream, chances are that you don't approve of your own behavior recently. Who are you flirting with? If it has a positive outcome, it could be a wish-fulfillment dream rather than a prophetic one.

floating

This can be an astral dream—your spirit actually could be floating. This is a very positive sign of good things to come; it means happier, more hopeful and joyous times.

flogging

To be flogged in a dream signifies that you feel you should be punished for something you've done or for treating someone badly. To see someone flogged in a dream indicates impending sadness and the need to settle some emotional issues in your life.

flood

A dream of a flood might suggest that you are being overwhelmed by a rising awareness of the unconscious aspects of your being. A dream of flooding can also serve as a warning that personal matters are spilling over into other areas of your life. Also, a flood in a dream can refer to sexual desires or a need for release.

flower

Flowers in a dream can symbolize love and beauty. Flowers can also be a symbol of the inner self. New blossoms suggest the opening of the inner self. Withered and dead flowers can mean disappointment and dismal situations. A wreath of fresh flowers means that a good opportunity will soon come your way and you need to take advantage of it.

flurry

To dream of snow flurries indicates joy and excitement soon to come. It also warns you to be expressive and communicative about your feelings in an upcoming discussion with a loved one.

fly (insect)

You may be having some pesky setbacks that are causing disappointment now. Try to be patient. It may take a little longer but things should go as planned. If you dream of being bitten by a fly, watch out for friends who aren't as they seem.

flying

A flying dream may suggest the dreamer is soaring, or flying high, as a result of a successful venture. Flying can also symbolize breaking free of restrictions or inhibitions. Flying itself can be a joyous experience in a dream, no matter what the symbolic meaning.

fog

Dreaming of foggy conditions indicates a lack of clarity in some aspect of your life. Fog can also symbolize something hidden or something you're not seeing. Keep in mind that fog is usually short-lived. When it lifts, you will gain a new sense of clarity.

foliage

A dream of foliage signifies concerns in love and in financial security. If the foliage is lush and green, it indicates good times ahead. If it is wilting, it may signify problems soon to come.

food

Because food is essential for survival, a dream of food has to do with nourishment of the mind—of ideas, thoughts, and relationships. It also has to do with acknowledging new ways of looking at things and their incorporation (digestion) into our lives.

fool

To dream of a fool indicates that there is something risky that you need to take a chance with to be successful. It means a leap of faith is necessary for the dreamer.

footprints

Footprints may signify envy. You long to emulate someone who is close to you. Perhaps you'd like to be as successful or as popular. It may also be a sign that you should watch where you're going in life.

forehead

A forehead in a dream signifies worry over a particular issue. Though things may be tough right now, this dream means that you'll soon find a resolution to the problem at hand.

forest

A forest suggests an exploration of the unconscious. It can also symbolize a need or desire to retreat from everyday life—to restore and revitalize your energies. To dream of a lush forest in complete foliage may mean prosperity and pleasure, although finding yourself in a dense forest may signify unpleasantness at home.

forest fire

A forest fire symbolizes the successful completion of your plans, with wealth and prosperity to follow. It can also symbolize a passion and healthy desire for a loved one. Be sure to note who else is in the dream.

forgery

There may be deceptive people around you—watch out! This symbol could also indicate contracts are not as they seem. Read the fine print. Forgery can also refer to unexpected money, such as an inheritance or lucky lottery number.

forked line/fork in the road

You'll have to make a decision soon. This is an indication that you should choose the simplest route for now.

fortune-teller

You seek good advice from someone you trust. You're not dealing with an important issue that could absolutely change your life. Weigh all the risks and make a list for yourself.

fortune-telling

An aspect of your life right now feels out of whack. You crave balance and security. Seek out the help of people you trust.

fountain

A dream of a fountain can suggest longevity and virility. Water is related to the emotions and unconscious, and a fountain can indicate an emotional surge. Also, a dream of a fountain can indicate an examination of your emotions. What is the condition of the fountain? A clear fountain suggests vast possessions and many pleasures. A dry and broken fountain symbolizes the end of pleasure. A sparkling fountain in the moonlight can indicate an ill-advised pleasure.

fox

If you're currently in an argument with someone, a fox dream may be a warning not to speak. Silence will help you get control over the situation. Also, be careful of those around you. Someone may not be as virtuous as she seems.

fragrance

To smell a fragrance in your dream is a good sign of happiness to come and good luck in love. It can also be a symbol of travel and of older women in your life coming to visit soon.

fraud

Dreaming of fraud can be a warning about yourself or others. Who is committing fraud in the dream? If you're the one committing fraud, it's possible you've shown a side of yourself to someone and it has made you feel vulnerable.

freedom

A dream about freedom can mean two completely opposite things. It could be that you feel repressed and are longing for more freedom to do the things you'd like to do. It could also mean that you are currently feeling good about the freedom you're experiencing in life.

freelance

To dream about freelance projects can be literal—you're involved or would like to be involved in these types of undertakings. It could also refer to the autonomy you'd like to express more often. Creative ideas should come to you more freely now.

friends

If you dream of a gathering of your friends and they are all happy, you will have a pleasant event to attend soon. If you dream of a gathering of your friends and they are sad and gloomy, call them—something is probably amiss.

frog

Frogs, like the prince who was turned into one, are transformative creatures. They start as tadpoles, grow legs and arms, and develop lungs. To dream of a frog may imply a major change or transformation in your life. Since frogs live part of their lives in water, a frog may also symbolize a leap into the unconscious.

frost

Frost, like ice, may represent an emotional state of the dreamer or a person in the dream. To see a friend or lover in frost could mean chilly feelings regarding the relationship.

frostbite

If you dream of frostbite, it could indicate that there's a part of you that feels stuck in a current situation or love relationship. It could also mean that you're not expressing yourself as well as you could or should.

fruit

Fruit, in your dreams, refers to health, long life, and knowledge. Are you yearning to take a class? It may be a good time to do so. Sometimes, fruit in dreams can be your unconscious giving you a literal warning to eat more healthfully.

fugitive

If you're on the run in your dream, chances are you're running from yourself. What aspect of your life are you unhappy with? Being a fugitive also refers to running away from your problems in love, at home, or at work.

funeral

Rather than death, this usually refers to saying goodbye to a way of thinking or a way of life. It indicates change and transformation. In rare cases, it can refer to worry over growing older.

fungus

Fungus in your dream can refer to a physical problem you currently have. It can also refer to a situation in your life that's growing out of control.

funnel

Funneling liquid from one container to another refers to sexual desire and the need to be intimate with someone close to you. Some people also have this dream when their bladders are full in real life.

fur

Dreaming of fur indicates warmth, nostalgia, and friends from long ago. Have you recently seen a friend from your past? Fur in dreams also tells you to prepare yourself for possible rough times ahead.

fur coat

Dreaming of a fur coat doesn't necessarily mean that you want one. Even if you're against the manufacture or ownership of a fur coat, its presence in your dream signifies luxury and easy living.

furnace

A furnace usually relates to security in love. Lighting up a furnace refers to new love and the possibility of marriage. An unlit furnace can hint at sadness in love and finding a good marriage partner.

furniture

The meaning of furniture in a dream depends on how you feel about that particular piece. If it's furniture from your childhood, are you reliving problems from the past? If it's a comfortable piece of furniture, do you long for more comfort or warmth from your home life?

fury

To be in a fury in your dream indicates a certain anger you feel toward yourself with regard to recent decisions you've made. If you feel fury toward another person in your dream, you may harbor resentment toward him you need to deal with soon.

fuse

If a fuse blows in your dream, this refers to the repressed anger you have with someone. It can also signify unexpected news to come; this news may shock you. Be prepared.

G

gambling

Dreaming of gambling suggests taking a chance. If you are winning, it may bode well for a risky business deal. If you're watching others win, the game may symbolize a fear of taking a chance. Whether you should be more daring or play it safe depends on other factors in the dream.

games

In order to translate a dream in which you're playing a game, take note of what kind of game it is and whether you win or lose. If it's a board game, you may feel a bit insignificant in your current dealings. If you win, it's a good omen of what is to come. If you lose, you may feel as if others are playing with you.

gang

If you encounter a gang in your dream, it means that you're feeling nervous about a situation you're currently in, and the need to escape is great. Confront the problem, and you'll cease having this unnerving dream.

garbage

To dream of garbage suggests a need to get rid of old, worn-out ideas or excess baggage in your life. Ask yourself if you are clinging to something or some condition that you no longer need.

garden

A garden sometimes indicates a need to bring more beauty into your life. It may be a metaphor for personal or spiritual growth, or a desire to cultivate a new talent or move into a higher realm of awareness. A garden with lots of weeds may symbolize a need to "weed out" old ideas or a desire to cultivate your spiritual self.

gardener

A gardener represents a person who takes care of things that should sprout and grow successfully; these could be relationships, financial endeavors, or personal happiness. Notice who the gardener is. Do you know this person? Chances are he or she has a positive influence on your life.

garnish

A garnish on top of a dish, in a dream, signifies the ultimate details in terms of your soul. Since food relates to spiritual nourishment, the garnish is the final touch. This is a sign that you're getting your life together—and it's going well.

gate

A gate may represent a portal from one state of being to another. Is there a gatekeeper? Do you meet the gatekeeper's criteria for passage to the next level?

gather

What is it you're gathering in your dreams? Flowers? Books? Whatever you're gathering is what you're hoping to reap from your efforts. Take note of the object, and look up the symbolic meaning in this glossary.

gathering

To dream that you're in a gathering can mean many things, depending on what the gathering is. Is it a happy occasion? If so, you'll soon receive good news and lots of opportunities to socialize. If not, you may have some sorrow that's weighing you down. Get out more and meet up with good friends.

ghost

An apparition or ghost appearing in a dream may suggest that something in your life is elusive or out of reach. If a person who has died appears in a dream, consider your past relationship with that person and what he symbolized in your life. A ghost of a living relative or friend in a dream may mean that someone you know could be dangerous to you. Or, if that ghost appears haggard, it may symbolize the breaking off of a friendship. Ghosts are not yet spirits—they don't realize that they're dead.

giant

Dreaming of a giant can mean two things. If you're scared of the giant, it signifies that you're aware of problems looming over you that you're unwilling to face. If the giant is friendly, it means that your popularity is increasing and you're aware of the good luck headed your way.

gift

If you're given a gift in your dreams, it's a good sign. You probably feel that you're being rewarded for a job well done. If your gift is broken or damaged, however, you may feel that you're not getting enough attention from loved ones.

girl

To dream of a little girl can signify a longing for innocence or more purity in your life. It could also refer to femininity and the need to be taken care of. If you see yourself as a little girl, it means that you're feeling very vulnerable lately and you need to set others straight.

glass

Glass is suggestive of separation and passive observation. Looking through glass in a dream may symbolize bitter disappointment clouding your brightest hopes. Receiving cut glass in a dream may suggest a reward for your efforts.

glasses

To dream of glasses is a warning that you're not seeing things as clearly as you should. Take note of what's happening around you and who is in the dream. Perhaps this person is trying to tell you something? (See **eyeglasses**.)

glassware

Glassware represents your home life. If the glass breaks, it could indicate a recent or upcoming dispute at home. If the glass is beautiful or if you're drinking from it, it indicates stability and good luck with family matters.

glider

Flying in a glider signifies hopefulness and optimism toward the future. Possibly, you feel like you've been recently liberated from an oppressive situation. This could also refer to the positive progress of a new love in your life.

globe

A globe, in a dream, signifies wisdom, world consciousness, and politics. It can also refer to upcoming travel. Also, a globe is a circle, which signifies wholeness. You're searching for completion in a project or venture.

gloom

If the scene around you in your dream is gloomy, this is how you feel about your current state of affairs. What's depressing you? Look to the other figures in the dream and examine whether or not they're actually positive influences in your life.

gloves

If you dream of wearing gloves, regardless of the weather, it means that caution should be exercised in your upcoming financial dealings. To dream of old, ragged gloves means that you may suffer a loss or betrayal soon. To dream of finding a pair of gloves can mean that a new love affair (even with your current partner) may start soon.

glue

Glue, in a dream, may signify your wish to bind something or someone to you. Do you want to be closer to someone? If you dream that the glue is an annoyance, it may be that you feel stuck in a current situation or that someone is not sticking to a promise he made you.

goat

A goat signifies nature and femininity—caregiving. If the goat is eating in the dream, it means that you long to find more solid ground in your relationships. The goat also refers to the month of January and the symbol Capricorn.

God

If you hear the voice of God, honorable people will soon praise you for your unselfishness and generosity. To see God in your dreams indicates exceptional happiness soon to come. If God is angry with you, it means you are unhappy with a choice you've recently made.

gold

Dreaming of gold jewelry, coins, or a gold object indicates that success is forthcoming. To dream of a room filled with gold suggests that things may not be as they seem. Be careful.

gold dust

Seeing or feeling gold dust usually indicates regret over the loss of a treasured liaison or partnership. If the dust sifts through your fingers, you are meditating about the loss in your dream. If you see the gold dust at a distance, you feel that this loss is for the best.

goose

A goose is often associated with a golden egg; dreaming of one is a symbol of abundance. On the other hand, a goose in the oven or on fire suggests that your goose is cooked—you're in trouble. Alternately, a big goose egg can mean "zero" reward for your efforts.

gossip

If people are gossiping about you in your dream, you're concerned with your recent behavior and are worried what people may think of you. If you're the one gossiping, you may feel that the power you have over someone isn't quite as strong as it seems.

grains

Grains indicate birth and rebirth. They also refer to the start of a new project or undertaking.

Dreaming of grains can also signify abundance and fruition in financial ventures.

grandmother

Notice the aspects of this dream. Are you dreaming of a grandmother who has passed on? If the dream is vivid and in color, chances are that you're having an astral visit with her. Perhaps she wants to let you know she's fine or she has advice for you. If you dream of someone else's grandmother, you probably long to be close to a maternal figure.

grandparents

A dream about grandparents may signify that you're looking for recognition and approval of your current efforts. If your own grandparents have passed away, check to see if this is an astral dream. Normally, you will receive visits from the Other Side from one grandparent at a time.

grapes

Grapes in a dream indicate fun, joyous times ahead. Don't be so pragmatic—go with the flow. Be spontaneous and things will turn out for the best. Grapes also indicate longing for love and flirting. It can also be a warning to be careful what you spend money on in the upcoming months.

grass

To dream of green grass signifies good things will happen in your life. If you are in business,

you may soon be wealthy. If you are an artist, you may soon become well known. If you are about to marry, you will have a safe, happy life with your partner. If the grass is wilted, it means you need to reassess your financial situation.

grave

Like many dream symbols, a grave is one that grabs your attention, especially if it's your grave. A grave may portend a death, just not necessarily a physical one. It may mean that you're leaving the old behind, moving on to something new. As a metaphor, a grave suggests that you may be dealing with a grave (serious) matter.

grease

This is a warning to watch where you're going in terms of love. The road ahead could be slick and slippery. Make sure you can trust your significant other. Even if his intentions are good, is he doing what's best for you?

green

When green is a dominant color in a dream, it can be interpreted symbolically. Green is a color of healing, growth, money, and new beginnings. It suggests positive movement.

grief

Grief, in a dream, can be a good thing because it helps you deal with a problem you're facing in waking life. Normally, the dreamer is actually suffering from something harsh in both the dream and in real life. This can also be a warning dream to get a checkup.

grocery store

Dreaming of a grocery store refers to the many upcoming choices you need to make. Take note of what you purchase in the store. Is it a practical food, a staple such as rice or corn? Or is it a more fun, sweet food such as cookies or cake? This is a warning against making the wrong decision.

grotesque

Dreaming of something grotesque refers to the fear you have within yourself. What is grotesque in the dream? Does it signify something for you? Notice the object that is grotesque, and then look up the symbolism for it in this glossary.

group

Dreaming of a group can have two meanings. How do you feel toward this group? Are you included? It may be that you're feeling left out in your personal relationships if you long to be part of this group. If the group annoys you, it means you resent having to join or follow the pack.

growing

Growing, in a dream, refers to your emotional state. Are you the one growing? Are you watching something grow? If you're growing straight and tall, it's a sign of positive things to come. If your growing is distorted in some way, it means you'll have some struggles, emotionally, but that you'll come out of it a better, stronger you.

guard

Seeing a guard in your dream may signify that something you deem valuable is being kept away from you. What is it that isn't within your grasp? Does it have to do with emotions or with a valuable object? Most likely, the thing you crave most is affection or love from a person close to you.

guest

Having a guest in your house can signify two things. Is this person someone you know? If he is, it's someone you'd like to bring closer, within your circle. If the guest is a stranger, you'd like to feel freer with your choice of friends and within your social circle.

gun

A gun in your possession can symbolize protection, but it is also a phallic symbol and a sign of aggression. If you shoot yourself, the act is what's important, not the gun (see **suicide**).

gushing

Gushing water or fluid often refers to release—mostly sexual. For a woman to dream of gushing water indicates repressed sexual desire. Gushing water from a fountain can also mean upcoming joy and happiness.

gymnastics

Performing gymnastics in a dream signifies that you're feeling happy and liberated or that you'd like to feel this way. If you're watching the gymnastics, it indicates a longing for simpler, happier times.

gypsy

Gypsy dreams can translate differently, depending on how you feel about the gypsy. A gypsy can signify mistrust, misunderstanding, and misplaced values. But she can also signify adventure, freedom, and spontaneity. Analyze how you feel toward the gypsy, and you'll get to the root of these issues at hand.

H

hail

To dream of being in a hailstorm, or to hear hail knocking against the house represents being besieged by a troubling matter, thoughts, or emotions. However, if you dream of watching hail fall through sunshine and rain, it may suggest that fortune and pleasure will shine on you after a brief period of trouble or misery.

hair

To dream that you have a beautiful head of hair and are combing it indicates thoughts of appearance over substance. To see your hair turn unexpectedly white suggests sudden misfortune and grief over a situation. A dream that you have a full head of white hair suggests a pleasing and fortunate passage through life. For a man to dream that his hair is thinning suggests bad luck due to generosity, or illness through worry. To see yourself covered in hair represents an indulgence in vice, and a dream of tangled and unkempt hair suggests trouble or concern over a matter at hand. For a woman to compare a white hair with a black one taken from her head symbolizes a hesitation between two paths.

hallway

A hallway can signify many things, but it usually refers to the many choices (of doorways) along your path. If a hallway is empty, without doorways, it means that you feel your path was chosen for you. If the doorways are open along the way, it means that you haven't yet found your way—but you will.

halo

Dreaming of a halo refers to a longing to return to innocence and spiritual purity. What is it in your life that you feel needs refining. Chances are, you're dreaming of a person or place from the past that you once deemed perfect.

halter-top

Strangely enough, a dream of putting on or wearing a halter-top refers to a need to celebrate youth. Or perhaps you're too caught up in the need to be beautiful, and your unconscious is aware of this. How far will you go to stay young?

hammer

A hammer may suggest strength or power. However, because it can be used for either constructive or destructive purposes, the way the hammer is used is the key to its meaning in the dream.

hand

A dream of a hand (or hands) is open to numerous interpretations, depending on what the hand is doing and the surrounding circumstances. Shaking hands is an act of friendship or an agreement. Hands folded in prayer may suggest you are seeking help or pursuing religious or spiritual urges. A grasping hand may suggest a fear of death. Something important could be "at hand." Beautiful hands signify feelings of great honor and rapid advancement. Ugly and malformed hands point to disappointment and poverty. A detached hand represents solitude—people may fail to understand your views and feeling in a matter. Burning your hands suggests that you have overreached your abilities and will suffer some loss because of it. A dream of washing your hands indicates participation in some joyous affair.

handbag

If you dream of a handbag, it indicates that you're trying to work out day-to-day problems. You're concerned with the details—appointments, bills you have to pay, and so on. A lost handbag alludes to confusion over sexual issues.

handkerchiefs

Dreaming of a handkerchief or handkerchiefs could mean that you'll soon embark on a flirtatious affair. If you dream of losing a handkerchief, a problem in love may possibly occur. A torn handkerchief signifies a lovers' quarrel, and reconciliation may be impossible. A dream of silk handkerchiefs means that you have a pleasing and magnetic personality that will help you succeed in life.

handyman

For a woman to dream of a handyman signifies that she feels some aspect of her love life is not being fulfilled. Perhaps she longs for a deeper emotional connection with a significant other or she hopes for a new love to come along.

hang

If you see someone being hanged in your dream, it means that you are afraid of being judged without the chance to explain yourself. If you dream that you're being hanged for something you've done, it means that you have enormous guilt. This is a warning to stop being overcritical of yourself.

hangover

To dream of a hangover signifies that you've been overdoing some unhealthy aspect of your life. It could be smoking too much or even thinking too much. Your unconscious recognizes this as a vice you would do better without.

happy

To dream of being happy in your dream signifies that you're optimistic about what is to come. It also means that you're aware of the positive energy surrounding you now. Go with it. Luck is on your side.

harbor

To dream of a harbor suggests that the unconscious is digging for answers to a current situation. You long for peace and tranquility in your life. Also, a harbor can sometimes predict good financial prospects ahead and the chance to travel soon.

harem

To dream of being in a harem can mean two things: either you long to be more open sexually or you may suspect your partner is being unfaithful. To see a harem may signify that you're now open to try more creative things in life.

harvest

A harvest represents completion and abundance, and it may indicate that your reward is due. As with all symbols, personal connotations are important. For instance, if you grew up on a farm, a harvest dream could mean a longing to return to the past or to simpler times.

hat

A hat can suggest concealment, as in "keep it under your hat." Dreaming that you have a feather in your hat indicates achievement. A hat in your dream also indicates that a new friend you're soon to meet will be important in your life. A tall hat signifies responsibility and authority.

havoc

If you dream there is havoc or bedlam around you, you're feeling overwhelmed in your finances and career. If you're causing the havoc in your dream, it means that you are aware that others deem your behavior less than satisfactory.

Hawaii

A dream of Hawaii or things associated with Hawaii is most likely a wish-fulfillment dream. Perhaps things have become too staid and predictable in life. You long for some fun and excitement. Maybe it's time to take a trip?

hawk

A hawk is a creature with keen sight. A soaring hawk in a dream might suggest the need for insight. It also might mean that the dreamer should keep a hawk's eye on someone or a situation.

head

Dreaming of a human head could indicate that you are ahead, or successful, on a matter of importance. A head also symbolizes a source of wisdom.

hearse

If you dream of seeing a hearse, it may indicate that you sense some financial problems ahead. If you dream of riding in a hearse, it signifies that you're saying goodbye to a certain part of yourself. Be ready for new things to come.

heart

To see a heart might relate to romantic inclinations. Is there a heartthrob in your life? Alternately, the image might suggest you get to the heart of the matter. On the negative side, if your heart is bleeding, it may mean that excessive sympathy is becoming a burden for you or the recipient, or both.

heaven

If you dream of heaven, it could be that you're aspiring to new heights in your love life or career. Examine who else is in the dream and what they're doing there.

heel

The heel of your foot or shoe may symbolize vulnerability, like in the Achilles' heel story. It might also stand for an oppressive situation, as in "under someone's heel." Are you dealing with someone who is not trustworthy? He or she could be the heel in question.

heights

To dream of being afraid of heights signifies that you're not doing enough in your career. You may have a fear of success, and your own ambition is being thwarted for it.

helmet

Wearing a helmet in a dream denotes protection. The helmet could also symbolize a need to guard your time, thoughts, or ideas.

hemorrhage

To dream of hemorrhaging denotes a dissatisfactory social or love life. Someone is emotionally draining you to the point that you feel your energy is being depleted.

hermaphrodite

To dream of a hermaphrodite could mean two things. Either you're trying to get in touch with a more emotional side of yourself, or you've been presented with two choices and you have an important decision to make.

hermit

Dreaming of a hermit is a sign that you need to be patient and wait for things to right themselves. Now is not the time to take action. It also means that you enjoy the time that you spend alone.

hero

To dream of a hero signifies that you'd like more recognition in your career. If you dream that you are the hero, it means that you're feeling good about yourself and can sense that things are now going your way.

hiccup

Most likely, some plans that you had or will have in the near future have been thwarted and you're searching to find out why. Hiccupping, in a dream, also refers to making too much out of trivial matters.

hiding

If you're hiding in a dream, it signifies that you're embarrassed or may feel guilty about some of your recent behavior. It could also point to a new sense of getting away from the daily rigors of life.

high tide

To dream of a high tide symbolizes that a change, usually favorable, is in order—the tides are turning.

hill

If you dream of going up a hill, it's your unconscious telling you that you need to strive for more in life and love. If you dream of going down a hill, it may be that you're afraid of financial setbacks soon to come.

hitchhiking

To dream of hitchhiking is a warning that you've been too dependent on others recently and you need to take more responsibility for your actions. It may also be a warning that you've put yourself in danger and should be more careful in the near future.

hitting

If you dream of being hit in a dream, it means you feel others around you are taking advantage of you and are judging you harshly. If you dream of hitting someone or something, it means you may have resentment or anger bottled up that you need to express.

hogs

A fat hog in a dream may suggest abundance, while a lean, hungry hog may foretell a troubling situation. If the hogs are wallowing in mud, the indication might be that you've lowered your standards regarding a matter, or that you are groveling. A squealing hog suggests that something distasteful has occurred or will soon occur.

hole

Seeing a hole in a dream can refer to fear of the unknown. It may also refer to sexual desire and the need for sex in order to feel complete. A hole in your clothing portends financial success soon to come.

holiday

Dreaming of a holiday is usually a wish-fulfillment dream. Perhaps things have been a bit boring lately or a little too hectic. This is the way your unconscious has of saying you need to take a break.

home

To dream of a home usually points to how the dreamer feels about herself at the time of the dream. It can also refer to family life. Was the home cozy or a mess? Did you feel good in it? Who was there?

homesickness

Being homesick in a dream is usually quite literal—you long for the way things were in days past. It can also portend a call or visit from someone you once knew and haven't heard from in a while.

homosexuality

Dreaming of being homosexual rarely has to do with your sexuality, unless this is a particular concern for you. More likely, it has to do with an emotional part of you that you've recently discovered.

honeymoon

To dream of a honeymoon can be literal, as in wish fulfillment. But dreaming of a honeymoon can also refer to a partnership in business. It's a good sign of positive things to come. If the honeymoon goes badly, it could be that you're nervous about the intentions of a new person in your life.

horse

A horse symbolizes strength, power, endurance, majesty, and virility. A man dreaming of a horse might desire virility and sexual prowess; a woman might be expressing a desire for sexual intercourse. Riding a horse suggests one is in a powerful position. White horses represent purity, while black horses represent a postponement of pleasure.

hospital

Finding oneself in a hospital suggests a need for healing or a concern about one's health. Seeing someone else in a hospital might indicate that the person is in a weakened condition. If you work in a hospital, the meaning of the dream may relate to work matters. In the latter case, other circumstances in the dream should be examined.

house

Houses are common forums for dreams and may be of little consequence unless the house itself is the focus of the dream. If so, examine the type of house and its size. Discovering new rooms in a house or following secret passages in an old house can relate to an exploration of the unconscious. A small house might suggest a feeling of confinement. If a house is under construction, it could symbolize growth. If it's dilapidated, it suggests improvements are needed in some part of the dreamer's life.

hugging

To dream that you're hugging a stranger suggests that you crave affection. If you know the person you are hugging, the interpretation will depend on your relationship to that person.

humidity

Dreaming of humidity represents the presence of an oppressive situation, either in work or at home.

hurricane

Destructive and unpredictable, hurricanes in dreams can have different meanings depending on the context. A coming hurricane symbolizes torment and suspense. Possibly, you're trying to avert failure. Looking at a hurricane's debris suggests that others will save you from calamity. A dream in which you are in a house that is shattered by a hurricane or in which you are trying to save someone caught in the rubble may mean that your life will suffer many changes but that there is still no peace in domestic or business matters. To see people dead and wounded suggests that you are concerned over the troubles of others.

I

ice

Ice may symbolize an emotional state of the dreamer or a person in the dream. Are you being given an icy reception? If you are in a tenuous situation, you could be skating on thin ice. In a sexual context, you could be acting coldly toward your partner. To dream of ice floating in a clear stream signifies an interruption of happiness. Dreaming of eating ice portends sickness.

iceberg

To dream of hitting an iceberg in your dream means that things have been rocky financially, or you sense that they soon will be. It's a good indication that, though there are obstacles to overcome, you'll be all right if you look for the warning signs.

ice cream

A dream of ice cream, especially melting ice cream, may suggest that obstacles are being removed and that there is reason to celebrate. If ice cream is your favorite dessert, then the dream suggests you're being rewarded or have reason to treat yourself. It can also stand for a desire for sexual fulfillment.

icicles

Icicles represent danger or your concern over a matter that is hanging over you in some way. To dream of icicles falling off trees or the eaves of a house may suggest that some misfortune will soon disappear. To dream of icicles on evergreens symbolizes that a bright future may be overshadowed by doubt.

idiot

To dream of seeing an idiot in your dream signifies that your unconscious is aware that you're about to make a very foolish decision. If you dream of being an idiot, it means that your self-confidence is low right now and you need to do something to bolster it.

illiteracy

Dreaming that you can't read or write in a dream has two meanings. Either you're having trouble expressing yourself in waking life, or there's a breakdown in communication with someone you're close to.

illness

If you dream of being ill, ask yourself if you're in need of being cared for or pampered. This dream might also be a message to watch your health.

immortality

To dream of being immortal signifies your need to rise up to your own and others' expectations. Also, this dream can point to anxiety or an acute fear of getting older.

impersonation

To dream of impersonating someone, or that someone is impersonating you, refers to envy you may be feeling toward someone you're close to. Also, it signifies that your sense of self is being threatened in life.

impotence

A dream of impotence means that you are feeling insignificant and out of control in terms of finances. Rarely does this dream actually refer to sexual problems.

incest

A dream of a sexual encounter with someone within your family is not necessarily a warning about incest. Examine your relationship with the person in question. If you've recently been alienated from this family member, the dream may be an expression of your love or need for love in a shocking way that will catch your attention.

indifference

This dream is indicative of how you think others view you. If someone is indifferent toward you in a dream, it could mean that you worry this is how he really feels. More likely, though, this is how he really feels about you, and your unconscious is spelling it out.

infants

Seeing infants in a dream suggests that pleasant surprises are near. Seeing an infant swimming represents a fortunate escape from some bad endeavor.

infidelity

Many times, dreaming that your partner is being unfaithful is simply a fear you have of being abandoned or cheated on in waking life. However, sometimes this is a warning sign that the deed is actually being done.

inheritance

Dreaming that you come into an inheritance is a good sign of opportunities soon to come. In fact, you'll be successful in your pursuits if you shoot for the stars. Dreaming of disinheritance denotes some rough times ahead. If you dream of a will or making your own will, momentous occasions should soon occur.

initiation

Initiation suggests that a new path is opening for you. It could be a career change or advancement. Often, initiatory dreams relate to a spiritual quest.

injured

If you dream of being injured, it refers to your current emotional state. Perhaps someone has used harsh words with you lately or has let you down in some way that has affected you deeply.

inquiry

If someone keeps asking something of you, in a dream, chances are that you're aware you need to get this one thing done. If you answer her, it means you've decided to go ahead and do it. If you don't, it means you're not willing to deal with it yet, but you know you need to.

insects

What's annoying or "bugging" you? If you dream of ants, you may be feeling "antsy" about a matter (see **ant**).

insults

To be insulted in your dream is actually you being hard on yourself. What are the insults? Do you feel this way toward yourself? Many times, if you're insulting someone in your dream, this is how you feel toward the person you're insulting.

intercourse

Many times, this dream is wish fulfillment and release. If you'd like to be more adventurous in life, you can also have this dream. The partner in the dream is less important than how you feel about the actual lovemaking.

interview

Being interviewed in a dream is similar to taking an examination. It suggests that you feel you're being judged. If you're surprised by the interview, it may indicate that you are feeling unprepared in a business or family matter.

intestines

Dreaming of intestines actually relates to your courage. This body part symbolizes strength of will and the gumption to move on ahead in the face of adversity. Notice in the dream how you feel about the intestines. Are they strong and healthy, or weak?

invalid

A dream of an invalid may indicate that you (or someone else) feel weak or incapable of living independently. It's an indication that you need to take charge of your life.

invisibility

To dream that you're invisible is metaphoric. You may feel that you're being ignored by others and would like to be recognized more for who you are than who others think you are.

invitation

If you receive an invitation in your dream, it could be that you'd like to get out more and be more social. If you send out an invitation in your dream, you're looking for guidance from someone close to you.

ironing

Ironing in a dream signifies getting all of the little things done in your life—paying bills, going to the doctor, and so on. Some also say that ironing refers to turning things around and making them go more smoothly.

island

An island can be viewed as an exotic place or as a separate, isolated land. Dreaming of an island might mean that a vacation is due, especially if going to the islands refers to your vacation destination. Alternately, finding yourself on a desert island may suggest you are cut off from others or from your inner self.

itching

If you have an itch in waking life, it could translate into your dream. As a metaphor, itching in a dream refers to little nagging problems you need to deal with as soon as possible.

ivy

Dreaming of ivy growing on trees or a house indicates you will have excellent health and success. Many joys in your life could follow this dream. For a young woman to dream of ivy clinging to a wall in moonlight portends she will have a secret affair with a young man. Beware of dreaming of withered ivy. It indicates broken engagements and sadness.

J

jail

A jail may indicate that you're feeling restricted or confined and fear being punished. Or you may believe that you *should* be punished. Dreaming of being a jailer suggests the desire to control others or to gain more control of your own life. Some people claim that jail dreams refer to a past life. Who was your jailer? Do you know him in this life?

January

To dream of this month may mean that you will be associated with unloved companions or children.

jaws

Do you feel like you're under attack? Jaws can be the entry point to an archetypal journey into the underworld. Such a dream might also translate as a disagreement with a close friend, family member, or partner.

jealousy

Who are you jealous of in the dream? Is it someone you know or is it a stranger? If it's someone you know, this may be a literal dream. If it's someone you don't know, it may be that you are feeling a strong sense of inadequacy. Go pamper yourself.

jewelry

In a material sense, jewelry can symbolize affluence, but look to other aspects of the dream for confirmation. Jewelry can also stand for inner wealth, psychic protection, or healing.

jewels (gems)

Dreaming of jewels signifies good luck to come. To dream of owning emeralds means you may inherit property. Dreaming of a sapphire denotes continuous good fortune. For a woman to dream of emeralds means she will soon make a smart choice (or has already) in selecting a husband. (See **pearls** and **diamonds.**)

job

Dreaming that you are at work may indicate that you're overworked, you're deeply focused on some aspect of your job, or you want to work harder and achieve more.

joke

If you're the butt of the joke, you may feel that you're being taken advantage of or that people are talking badly about you. If you're telling a joke in your dream, you're craving the spotlight and you need to go out more often.

judge

If you're the judge, the dream suggests that you have a choice to make. A judge can also represent justice or fairness. Alternately, a judge may stand for a part of you that criticizes your impulsive behavior. Or perhaps you're concerned that you're being judged. Who is judging you?

juggler

Dreaming of a juggler or having a dream in which you're juggling implies that you've been spreading yourself too thin lately. It also indicates some worry in terms of finances. Concentrate on one thing.

July

A dream that takes place in this month symbolizes a depressed outlook that will suddenly change to unimagined pleasure and good fortune.

jumping

Pick your metaphor. Are you "a jump ahead," "jumping to conclusions," "jumping the gun," or "jumping for joy"? A series of jumps may be the take-off point for a flying dream. A great leap can also symbolize success or achievement—"a leap of faith."

June

For a dream to take place in June symbolizes unusual gains in all undertakings.

jungle

A jungle may represent a hidden, dark part of the self that you've been avoiding. Your unconscious may be telling you of a need to explore this part of yourself. It may also represent a great, untapped fertility within you for spiritual growth.

junk

If you dream of junk or clutter, ask yourself if you're clinging to the past—to things or ideas that are no longer useful. If something you value appears as junk in a dream, it may indicate that you need to reassess your values.

jury

Being in front of a jury in your dream simply means that you feel that someone is judging you too harshly. To be on a jury indicates that you have some important decisions to make.

K

kangaroo

To see a kangaroo may suggest that you're hopping mad about something. It could also mean that you have the ability to "hop to" a particular matter that is pending.

karate

To dream of karate indicates one of two things: either you feel that someone is opposing you strongly and you need to defend yourself emotionally, or you have recently felt physically in danger and you want to be prepared.

ketchup

To dream of ketchup signifies a certain element of sweetness in your life that you've been ignoring. Possibly, you've been too hard on someone close to you. Learn to open up to this person, and your life will be better for it.

key

A key can stand for a part of yourself that you've locked away or something that you can now access if you have the key. Such a dream may also indicate you hold the key to your own concerns.

kicked out

To get kicked out of a place denotes sadness about not fitting in to a group or social situation. In waking life, this may also refer to you pushing people's buttons or limits too much and too often.

kicking

Kicking, in a dream, represents hostility and anger. Are you the one kicking or is someone kicking you? Kicking also indicates a desire to get revenge on someone who has wronged you.

killing

A dream of killing someone is not a warning that you might turn into a killer. Instead, the meaning is more likely a symbolic act of aggression. Whom you kill and how that person is involved in the dream may symbolize killing off an unwanted part of yourself. What bothers you about this person?

kindergarten

If you see a kindergarten, it means that you're sick of people's childish behavior around you. If you have children, dreaming of kindergarten often means that you want the best education for them. To dream of being in kindergarten means you long for simpler times.

king

A king is a ruler and a powerful authority figure. Dreaming of a king may mean you are seeking status or support. The king may represent your father or some other powerful figure in your life. If you're the king, the indication is that you have achieved a high level of authority or are a highly capable individual.

kiss

A kiss suggests a romantic involvement, but it can also be a metaphor, as in "kiss and make up" or the "kiss of death." For married people to kiss each other symbolizes harmony in the home life. Is it dark or light out during the kiss? The former suggests danger or an illicit situation while the latter represents honorable intentions. To dream of kissing someone on the neck symbolizes a passionate inclination toward that person.

kitchen

Going to a kitchen in a dream suggests some part of your life is in need of nourishment. Alternately, a kitchen might suggest that something is in the process of being "cooked up," like a new project. Notice what you're doing in the kitchen.

kite

Flying a kite in your dream usually refers to a work or social situation that is taking off—you're finally having success with it or you're just about to.

kitten

To discover kittens in a closet or a basement suggests the awakening of hidden aspects of the self. It can also relate to new ideas and projects.

kneeling

Kneeling down in a dream usually means you feel guilty. It also indicates that there may be someone you're hoping will accept your sincere apology.

knife

A knife is a symbol of aggression and a phallic symbol. Examine the other aspects of the dream. Are you being stabbed in the back? Do you hold the knife, or is someone threatening you with it? A rusty knife may symbolize dissatisfaction, while a sharp knife means worry and a broken knife, defeat.

knight

A knight signifies honor and high standing. Are you searching for a knight, or are you acting like a knight? Knights are also armored and stand for protection.

knitting

Knitting, in a dream, can refer to the small details in life or peace within the home and with family. A dream about knitting is a warning to check the emotional state of those close to you and make sure everyone is happy and doing well.

knob

A knob appearing in a dream may imply a need to get a handle on a matter. Knobs also signify a means of passing from one room to the next, or one way of life to another.

knot

Dreaming of knots suggests that you're all tied up about something—worries and anxieties are troubling you. You may feel as if you're tied in a knot. Alternately, if you or someone close to you is tying the knot, the dream might signify concern over an upcoming marriage.

L

laboratory

A laboratory is a place where experiments are conducted. The implication is that the dreamer is unsatisfied with a present situation and is experimenting with something new. The dreamer might also be testing a relationship with someone.

labyrinth

A dream of a labyrinth may indicate that you feel trapped in a situation or a relationship and are looking for a way out. It may also refer to the intricacies of a spiritual journey.

lace

Dreaming of lace indicates unrequited romantic feelings and a strong desire to feel more feminine. For a man to dream of lace means he has feelings for the woman wearing the lace.

ladder

Are you going up or climbing down the ladder? An ascent may symbolize a higher step into an inner realm or a promotion to a higher status in one's career. A ladder also means that you should be patient—destiny is guiding you.

ladle

Serving something in a ladle in your dream indicates that you may feel restless and are currently annoyed with your job as a caretaker or mother. It signifies a need for change and less responsibility. Take a break.

lagoon

Lagoons symbolize doubt and confusion over an emotional matter or a stagnant situation.

lake

In the Freudian interpretation, a lake is symbolic of the vagina. In the Jungian world, lakes and other bodies of water stand for the unconscious or emotions. In one interpretation, the dreamer who dives into a lake is returning to the womb. In the other, the dreamer explores the unconscious. But if neither interpretation fits, examine the other elements in the dream. Is the lake clear or muddy? The former suggests lucidity and strength of purpose, while the latter may represent muddled feelings and an unsure direction in a matter at hand.

lamb

A lamb may stand for gentleness or vulnerability, as in "a lamb to the slaughter." Or it may be a spiritual symbol, as in "sacrificial lamb" and "lamb of God." However, a dream of a lamb may simply symbolize a general love of animals. On another note, is this animal your totem?

lamp

A lamp, like a lantern, represents light or illumination and suggests the dreamer is searching for truth.

lance

A lance, by Freudian standards, is a phallic symbol and one of masculinity and aggression. Who is using the lance in your dream? Do you have intimate feelings about this person in waking life?

landing

Dreaming of landing in an airplane, for example, indicates the dreamer's wish to finish a current project successfully. If the landing goes well, it's a good indication that it will.

language

Hearing another language spoken indicates a desire to meet more people and, perhaps, to travel to foreign lands. It also signifies an open heart—you're ready for love.

lantern

Holding a lantern or seeing one in your dream means that you'd like to shed some light on a current issue. Perhaps you're aware that you're not getting the full truth.

lap

This is a symbol of security, the "lap" of luxury. To dream of sitting on someone's lap signifies safety from a troubling situation. To dream of a cat in a lap represents danger from a seductive enemy.

lasso

If a lasso is used on you, it means that someone or something is holding you back. If you're the one using the lasso, it portends good financial luck coming your way.

launch

To launch a boat or even a space rocket, in a dream, signifies the successful start of something new. Usually, it refers to new ideas or to financial projects. Examine how the launch goes. Does it go well?

lawsuit

Dreams of legal matters suggest the dreamer feels he or she is being judged.

leeches

Leeches are nightmarish creatures that suck blood. Is there someone in your life who is draining your energy?

legs

Legs are frequently seen in dreams, and interpretation depends on the context. Admiring well-shaped legs suggests a loss of judgment; misshapen legs represent unsuccessful endeavors and ill-tempered friends. A wooden leg represents deception of friends, while a wounded leg suggests a loss of power and standing. A young woman who admires her own legs indicates vanity, and if she has hairy legs, then it may indicate feelings of domination over her mate. Dreaming that your own legs are clean and shapely represents a happy future with faithful friends.

leopard

If you dream of a leopard attacking you, your future may suffer many difficulties. But if you kill the leopard, you will be victorious in life. If you dream of a caged leopard, it means that, although your enemies surround you, they will fail to injure you.

letter

A letter sometimes symbolizes a message from your unconscious to you. If you're unable to read the letter, look at other aspects of the dream for clues. An anonymous letter may signify concern from an unspecified source. Blue ink symbolizes steadfastness and affection. Red ink may suggest suspicion and jealousy, and a letter with a black border may represent distress and death of some kind. Receiving a letter written on black paper with white ink may suggest feelings of misery and disappointment over a matter. If this letter is passed between husband and wife or lovers, then concerns over the relationship may be present. A torn letter may suggest concerns that hopeless mistakes may ruin your reputation.

lightning

A dream of lightning indicates a flash of inspiration or sudden awareness about the truth of a matter. Lightning can also mean a purging or purification, or fear of authority or death.

lion

To dream of a lion signifies that a great force drives you. Subduing a lion indicates victory in a matter. If the lion overtakes you, the dream suggests that you may be vulnerable to an attack of some sort. A caged lion may mean that you will succeed as long as the opposition is held in check.

loss

To dream of losing something in a dream often means that your unconscious is working out the loss of something very real in your waking life. What is it you feel you're parting with? Is it a healthy thing or something you actually still need? The thing in question in the dream is often not literal—you use substitutions for the actual lost object, relationship, or opportunity.

lottery

To dream of a lottery signifies chance or throwing your fate to luck. If you dream of holding the winning number, then luck and good fortune in a matter at hand may follow. To see others winning in a lottery may suggest that many friends will be brought together in a pleasing manner. A young woman dreaming of a lottery may indicate a reckless attitude.

luggage

Luggage stands for your personal effects or what you carry with you on a journey. What happens to the luggage? Lost luggage might be a concern about your identity or about being prepared for the journey. Stolen luggage might suggest that you feel someone is interfering with your attempt to reach a goal.

M

magic

This could point to the magical aspects of creativity or, on the darker side, to deceit and trickery.

mailbox

A mailbox is a symbol of authority. Consequently, putting a letter in a mailbox may mean you are submitting to authority or feeling guilt over a particular matter.

man

To dream of a strange but handsome man represents an enjoyment of life. If the man is disfigured, then perplexities and sorrow may involve you in a matter at hand. For a woman to dream of a handsome man can suggest that distinction will be offered.

manuscript

A manuscript represents the collection of your hopes and desires. To interpret the dream, note the shape or appearance of the manuscript. Is it finished or unfinished? Are you at work on it? Did you lose it?

map

You're searching for a new path to follow or are being guided in a new direction.

March

A dream that occurs in this month may symbolize unsatisfactory results in a business matter.

mask

A mask hides your appearance and your feelings from others, but the dream may signify that you are hiding your emotions on a particular matter from yourself. If others are wearing masks, then perhaps you are confronted with a situation in which you think someone is not being truthful.

May

A dream of May indicates fortunate times and pleasures for the young. To dream of a freakish appearance of nature suggests sudden sorrow and misery.

medicine

Taking medicine in a dream can be a potent symbol of healing your wounds. It also suggests that you have to "take your medicine" and do what is necessary or required of you.

merry-go-round

A merry-go-round suggests that you are going around and around in life and never moving ahead.

meteor

A meteor or falling star may symbolize that your wish will come true, or it could suggest that you are engaged in wishful thinking. Look at the other elements in the dream and decide which possibility is true for you.

microphone

A microphone may symbolize the desire to draw attention to yourself or to gain power over others. Alternately, a microphone may suggest a concern that you are not forceful enough and need help in projecting yourself.

microscope

A microscope symbolizes the need or wish to find something that's out of sight or hidden from you.

milk

Milk symbolizes nurturing. It can also represent strength and virility. To dream of milk portends prosperity and happiness. To dream of giving milk away may mean that you are too generous for your own good. Dreaming of sour milk means you'll soon be upset over a friend's distress.

mist

Like fog, mist indicates a period of temporary uncertainty. Seeing others in a mist may mean that you will profit from their misfortune and uncertainty.

mistletoe

To dream of mistletoe signifies great happiness and honor coming your way. If you are young and dream of mistletoe, it indicates you will have many pleasant times in your future. To kiss someone under the mistletoe indicates that this person may, indeed, return your feelings.

money

Money represents energy, power, and influence. Dreaming of gaining money suggests abundance; losing sums of money symbolizes a draining of physical and emotional resources. To dream of stealing money suggests danger.

moon

Your emotions are running high right now. Try not to make too many impulsive decisions. Wait until you're calmer. The moon also indicates obsession or an unhealthy relationship you need to escape.

morning

Morning represents a fresh start or a sudden change of fortune for the positive. To dream of a cloudy morning indicates that heavy matters may overwhelm you.

mother

To see your mother symbolizes pleasing results from any endeavor. What is the context in which she appears? To converse with her suggests you may soon receive good news. To hear your mother calling to you means that you are in need of a correction in your life.

mother-in-law

A dream in which your mother-in-law appears suggests that a pleasant reconciliation of a serious disagreement is on the way.

mountain

A mountain represents a challenge. If you're climbing the mountain, you're working to achieve your goals. Descending a mountain suggests that things are easier now; your success may ensure your future.

mule

Mules are known for their contrary behavior, as in "stubborn as a mule." To dream of a mule suggests that the dreamer may be acting in a stubborn manner that others find annoying. Mules are also work animals. Consider whether you are rebelling against some aspect of your job or career.

murder

Murder symbolizes repressed anger, either at yourself or others. If you murder someone you know, consider your relationship with that person. If you're the murder victim, then the dream may symbolize a personal transformation.

music

Music in a dream symbolizes emotional matters. Consider the type of music you heard and how you related to it. Did it fill you with joy? Did it make you sad or angry?

N

nail

A nail in a dream can have a variety of meanings. To "nail it down" suggests putting something together or holding it together. If you hit the nail on the head, your intuition is right on the mark. If you step on a nail in your dream, it's a warning to be more aware of your surroundings. Also, if you break a fingernail, you need to take better care of yourself, physically.

naked/nudity

Being nude in a dream can symbolize a wish for exposure—to be seen or heard. It can also relate to a need to bare the truth. Alternately, a dream of nudity can be sexually related and suggests that the dreamer is no longer inhibited. To dream of swimming naked may represent an illicit affair that will end badly or that you have many admirers.

name

Hearing your name called in a dream can mean one of two things: either someone is trying to get your attention in waking life, or you are trying to alert yourself to something important happening around you.

napkins

Napkins in a dream signify being emotionally content with your friends and, perhaps, your love life. On the other hand, it can also be that you feel you still need to clean up your life.

navigating

To dream of navigating a spaceship or a boat indicates the dreamer's desire to come out on top in a current situation. This dream says that, although there will be obstacles, if the dreamer is careful, he can be victorious.

neck

A neck can be a sexual symbol related to the slang term "necking." A neck can also represent taking a chance, as in "sticking one's neck out." Alternately, if there is pain related to this part of the body, something might be a "pain in the neck."

necklace

To dream of receiving a necklace signifies good luck in love and marriage. To dream about losing a necklace means that you're having problems with love or that they're soon to come. This can also be a literal dream—you fear losing a particular necklace.

needle

A dream of a needle and thread might indicate that a matter is being sewn up or that a deal is being completed. A needle might also suggest that someone is needling you. To dream of threading a needle symbolizes that you may be burdened with caring for others, and to look for a needle alludes to useless worries. To break a needle in a dream signifies loneliness and poverty.

neighbor

If you dream of a neighbor, be prepared to spend hours ironing out problems due to unwarranted gossip. If you dream your neighbor is sad, watch out. You may soon quarrel with that neighbor.

nest

A nest is a symbol of home and might relate to the desire to return home. If you are moving, it might relate to your concerns about your new home. If there is an egg in the nest, the dream might relate to a concern about your savings or "nest egg." To dream of a nest full of eggs is a good omen; an empty bird's nest may denote some tough times ahead in business.

newspaper

If you dream of a newspaper, chances are that you feel out of the loop, and your unconscious knows that you need to be more on top of things. This is also a good and positive omen of brighter times to come.

night

A night setting for a dream might suggest something is hidden or obscured. There might be a need to illuminate something. Being surrounded by night in a dream suggests oppression and hardship.

nose

A nose can be a symbol of intrusive behavior, as in "sticking one's nose into someone else's business." Dreaming of a nose may suggest that someone is interfering in your life or that you are being nosy.

November

November dreams usually suggest a season of indifferent success in all affairs.

nurse

A dream of a nurse suggests that you are being healed or are in need of healing. It also implies a desire to be pampered or nursed. The dream could also relate to a relationship or a project that you are nursing along.

O

oak

An oak tree represents strength, stability, endurance, truth, and wisdom. A dream of an oak may suggest that a strong, proper foundation has been established in a matter.

oar

An oar can represent masculinity and strength; it dips into the water, the emotions. To row vigorously suggests a need for aggressiveness or that you are moving through an issue. If you have only one oar and are rowing in a circle, it might suggest frustration with a lack of forward movement in life.

oasis

An oasis suggests that you've arrived at a place of sustenance—that you are being nurtured. Or it might suggest that you're taking a break from your journey or have succeeded in reaching one destination on the journey. Alternately, the dream might imply that you need a vacation—a break.

objects

If there are many objects in your dream, you need to analyze each object and what the symbolism is in regard to it. Many times, the objects represent how you the dreamer are feeling about yourself.

obstacles

Obstacles in dreams always translate metaphorically. In other words, the dreamer has placed a burden or problem in front of him, and all he needs to do is step back and see the picture more clearly in order to solve the dilemma.

ocean

The ocean often represents the emotional setting of your life. The context of the dream is important here. Sailing through rough seas suggests you are capable of dealing with life's ups and downs. Large waves can also represent untapped powers or the unconscious. Catching a large fish in the ocean can suggest opportunity or that you are delving into the wealth of your unconscious. To be lost at sea may suggest that you are in need of direction. To be anchored in the ocean may indicate you have found a place in life.

October

To dream of October portends success. New friendships or business affairs will ripen into lasting relationships.

odor

If you smell an odor in your dream, it could be literal. The dreamer smells the odor in waking life and it filters into the dream. Otherwise, good odors signify good luck and bad odors signify the opposite.

officer

An officer, whether military, police, or otherwise, represents an authority figure. Dreaming of an officer, especially if you don't know the person, can suggest a fear or wariness of authority figures or a need for guidance from an authoritative person.

oil

A dream of oil represents great wealth or inner wealth, as in a dream of pumping crude oil to the surface. Using aromatic oils in a dream can represent sacred matters. A person associated with oil might be slick, or a smooth talker.

old man

If the old man guides or directs you in some way, he is, in Jungian terms, an archetypal figure. If the man appears to be weak or injured in some way, he could symbolize some part of yourself that needs attention or someone in your life who needs your help. It may also mean that you need to redefine your beliefs about aging.

old woman

In Jungian terms, an old woman is an archetypal symbol of feminine power, or the gatekeeper between life and death. If she is weak or injured, she may represent a part of yourself that needs attention or someone in your life who needs help.

operation

To dream of an operation could mean that you're worried about some aspect of your health and you'd like to become more physically fit. It also represents change from a current situation.

oven

An oven might represent a gestation period. It also symbolizes the womb and feminine energy. A dream of an oven could relate to a pregnancy.

owl

An owl represents both wisdom and mystery and is a symbol of the unconscious. If you hear an owl screech in your dream, it could mean that bad news is coming.

ox

To dream of an ox implies great strength and endurance and an ability to carry on against great odds.

P

painting

If a wall is being painted, the act may suggest that something is being hidden or covered up. Painting at an easel may indicate artistic or creative talents are ready to be expressed.

paper

To see papers piled high indicates a certain level of stress in waking life. Perhaps you feel that your responsibilities are not being taken care of. If you're signing papers in the dream, it indicates that you'll soon have a financial decision to make—and that you'll make the right one.

paradise

If you dream you're in paradise, it's a good indication that all your close friends are loyal. If a mother dreams of paradise, it means her children will be fair and obedient. To dream of Adam and Eve in paradise is a warning to tread carefully in the upcoming months.

park

Dreaming of a park may suggest a wish to relax and enjoy life. Walking in an unlit park at night may mean that you are delving into areas of darkness and danger or that you are dealing with hidden or mysterious matters.

party

To dream of yourself at a party suggests that a celebration is in order. If you are concerned about a particular matter that remains unsettled, the dream may indicate a favorable resolution.

peacock

A dream of this bird suggests that you have a reason to be proud, just as the peacock displays its colorful tail feathers.

pearls

If you dream of owning pearls, you will have success in business and be highly regarded in society. If a woman dreams she receives pearls from a lover, she should be prepared for festive occasions ahead. It also means she will select a faithful and loving husband. If a string of pearls breaks in your dream, you should be on the lookout for impending sadness and problems of the heart.

pepper

If you dream of pepper burning your tongue, it could mean that you'll soon suffer from friends gossiping about you. To sneeze from pepper indicates that something you currently suspect is true.

photograph

Since a photograph is an image of a person or object rather than the real thing, a dream of a photograph hints at deception. If you recognize a person in a dream photo, be careful in your dealings with the person and look for hidden meaning in the person's actions. To dream of having your own photograph taken suggests that you may unwittingly be the cause of your own troubles.

physician

A physician appearing in a dream might indicate that a healing is at hand. A physician is also an authority figure who might be offering a diagnosis on some matter. Sometimes, a physician may take the form of a trusted friend who isn't a doctor but whose nurturing traits are healing.

piano

Music in general represents joyous or festive feelings. Note the condition and type of music coming from the piano. A broken piano symbolizes displeasure in your achievements; an old-fashioned piano suggests neglect.

pill

Taking a pill in a dream suggests that the dreamer may be required to go along with something unpleasant. But positive results should follow. If the pill is birth control, it's a warning to pay attention to current sexual activities.

pilot

A pilot symbolizes someone soaring high and in control in spite of the fast pace. A dream of a pilot may represent that you're in the pilot's seat concerning some issue in your life.

planet

Seeing a planet or visiting another planet in a dream may indicate a new adventure, a new way of thinking, or a new dimension of creativity.

plums

If you dream of ripe plums, you will soon have a joyous occasion to attend. If you dream of eating plums, you can expect a flirtatious affair. If you are gathering plums in your dream, it signifies that you need only work a little to secure your heart's desires.

polar bear

These creatures may mean that trickery or deceit is upon you. Maybe one of your enemies will appear as a friend to overcome you. However, seeing the skin of a polar bear suggests that you will successfully triumph over adversity.

police

Police officers represent authority; they uphold the law. A dream of police may serve as a warning against breaking the law or bending rules. It might suggest a fear of punishment. Alternately, the dream may indicate a desire for justice.

pond

A pond signifies tranquility and a placid outlook in either the dreamer or a person in the dream.

pregnant

If a woman dreams of being pregnant, it could indicate a desire for a child or the onset of the condition. A pregnancy could also symbolize something new coming into the dreamer's life—an idea or project that is gestating.

president of the United States

Not as uncommon as it may seem, to talk with the president of the United States in a dream may represent an interest in lofty ideals or political matters, or a strong desire to be a politician.

priest

A priest represents a benign spiritual authority serving as a guide. Alternately, a priest might symbolize a dictatorial figure or one who judges and condemns. A dream of a priest may indicate the need to follow or eschew conventional religion. Look to surrounding details for clarification.

prison

Constraint and restriction are implied. If you see yourself at work in a prison, the dream might suggest that you've limited your creativity or that you feel it's difficult to escape your job for a better one.

professor

A professor may represent knowledge, wisdom, and higher education.

prophet

A prophet provides knowledge, guidance, and perhaps a peek at the future. The symbol may also indicate that you're in need of guidance.

puddle

Stepping into or stomping through puddles represents a parting or clearing away of troubles, with good times to follow. To dream that you are just wetting your feet in a puddle may mean that trouble will follow a pleasurable experience.

pump

To see a pump in a dream denotes that energy is available to meet your needs. A functioning pump could also symbolize good health. A broken pump signifies a breakdown or disruption of the usual way of doing things.

puppet

A dream of a puppet might indicate that you are feeling manipulated in some aspect of your life. Alternately, if you are behind the puppet, the dream may indicate that you're acting in a manipulative manner.

Q

quarrel

A dream of a quarrel may indicate that an inner turmoil is plaguing you. If the person you're quarreling with is identifiable, look at your relationship with the person and see if you can identify the area of disagreement. There could be clues in the dream that indicate a way to resolve the differences.

queen

Both an authority and a mother figure, the queen is an archetypal symbol of power. If you are the queen, the dream may be suggesting a desire for leadership. If someone else is the queen, the dream may indicate that you see the woman as capable and powerful.

quest

A dream of a quest may indicate a desire to achieve a goal or embark on an adventure.

quicksand

A dream of quicksand indicates that you need to watch where you are headed. If you're already in the quicksand, then you're probably mired in an emotional matter and feel as if you can't escape. It could refer to either business or personal matters.

quill

A quill or fountain pen is a symbol of masculinity and signifies that you need to follow your heart's desire. It's also a sign to stay steadfast in your convictions.

quilt

A quilt suggests warmth and protection. A patchwork quilt symbolizes the joining together of various aspects of your life to form a protective covering.

R

rabbit

The rabbit is a symbol of fertility and magic, like the rabbit pulled from the magician's hat. Although fertility could relate to the conception of children, it might also concern financial abundance, the success of a particular project, or other matters. A white rabbit may signify faithfulness in love.

race

If you are racing in a dream, then perhaps you're involved in an overly competitive situation or you're in a rush. The message might be that it's time to slow down and relax.

rain

A fresh downpour symbolizes a washing or cleansing away of the old. Alternately, a rainy day may indicate a gloomy situation. To hear the patter of rain on the roof may signify domestic bliss, while seeing a downpour of rain from inside a house may represent requited love and fortune. Seeing it rain on others may mean that you are excluding friends from your confidence.

rainbow

Usually seen after a storm, a rainbow in a dream may mean that favorable conditions will arise after a brief period of unpleasantness. Seeing a low-hanging rainbow over verdant trees may signify success in any endeavor.

rams

If you dream of a ram charging you with its head down, it indicates that you are under attack. If the ram is near, it may indicate that the attack is near or that you will have little time to react. A ram charging from a distance suggests that you will have time to respond to the situation.

Consider whether someone in your life is trying to "ram" something down your throat. If the ram is quietly grazing in a pasture, the indication could be that you have powerful allies on your side.

rapids

Rapids represent danger and a fear of being swept away by emotions.

rat

Rats are generally associated with filth and dilapidation. Dreaming of a rat or rats may suggest the deterioration of a situation. Ask yourself who the rat is in your life.

red

The color red is often associated with vitality and energy, the heart, and blood. The color red in a dream can also mean anger or strong emotions, as in "seeing red." Red often indicates that the dream originates from the deepest level of your being.

referee

A referee in a dream can symbolize an inner battle, or it can relate to conflict in your daily life. Can you identify the issue? If so, weigh the two sides, negotiate, and reach a settlement. Sometimes working with an unbiased third party can help.

religion

To dream of religion—discussing it or practicing it—indicates that you may have some problems in the near future with business. Watch out for adversity and conspiring coworkers or partners. Dreaming that you're attending a religion conference signifies an impending family disturbance. However, if you're a farmer or in a business that requires you to work with your hands, a dream of being religious signifies abundance and money ahead.

ribbons

If you should dream of ribbons floating, you will have happy and pleasant friendships, and your everyday cares shouldn't be that troubling. To dream of buying ribbons indicates a predestined happy life. Dreaming of decorating yourself with ribbons can signify a good marriage offer.

rice

Rice is the dietary staple of the majority of the world's population. To dream of rice is a symbol of fertility and good fortune.

river

A dream of floating down a river might indicate a lack of motivation. Are you allowing surrounding circumstances to direct your life, rather than taking charge? A dream of a surging, frothing river may relate to deep-seated anger. In mythology, a river sometimes relates to death or the passing from one state to another.

road

A road is a means of getting from one place to another. What is the condition of the road in your dream? A smooth and straight road suggests the path ahead is easy. A road with dips and curves may indicate that you need to be aware, flexible, and ready for change. A roadblock suggests that there are detours in your path.

rose

A rose symbolizes the feminine and is associated with romance, beauty, and love. A dream of someone handing you a rose may indicate an offering of love. A rose can also relate to good and evil. If someone crushes a rose, that person's intent might be evil.

ruins

To dream of something in ruins suggests the deterioration of some condition in your life. Keep in mind that when things fall apart, an opportunity to rebuild inevitably appears. If you are planning a trip, especially one to another culture, a dream of ancient ruins could symbolize the adventure of the journey ahead. Alternately, it could signify that you have the ability to access knowledge or wisdom from the past.

running

When you run in a dream, you may be in a hurry to escape from something (usually yourself or a current dilemma) or to reach a goal. The dream may indicate that you need to hurry or that you're rushing around too much and need to rest. Are you running alone or with others? The former may symbolize that you will overcome your competition in business matters, while the latter may represent participation in a joyous occasion. If you dream of running for exercise, it means that you are moving toward a pleasant and successful life. Running and not getting anywhere indicates a feeling in your waking life that you've lost control of a certain situation.

S

sacrifice

To see yourself sacrificed in a dream suggests that you're giving up something important for the sake of others. Closely examine your feelings about the matter. Decide what changes, if any, need to be made.

sailor

A dream of a sailor suggests that you are working on a ship. Symbolically, it could mean that you are working on matters dealing with the unconscious or emotions (see **ship** and **water**).

saint

A saint in a dream indicates that you're being guided or are seeking guidance from a higher source. Pay attention to what he says or does, and take his advice.

salt

Dreaming of salt generally indicates unpleasant situations or unhappy surroundings. Are you due for a move or a change in career? To dream of eating salt means that quarrels may arise now within your family. Traditionally, if a young woman dreamed of eating salt, it meant that her lover would desert her for a more beautiful woman.

school

A school dream may indicate that you are gaining a deep level of knowledge or that your unconscious is processing lessons from your waking life. What happens in the school is important in the interpretation. If you're late to class or show up to take a test without ever having gone to class, the dream is a common symbol for feeling unprepared for something in your life. If you're looking for a school or classroom, it may be time to continue your education.

scissors

Is there something in your life you want to cut off? Scissors also indicate a need to "cut it out." Or the person with the scissors may be acting "snippy."

scrapbook

Scrapbooks are full of things from the past that are filed away and forgotten. Note the other details of the dream. Are you viewing a scrapbook with someone? What are you placing in the scrapbook? It may suggest an unpleasant situation that needs to be put in the past.

sea

Dreams of the sea represent unfulfilled longings or unchanging emotions.

September

Dreaming of September represents good luck and fortune.

shadow

Dreaming of your shadow may suggest that you need to address hidden parts of yourself. Perhaps you do not accept these darker aspects of your personality and project them onto others. The dream may also suggest that you need to incorporate the shadow side into your psyche.

shaking hands

The handshake marks either a new beginning or an ending to a situation. Are you saying farewell to someone in a dream? Then perhaps you are saying goodbye to a matter at hand. To dream of shaking hands with a prominent leader may mean strangers will hold you in high esteem.

shaving

Is there something in your life that needs cleaning up or removal? To dream of shaving yourself connotes that you are in charge of your future. Shaving with a dull razor suggests a troublesome or painful issue. A clean-shaven countenance suggests a smooth journey.

sheep

Do you perceive yourself as one of a flock? This can be a comforting image in terms of being part of a community. Or it may indicate that you lack individuality or the will to strike out on your own.

shell

A shell usually symbolizes a womb. Depending on the circumstances of the dream, it can portend the birth of a child or a new project. A shell can also symbolize protection.

ship

Since a ship travels on water, the dream may signify a voyage through the unconscious or a journey involving your emotions. The state of the ship and the condition of the water should be considered in the interpretation. To see a ship in a storm may indicate your concern over a tempestuous or unfortunate affair, either in business or personal matters. To dream of others shipwrecked may symbolize a feeling of inadequacy in protecting friends or family.

shoes

Shoes are a means of moving ahead. Shiny, new shoes might suggest a journey is about to begin. Well-worn shoes, on the other hand, might indicate that one is weary of the journey or that it is near completion. Mismatched shoes could indicate that the journey is multifaceted. Consider the old cliché, "If the shoe fits, wear it."

shovel

A tool for digging, a shovel in a dream may indicate that you are searching for something or are about to embark on a quest for inner knowledge. A shovel might also represent labor or hard work ahead. A broken shovel could mean that you are experiencing frustration in your work.

shower

To dream of taking a shower may symbolize a spiritual renewal. It might also signify a bonus or reward being showered upon the dreamer.

sickness/illness

If you dream of being ill, ask yourself if you're in need of care and pampering. This dream might also be a message to watch your health. To dream of a sick family member represents some misfortune or issue that is troubling your domestic life.

singing

Hearing singing in a dream signifies a pleasant and cheerful attitude. You may hear promising news soon. If you are singing in the dream, note the type of song you are singing.

skating

Dreaming of skating may signify that you are gliding over a matter at hand, or that you may be skating on thin ice. Make note of all the aspects within the dream. Are you headed toward something? Are you skating away from something?

Skating can be liberating but it can also be frightening, if you're not sure how to do it. (See **walking** and **running**.)

skull

To dream of a skull and crossbones is a traditional sign of danger and possible death—a warning.

sky

Dreaming of the sky symbolizes hope, vitality, and a creative force.

smoke

If you dream of smoke filling a room, it suggests that a situation is being obscured. On the other hand, if the smoke is clearing, clarity is imminent.

snake

A snake is an archetypal image that can have numerous interpretations. Snakes are symbols of wisdom, healing, and fertility, and—in their shedding of skin—renewal. Snakes can also symbolize the dangers of the underworld. In Christianity, the snake symbolizes temptation and the source of evil. In some Eastern traditions, the snake is related to a power that rises from the base of the spine and can be a symbol of transformation. The Freudian interpretation relates snakes to the male genitalia.

snow

Snow can represent purity if seen in a pristine landscape. Since snow is a solidified form of water, it can also stand for frozen emotions. If the snow is melting, the suggestion is that frozen feelings are thawing. To find yourself in a snowstorm may represent uncertainty in an emotional matter or sorrow in failing to enjoy some long-expected pleasure. Dreaming of snowcapped mountains in the distance suggests that your ambitions will yield no advancement. Eating snow symbolizes a failure to realize ideas.

spaceship

A spaceship in a dream may suggest a journey into the unknown or a spiritual quest.

spear

Thrusting a spear at someone in a dream may represent an effort to thrust your will on another person. If the spear is hurled over a field, toward a mountain, or an ocean, the dream may mean that you are making a powerful statement to the world.

spider

Spiders may symbolize a careful and energetic approach to your work and that you will be pleasantly rewarded for your labors. To dream of a spider spinning its web signifies that your home life will be happy and secure, while many spiders represent good health and friends. A confrontation with a large spider may signify a quick ascent to fame and fortune, unless the large spider bites you, in which case it may represent the loss of money or reputation.

squirrel

To see these creatures may mean that pleasant acquaintances will soon visit, or that you will advance in business.

stairs

Climbing a stairway in a dream can mean that you are on your way to achieving a goal. Descending a stairway, or falling down one, might indicate a fall in prestige or economic status. To sit on a step could suggest that you are pausing in your everyday life to consider where things stand.

statue

Dreaming of a statue or statues could signify a lack of movement in your life. Statues are also cold and can symbolize frozen feelings.

stillborn

To dream of a stillborn infant indicates a premature ending or some distressing circumstance in a matter at hand.

stones

Stones can represent small irritations or obstacles that must be overcome. Seeing yourself throw a stone in a dream may mean that you have cause to reprimand someone.

storm

To dream of an approaching storm indicates emotional turmoil in some aspect of your life.

Dark skies and thunder may also be a warning that danger is approaching. Alternately, a storm could symbolize rapid changes occurring in your life.

suffocation

To dream of being suffocated may have to do with the way you're sleeping. Is your breathing being obstructed in some way—a cold, asthma, or a blanket? If not, it's possible that you fear being bossed around or caged in.

suicide

A dream of killing yourself probably is a symbolic reflection of what's going on in your conscious life. Such a dream might reflect a personal transformation, divorce, career change, or other major life shift. You are essentially killing your past—becoming a new person.

sun

Dreaming of the sun is usually fortuitous. The sun is the symbol of light, warmth, and energy. In Native American lore, the sun symbolizes the father or the masculine principle.

swimming

A dream of swimming suggests the dreamer is immersed in an exploration of emotional matters or the unconscious.

sword

A sword is a symbol of strength and power. It also can cut to the bone. Dreaming of a sword might suggest that aggressive action is required.

T

table

To dream of an empty table might suggest a concern about a lack of possessions, while a table covered with food may symbolize a time of abundance.

tambourine

The appearance of a tambourine symbolizes pleasure in some impending unusual undertaking.

tattoo

Tattoos are associated with the strange and exotic. To dream of seeing your body tattooed suggests that some difficulty will cause you to be long absent from home or familiar surroundings. Dreaming that you are a tattoo artist suggests that your desire for some strange experience may alienate you from friends.

teeth

Teeth are what you use to bite. If you lose your bite, you lose power. Losing teeth might also symbolize a loss of face. It could also be a metaphor for loose or careless speech. To examine your teeth suggests that you exercise caution in a matter at hand. To clean your teeth represents that some struggle is necessary to keep your standing. Admiring your teeth for their whiteness suggests that wishes for a pleasant occupation and happiness will be fulfilled. To dream that you pull your own teeth and then feel around the cavity with your tongue signifies your trepidation about a situation you're about to enter into. Imperfect teeth connote bad feelings about appearance and well-being.

telephone

A telephone might symbolize the attempt to contact the unconscious. If the phone is ringing and no one is answering, the dream might suggest that you are ignoring the call of your unconscious. If you have trouble hearing the person on the other line, it suggests that you're having problems communicating in a love relationship.

tent

A tent provides shelter and is usually associated with camping. A dream of a tent could indicate that you are in need of a getaway—a retreat from everyday life.

thaw

Thawing represents a rebirth or return to pleasant conditions. To dream of seeing ice thaw may mean that something or someone giving you trouble will soon yield pleasure and profit.

thief

If you dream of someone stealing something, the implication is that something is being taken from you. It could be a boss or colleague who is stealing your energy or ideas, rather than an actual theft of goods. If you're the thief, the message may be a warning that you are taking what you don't deserve and that you should change your ways.

thirst

A dream in which you are thirsty suggests that you are in need of nourishment, whether physical, mental, or emotional. To see others relieving their thirst suggests that this nourishment may come from others.

thorn

A thorn may represent an annoyance of some sort—"a thorn in your side."

tiger

Aggressive and fierce in the wild, the appearance of these animals may mean that you are under persecution or will be tormented. However, if you see yourself fending off an attack, this may mean that you will be extremely successful in all your ventures.

tornado

Swift and terrible agents of destruction in nature, tornadoes in dreams suggest that your desire for a quick resolution to a matter at hand may lead to disappointment.

torrent

To dream of a seething torrent of water suggests a profound unrest in the emotional state of the dreamer or a person in the dream.

totem

This is the term for your animal or spirit guide. Usually, your totem is the animal to which you have the deepest connection. If you're afraid of an animal in your dream, it is not your totem.

tower

To dream of a tower could symbolize vigilance, as a watchtower, or punishment or isolation, as a guard tower. Dreaming of being in an ivory tower indicates that you or the subject of your dream is out of touch with the everyday world.

train

A train symbolizes a journey. If the train isn't moving, the dream might be suggesting some impediment in your life. If you can't find your luggage, you might be concerned that you're not ready for this journey. If you are on a smoothly running train, but there are no tracks, you might be concerned over some affair that will eventually be resolved satisfactorily. Traveling on the wrong train may indicate your journey is in need of a correction.

treasure

A dream of a treasure may suggest a hidden talent or hidden abilities that you can now unearth. It could indicate latent psychic abilities.

tree

A tree is a symbol of strength and foundation. It may also symbolize inner strength. A tree grows both below the earth and above it. In that sense, a tree transcends the sky above and the earth below and stands for the realms of nature and the spirit. To dream of a tree in new foliage represents a pleasant outcome to your hopes and desires. Tree-climbing dreams may signify a quick ascent in business. Newly felled green trees portend unexpected unhappiness after a period of prosperity and delight.

trial

A dream of being on trial suggests that you are being judged or are afraid of being judged. Alternately, a trial in a dream could indicate that you are judging others too harshly.

triplets

To dream of triplets indicates success in a matter where failure was feared. For a man to dream of his wife having triplets represents a pleasing end to a situation that has long been in dispute. To hear newly born triplets crying suggests a disagreement that will soon be resolved in your favor.

tunnel

From a Freudian perspective, a dream of a tunnel suggests a vagina, and a train entering the tunnel represents sexual intercourse. A tunnel may also be a link between two conditions. When you exit the tunnel, you will enter a new state of mind.

turtle

While dreaming of a turtle might symbolize slow, painstaking movement, the shelled creature is also a symbol of spiritual development.

twins

A dream of twins may mean that there are two parts to a matter of concern or two aspects to your personality. Seeing twins in a dream symbolizes security in a business matter and faithfulness in a domestic issue.

U

umbrella

An umbrella represents protection against adverse conditions or an emotional flood from the unconscious. If the umbrella is closed and a downpour is soaking you, the indication is that you are open to your emotional needs.

underground

To dream of being underground often symbolizes contact with your subconscious. Other images in the dream will provide more meaning to the nature of the contact. Ask yourself how you feel about the situation. Is there something you've been hiding that should be brought to the surface? Do you feel protected by the underground cavern or room? Or are you hiding or being held prisoner? Dreaming of an underground railway could indicate passage to another state of being—a personal transformation.

underwear

A dream of underwear may symbolize that you are exposing something that is under cover or hidden. It could indicate that you're bringing matters from the unconscious to the surface.

unicorn

To dream of a unicorn is always a good sign—it means that happy circumstances will soon be yours. Unicorns protect you and cancel out the bad omens around them. To touch the unicorn's horn means you'll have luck for months. Dreaming of flying on a unicorn means you'll have true friendships and good health.

unicycle

If you are riding a unicycle in a dream, you may be concerned about balance. Alternately, you're the "big wheel" and on your own.

urination

A dream in which you urinate may simply indicate that you need to wake up and go to the bathroom. Symbolically, the dream may indicate a desire to eliminate impurities from your life.

V

vagrant

Are you afraid of losing your home, stability, or livelihood? Perhaps you want to break away from social regimentation.

valuables

Uncovering valuables may symbolize the discovery of self-worth or inner resources.

vampire

To dream of a vampire may indicate that someone is draining energy from you or taking advantage of you. The message is to guard against people who take too much of your time or energy. To dream of battling or staking a vampire suggests a positive outcome versus someone with harmful intentions.

vault

A vault usually holds valuables. Your ability to open it determines the nature of the dream. If you hold the key, the vault may be a symbol of wealth and prosperity. If you are unable to open it, then the dream may signify that you are being frustrated in your effort to achieve wealth or a specific goal.

veil

A dream in which someone or something is veiled suggests that you're hiding something or something is being hidden from you.

ventriloquist

If you dream of a ventriloquist, you should beware of deception and fraud. Dreaming of a ventriloquist can also mean that a love affair may not turn out so well.

victim

A dream of yourself as a victim may indicate that you're feeling helpless regarding a situation. If someone rescues you, the dream suggests that help is available.

violin

A violin played in a dream portends a romantic interlude—a time of love and harmony. It can also mean that you or someone else is high-strung.

visitor

Encountering a visitor in a dream indicates that a new condition is entering your life. If you welcome the visitor, the change may be for the better. If you turn away the visitor, you're unwilling to change or you don't accept what is being offered.

voices

Dreaming that you are hearing pleasant voices indicates joyous reconciliations will happen in your future. If the voices are angry, expect disappointments. If the voices are weeping, expect to have a sudden outburst of anger.

volcano

The eruption of a volcano or a smoking volcano may suggest that your strong emotions are rising to the surface and need to be expressed before you explode.

vomit

To vomit in a dream may be a dramatic exhibition of a need to rid yourself of something or someone. To dream of vomiting a chicken suggests a relative's illness will be a cause for disappointment. To see others vomiting symbolizes that someone's false pretenses will soon be made apparent.

vulture

There is a scheming person out to injure you if you dream of vultures. But this evildoer will not succeed if you dream the vulture is dead. A woman dreaming of a vulture indicates she may soon be overwhelmed by slander and gossip.

W

walking

A dream of walking in the woods means you will have business difficulties. Dreaming of walking at night means you will have struggle and difficulty. Dreaming of walking in pleasant places indicates good fortune and favor. Walking and not getting anywhere indicates a static situation you need to change.

wallet

A wallet carries personal effects, such as your identification. It is also where you carry financial resources. If you dream of losing your wallet, it may relate to a concern about your sense of self or about your finances. What happens in the dream and how you react can help you determine its meaning.

war

A dream of war could relate to reliving your past in the military. Whether you've served in the military or not, a dream of war might symbolize internal turmoil or a need to make peace with yourself or others. By examining other elements in the dream, you may determine the message behind the aggressive behavior.

washing

If you are washing something in a dream, you may be attempting to cleanse or purify the self. If a stain won't come out, the dream may relate to a concern about something from your past connected with feelings of guilt.

water

A dream of water can relate to the emotions or the unconscious. In the Freudian perspective, water relates to sexual matters, usually the female genitalia (see **lake, ocean, river,** and **waves**). If you dream of clear water, you can expect joy. To dream of muddy water, however, means that you may experience some sorrow in the near future. For a young woman to dream of wading in clear water means she will have her heart's desire. To dream of children wading in water signifies future happiness. Rocky water connotes problems of the heart and problems communicating with a loved one.

waterfall

Water signifies the unconscious or the emotions, so to dream of waterfalls may represent a sudden or dramatic change in the dreamer's emotional state.

waves

Waves symbolize the power of the unconscious. Enormous breaking waves may represent powerful emotions, and gentle waves may suggest a tranquil state of mind.

weapon

Weapons may signify the male genitals. The meaning of the dream is best determined by considering who is holding the weapon and how it is being used.

wedding

Weddings are a union between two people, and dreams of weddings may symbolize the joining or acceptance by your unconscious of an idea or emotion. To attend a wedding in a dream connotes an occasion that may bring about bitterness and delayed success. To dream of a wedding that is not approved by your parents suggests unrest among family members.

weeds

Dreaming of weeds suggests that something needs to be weeded out of your life. An overgrown garden might signify that something is being neglected in your life.

well

A well in a dream reveals that resources are available deep within you, although you may not be aware of them. To fall into a well symbolizes a loss of control regarding a matter at hand. A dry well indicates that you feel a part of your life is empty and needs to be nourished. To draw water from a well denotes the fulfillment of ardent desires.

wet

As in the saying "You're all wet," wetness represents uncertainty or a lack of knowledge. Maybe someone is giving you bad advice about a particular situation. For a young woman to dream that she is soaking wet symbolizes a disgraceful affair with someone who is already attached.

whale

A whale is an enormous mammal, and to dream of one might indicate that you are dealing with a whale of a project. On the other hand, a whale dream may suggest you are overwhelmed. Whales can also relate to water and the relationship of the self to the unconscious and the emotions.

whip

Being whipped in a dream refers to two things: your need to feel protected and dominated by a loved one, and your feeling that this person is taking advantage of you. The key is to find a balance between the two. If you dream of whipping someone, beware of your own manipulative or aggressive tendencies.

whirlpool

Water represents the emotions or the unconscious, so to dream of a whirlpool may indicate that your emotions are in a state of flux and can ensnare you unless caution is exercised.

whirlwind

A dream of a whirlwind suggests that you are confronting a change that threatens to overwhelm you. Pay attention to the other aspects of the dream. Are you facing this danger alone or with somebody?

wind

Dreaming of wind softly blowing means you may receive a considerable inheritance from a loved one and, after sadness, know happiness in the future. If you dream you are walking against a brisk wind, it indicates you are courageous, able to resist temptations, and determined. You will be successful. If, however, in your dream the wind blows you along against your wishes, it signifies you might have disappointments in love and in business. A dream of a gale means possible business losses.

window

If a window appears in a dream, it may symbolize a view of your life from the inside out. Are there changes you would like to make? If the view is illuminated, then the outlook is bright. If you are on the outside looking in, you may feel that you have been excluded from something.

wine

Drinking wine in a dream might be a sign of celebration. It can also represent an elevated or altered state of mind. In a spiritual sense, wine can symbolize a transformation. For an alcoholic or someone who has been affected by one, wine or other alcoholic beverages can represent a negative influence.

wings

Wings are a means of transport. They may suggest that you will soar to wealth and honor or that you are worried about someone who has gone on a long journey.

witch

The Halloween image of a witch might be symbolic of a scary or evil scenario. For those involved in Wicca or attracted to New Age ideas, a witch might relate to the worship and respect of nature and the earth.

wolf

In Native American lore, the wolf is good medicine, a symbol of the pathfinder—a teacher with great wisdom and knowledge. Dreaming of a wolf can be auspicious. Alternately, the wolf can be a symbol of a lone male aggressively pursuing a young female, as in the story of Little Red Riding Hood.

woman

The appearance of different types of women can symbolize different things in a dream. A dark-haired woman with blue eyes and an upturned nose may represent withdrawal from a matter at hand. A brown-eyed woman with a hooked nose may suggest that you will be lured into a speculative venture. A woman who appears with auburn hair alludes to your anxiety over an issue. A blond woman is symbolic of a favorable or pleasing outcome.

writing

Writing is usually difficult to read in a dream, so the message is usually symbolic. Writing could serve as a warning, as in "the writing is on the wall." Writing could also suggest that your inner self is seeking contact with your conscious self. Ancient writings in a dream indicate that the dreamer is seeking knowledge from the distant past.

Y

yard

Dreaming of a yard may relate to your childhood—a time when you played in the yard. The dream may symbolize a longing for a carefree time, more personal space, or something to fill the vacancy of the yard.

yellow

In the positive sense, yellow is the symbol of brightness, energy, and intellect. The color can also be linked to cowardly behavior.

youth

A dream of a youth might signify that younger people are energizing you. Seeing yourself as younger in a dream may point to youthful self-empowerment.

Z

zebra

Dreaming of zebras running fast indicates you are interested in fleeting enterprises. If you dream of a wild zebra in its native environment, you might try a pursuit that could bring unsatisfactory results. Beware of those with multicolored stripes.

zero

A symbol of many interpretations, zero can mean emptiness—a lack of something in your life. It also forms a circle and can stand for wholeness and completion, or even the mysteries of the unknown. In Freudian terms, the shape is reminiscent of a vagina and suggests a desire for sexual relations.

zoo

A dream of a zoo might relate to a feeling of being in a cage. It could also symbolize chaos: "This place is like a zoo." Alternately, it could recall a time of recreation, relaxation, and pleasure.

Appendix A

Dream Groups

The following are organizations, institutions, and publications involved in dream-related activities.

Alfred Adler Institute
594 Broadway
Suite 1213
New York, NY 10012
✍ *www.alfredadler-ny.org*

The Alfred Adler Institute provides training in psychotherapy and counseling along the theory of individual psychology as formulated by Austrian psychiatrist Alfred Adler.

American Sleep Disorders Association (ASDA)
1640 14th St. NW
Suite 300
Rochester, MN 55901

If you suffer from insomnia, night terrors, or any other sleep-related disorder, you might gain help from the ASDA. Referrals to sleep disorder centers in your area can be provided. These centers offer diagnostic and treatment services.

American Society for Psychical Research
5 W. 73rd St.
New York, NY 10023
✍ *www.aspr.com*

The American Society for Psychical Research conducts research activities into the paranormal, including the telepathic influences on dreams.

Association for Research and Enlightenment (A.R.E.)

215 67th St.

Virginia Beach, VA 23451

www.are-cayce.com

A.R.E., also known as the Edgar Cayce Foundation, offers an extensive research library based on the recorded readings of famed psychic Edgar Cayce. A.R.E. offers year-round seminars on a wide range of topics related to parapsychology, including dreams.

Association for the Study of Dreams (ASD)

ASD Central Office

P.O. Box 1592

Merced, CA 95341

www.asdreams.org

ASD provides an international forum for promoting research and dispensing information about the psychological and therapeutic aspects of dreams and their interpretation. The association offers a newsletter and sponsors conferences.

C.G. Jung Foundation for Analytical Psychology

28 E. 39th St.

New York, NY 10016

www.cgjungny.org

The Jung Foundation offers training and information on analytical psychology based on Jungian concepts. Archival material includes studies on archetypal symbolism.

Cleargreen, Inc.

11901 Santa Monica Blvd.
Suite 599a
Los Angeles, CA 90025

Cleargreen, Inc., was founded by Carlos Castaneda and his colleagues in sorcery to promote the teachings of Don Juan Matus, a Yaqui Indian and sorcerer who taught dreaming techniques to Castaneda. The organization promotes seminars in which "magical passes," called Tensegrity, are taught. Cleargreen, Inc., also publishes a newsletter called *Readers of Infinity: A Journal of Applied Hermeneutics.*

Common Boundary

5272 River Rd.
Bethesda, MD 20816

Common Boundary is an educational organization founded to foster support and communication for those in mental health, helping, and healing professions, and anyone interested in the interrelationships between psychology, spirituality, and creativity.

Dream Network
1137 Powerhouse Lane
Suite 22
Moab, UT 84532

Dream Network is a quarterly journal devoted to exploring the relationship between dreams and myths. Its stated purpose is to "demystify dream work and to integrate dream-sharing into our lives for the enhancement of our culture." *Dream Network* also provides information on ongoing dream groups.

National Sleep Foundation

1522 K St., NW
Suite 500
Washington, D.C. 20005
www.sleepfoundation.org

The National Sleep Foundation is an independent nonprofit organization dedicated to improving public health and safety by achieving understanding of sleep and sleep disorders and by supporting education, sleep-related research, and advocacy.

Omega Institute

150 Lake Drive
Rhinebeck, NY 12572
www.eomega.org

The Omega Institute offers seminars taught by the leaders in psychology, metaphysics, shamanism, the arts, and related fields.

Saybrook Graduate School

747 Front St., 3rd Floor
San Francisco, CA 94111
www.saybrook.edu

Founded and directed by Dr. Stanley Krippner, a renowned dream-researcher and author, Saybrook is an accredited graduate school that offers students many opportunities to study dreams.

Sleep Research Society (SRS)
c/o Wallace Mendelson
Cleveland Clinic S-51
Dept. of Neurology
9500 Euclid Ave.
Cleveland, OH 44195
✑*www.sleepresearchsociety.org*

The Sleep Research Society fosters scientific investigation, professional education, and career development in sleep research and academic sleep medicine. The organization also publishes the journal *Sleep*.

Appendix B

Books about Dreams

Castaneda, C., *The Art of Dreaming*. New York, HarperCollins, 1993.

Delaney, G., *Breakthrough Dreaming: How to Tap the Power of Your 24-Hour Mind*. New York, Bantam, 1991.

Faraday, A., *Dream Power*. New York, Afar Publishers, 1972.

Faraday, A., *The Dream Game*. New York, Harper & Row, 1974.

Garfield, P., *Creative Dreaming*. New York, Ballantine, 1974.

Godwin, M., *The Lucid Dreamer*. New York, Simon & Schuster, 1994.

Harner, M., *The Way of the Shaman*. New York, Harper & Row, 1980.

Jung, C., *Memories, Dreams, Reflections*. New York, Vintage, 1961.

Jung, C., *Man and His Symbols*. New York, Dell, 1964.

LaBerge, S., *Lucid Dreaming*. New York, Ballantine, 1986.

LaBerge, S. and Rheingold, H., *Exploring the World of Lucid Dreaming*. New York, Random House, 1990.

Lewis, J., *The Dream Encyclopedia*. Detroit, Visible Ink Books, 1995.

Maxmen, J., *A Good Night's Sleep*. New York, Warner, 1981.

McGuire, W. and Hull, R. (Eds.), *C.G. Jung Speaking*. Princeton, NJ, Princeton University Press, 1977.

Michaels, S., *The Bedside Guide to Dreams*. New York, Fawcett Crest, 1995.

Morris, J., *The Dream Workbook*. New York, Fawcett Crest, 1985.

Perkins, J., *PsychoNavigation*. Rochester, VT, Destiny Books, 1990.

Perkins, J., *The World as You Dream It: Shamanic Teachings from the Amazon and Andes*. Rochester, VT, Destiny Books, 1994.

Roberts, J., *Seth Speaks*. New York, Prentice-Hall, 1972.

Roberts, J., *The Nature of Personal Reality: A Seth Book*. New York, Prentice-Hall, 1974.

Roberts, J., *Seth: Dreams and Projection of Consciousness*. New York, Prentice-Hall, 1987.

Sanford, J., *Dreams and Healing: A Succinct and Lively Interpretation of Dreams*. New York, Paulist Press, 1978.

Ullman, M. and Krippner, S. and Vaughan, A., *Dream Telepathy*. Toronto, Macmillan, 1973.

Ullman, M., and Zimmerman, N., *Working with Dreams*. New York, Dell, 1979.

Villoldo, A., *Dance of the Four Winds*. New York, Harper & Row, 1990.

Villoldo, A., *Island of the Sun: Mastering the Inca Medicine Wheel*. San Francisco, HarperSanFrancisco, 1992.

Williams, S., *Jungian-Senoi Dreamwork Manual*. Berkeley, Journal Press, 1980.

THE EVERYTHING SERIES!

BUSINESS & PERSONAL FINANCE

Everything® Budgeting Book
Everything® Business Planning Book
Everything® Coaching and Mentoring Book
Everything® Fundraising Book
Everything® Get Out of Debt Book
Everything® Grant Writing Book
Everything® Homebuying Book, 2nd Ed.
Everything® Homeselling Book
Everything® Home-Based Business Book
Everything® Investing Book
Everything® Landlording Book
Everything® Leadership Book
Everything® Managing People Book
Everything® Negotiating Book
Everything® Online Business Book
Everything® Personal Finance Book
Everything® Personal Finance in Your 20s
     and 30s Book
Everything® Project Management Book
Everything® Real Estate Investing Book
Everything® Robert's Rules Book, $7.95
Everything® Selling Book
Everything® Start Your Own Business Book
Everything® Wills & Estate Planning Book

COOKING

Everything® Barbecue Cookbook
Everything® Bartender's Book, $9.95
Everything® Chinese Cookbook
Everything® College Cookbook
Everything® Cookbook
Everything® Diabetes Cookbook
Everything® Easy Gourmet Cookbook
Everything® Fondue Cookbook
Everything® Grilling Cookbook
Everything® Healthy Meals in Minutes
     Cookbook
Everything® Holiday Cookbook

Everything® Indian Cookbook
Everything® Low-Carb Cookbook
Everything® Low-Fat High-Flavor Cookbook
Everything® Low-Salt Cookbook
Everything® Meals for a Month Cookbook
Everything® Mediterranean Cookbook
Everything® Mexican Cookbook
Everything® One-Pot Cookbook
Everything® Pasta Cookbook
Everything® Quick Meals Cookbook
Everything® Slow Cooker Cookbook
Everything® Soup Cookbook
Everything® Thai Cookbook
Everything® Vegetarian Cookbook
Everything® Wine Book

HEALTH

Everything® Alzheimer's Book
Everything® Diabetes Book
Everything® Hypnosis Book
Everything® Low Cholesterol Book
Everything® Massage Book
Everything® Menopause Book
Everything® Nutrition Book
Everything® Reflexology Book
Everything® Stress Management Book

HISTORY

Everything® American Government Book
Everything® American History Book
Everything® Civil War Book
Everything® Irish History & Heritage Book
Everything® Middle East Book

HOBBIES & GAMES

Everything® Blackjack Strategy Book
Everything® Brain Strain Book, $9.95
Everything® Bridge Book
Everything® Candlemaking Book

Everything® Card Games Book
Everything® Cartooning Book
Everything® Casino Gambling Book, 2nd Ed.
Everything® Chess Basics Book
Everything® Crossword and Puzzle Book
Everything® Crossword Challenge Book
Everything® Cryptograms Book, $9.95
Everything® Digital Photography Book
Everything® Drawing Book
Everything® Easy Crosswords Book
Everything® Family Tree Book
Everything® Games Book, 2nd Ed.
Everything® Knitting Book
Everything® Knots Book
Everything® Motorcycle Book
Everything® Online Genealogy Book
Everything® Photography Book
Everything® Poker Strategy Book
Everything® Pool & Billiards Book
Everything® Quilting Book
Everything® Scrapbooking Book
Everything® Sewing Book
Everything® Woodworking Book
Everything® Word Games Challenge Book

HOME IMPROVEMENT

Everything® Feng Shui Book
Everything® Feng Shui Decluttering Book,
     $9.95
Everything® Fix-It Book
Everything® Homebuilding Book
Everything® Lawn Care Book
Everything® Organize Your Home Book

EVERYTHING® KIDS' BOOKS

All titles are $6.95
Everything® Kids' Animal Puzzle & Activity
     Book
Everything® Kids' Baseball Book, 3rd Ed.

All Everything® books are priced at $12.95 or $14.95, unless otherwise stated. Prices subject to change without notice.

Everything® Kids' Bible Trivia Book
Everything® Kids' Bugs Book
Everything® Kids' Christmas Puzzle
   & Activity Book
Everything® Kids' Cookbook
Everything® Kids' Halloween Puzzle
   & Activity Book
Everything® Kids' Hidden Pictures Book
Everything® Kids' Joke Book
Everything® Kids' Knock Knock Book
Everything® Kids' Math Puzzles Book
Everything® Kids' Mazes Book
Everything® Kids' Money Book
Everything® Kids' Monsters Book
Everything® Kids' Nature Book
Everything® Kids' Puzzle Book
Everything® Kids' Riddles & Brain Teasers Book
Everything® Kids' Science Experiments Book
Everything® Kids' Sharks Book
Everything® Kids' Soccer Book
Everything® Kids' Travel Activity Book

KIDS' STORY BOOKS

Everything® Bedtime Story Book
Everything® Fairy Tales Book

LANGUAGE

Everything® Conversational Japanese Book
   (with CD), $19.95
Everything® French Phrase Book, $9.95
Everything® French Verb Book, $9.95
Everything® Inglés Book
Everything® Learning French Book
Everything® Learning German Book
Everything® Learning Italian Book
Everything® Learning Latin Book
Everything® Learning Spanish Book
Everything® Sign Language Book
Everything® Spanish Grammar Book
Everything® Spanish Phrase Book, $9.95
Everything® Spanish Verb Book, $9.95

MUSIC

Everything® Drums Book (with CD), $19.95
Everything® Guitar Book
Everything® Home Recording Book
Everything® Playing Piano and Keyboards
   Book

Everything® Reading Music Book (with CD),
   $19.95
Everything® Rock & Blues Guitar Book
   (with CD), $19.95
Everything® Songwriting Book

NEW AGE

Everything® Astrology Book
Everything® Dreams Book, 2nd Ed.
Everything® Ghost Book
Everything® Love Signs Book, $9.95
Everything® Numerology Book
Everything® Paganism Book
Everything® Palmistry Book
Everything® Psychic Book
Everything® Reiki Book
Everything® Spells & Charms Book
Everything® Tarot Book
Everything® Wicca and Witchcraft Book

PARENTING

Everything® Baby Names Book
Everything® Baby Shower Book
Everything® Baby's First Food Book
Everything® Baby's First Year Book
Everything® Birthing Book
Everything® Breastfeeding Book
Everything® Father-to-Be Book
Everything® Father's First Year Book
Everything® Get Ready for Baby Book
Everything® Getting Pregnant Book
Everything® Homeschooling Book
Everything® Parent's Guide to Children
   with ADD/ADHD
Everything® Parent's Guide to Children
   with Asperger's Syndrome
Everything® Parent's Guide to Children
   with Autism
Everything® Parent's Guide to Children
   with Dyslexia
Everything® Parent's Guide to Positive
   Discipline
Everything® Parent's Guide to Raising a
   Successful Child
Everything® Parent's Guide to Tantrums
Everything® Parent's Guide to the Overweight
   Child
Everything® Parenting a Teenager Book
Everything® Potty Training Book, $9.95

Everything® Pregnancy Book, 2nd Ed.
Everything® Pregnancy Fitness Book
Everything® Pregnancy Nutrition Book
Everything® Pregnancy Organizer, $15.00
Everything® Toddler Book
Everything® Tween Book
Everything® Twins, Triplets, and More Book

PETS

Everything® Cat Book
Everything® Dachshund Book, $12.95
Everything® Dog Book
Everything® Dog Health Book
Everything® Dog Training and Tricks Book
Everything® Golden Retriever Book, $12.95
Everything® Horse Book
Everything® Labrador Retriever Book, $12.95
Everything® Poodle Book, $12.95
Everything® Pug Book, $12.95
Everything® Puppy Book
Everything® Rottweiler Book, $12.95
Everything® Tropical Fish Book

REFERENCE

Everything® Car Care Book
Everything® Classical Mythology Book
Everything® Computer Book
Everything® Divorce Book
Everything® Einstein Book
Everything® Etiquette Book
Everything® Mafia Book
Everything® Philosophy Book
Everything® Psychology Book
Everything® Shakespeare Book

RELIGION

Everything® Angels Book
Everything® Bible Book
Everything® Buddhism Book
Everything® Catholicism Book
Everything® Christianity Book
Everything® Jewish History & Heritage Book
Everything® Judaism Book
Everything® Koran Book
Everything® Prayer Book
Everything® Saints Book
Everything® Torah Book
Everything® Understanding Islam Book

All Everything® books are priced at $12.95 or $14.95, unless otherwise stated. Prices subject to change without notice.

Everything® World's Religions Book
Everything® Zen Book

SCHOOL & CAREERS

Everything® Alternative Careers Book
Everything® College Survival Book, 2nd Ed.
Everything® Cover Letter Book, 2nd Ed.
Everything® Get-a-Job Book
Everything® Job Interview Book
Everything® New Teacher Book
Everything® Online Job Search Book
Everything® Paying for College Book
Everything® Practice Interview Book
Everything® Resume Book, 2nd Ed.
Everything® Study Book

SELF-HELP

Everything® Great Sex Book
Everything® Kama Sutra Book
Everything® Self-Esteem Book

SPORTS & FITNESS

Everything® Fishing Book
Everything® Fly-Fishing Book
Everything® Golf Instruction Book

Everything® Pilates Book
Everything® Running Book
Everything® Total Fitness Book
Everything® Weight Training Book
Everything® Yoga Book

TRAVEL

Everything® Family Guide to Hawaii
Everything® Family Guide to New York City, 2nd Ed.
Everything® Family Guide to RV Travel & Campgrounds
Everything® Family Guide to the Walt Disney World Resort®, Universal Studios®, and Greater Orlando, 4th Ed.
Everything® Family Guide to Washington D.C., 2nd Ed.
Everything® Guide to Las Vegas
Everything® Guide to New England
Everything® Travel Guide to the Disneyland Resort®, California Adventure®, Universal Studios®, and the Anaheim Area

WEDDINGS

Everything® Bachelorette Party Book, $9.95
Everything® Bridesmaid Book, $9.95

Everything® Elopement Book, $9.95
Everything® Father of the Bride Book, $9.95
Everything® Groom Book, $9.95
Everything® Mother of the Bride Book, $9.95
Everything® Wedding Book, 3rd Ed.
Everything® Wedding Checklist, $9.95
Everything® Wedding Etiquette Book, $7.95
Everything® Wedding Organizer, $15.00
Everything® Wedding Shower Book, $7.95
Everything® Wedding Vows Book, $7.95
Everything® Weddings on a Budget Book, $9.95

WRITING

Everything® Creative Writing Book
Everything® Get Published Book
Everything® Grammar and Style Book
Everything® Guide to Writing a Book Proposal
Everything® Guide to Writing a Novel
Everything® Guide to Writing Children's Books
Everything® Screenwriting Book
Everything® Writing Poetry Book
Everything® Writing Well Book

- -

We have Everything® for the beginner crafter!
All titles are $14.95

Everything® Crafts—Baby Scrapbooking
1-59337-225-6

Everything® Crafts—Bead Your Own Jewelry
1-59337-142-X

Everything® Crafts—Create Your Own Greeting Cards
1-59337-226-4

Everything® Crafts—Easy Projects
1-59337-298-1

Everything® Crafts—Polymer Clay for Beginners
1-59337-230-2

Everything® Crafts—Rubber Stamping Made Easy
1-59337-229-9

Everything® Crafts—Wedding Decorations and Keepsakes
1-59337-227-2

Available wherever books are sold!
To order, call 800-872-5627, or visit us at *www.everything.com*
Everything® and everything.com® are registered trademarks of F+W Publications, Inc.